M000315772

Egypt in a Time of Revolution

This book considers the diverse forms of mass mobilization and contentious politics that emerged during the Egyptian Revolution of 2011 and its aftermath. Drawing on a catalog of more than 8,000 protest events, as well as interviews, video footage and still photographs, Neil Ketchley provides the first systematic account of how Egyptians banded together to overthrow Husni Mubarak, and how old regime forces engineered a return to authoritarian rule. Eschewing top-down, structuralist, and culturalist explanations, the author shows that the causes and consequences of Mubarak's ousting can only be understood by paying close attention to the evolving dynamics of contentious politics witnessed in Egypt since 2011. Setting these events within a larger social and political context, Ketchley sheds new light on the trajectories and legacies of the Arab Spring, as well as recurring patterns of contentious collective action found in the Middle East and beyond.

Neil Ketchley is Lecturer in Middle East Politics at King's College London. He was a Hulme Postdoctoral Research Fellow at Brasenose College, University of Oxford, from 2014–2016. He received his Ph.D. in Political Science from the London School of Economics.

Cambridge Studies in Contentious Politics

Editors

Mark Beissinger   *Princeton University*
Jack A. Goldstone   *George Mason University*
Michael Hanagan   *Vassar College*
Doug McAdam   *Stanford University and the Center for Advanced Study in the Behavioral Sciences*
Sarah Soule   *Stanford University*
Suzanne Staggenborg   *University of Pittsburgh*
Sidney Tarrow   *Cornell University*
Charles Tilly (d. 2008)   *Columbia University*
Elisabeth J. Wood   *Yale University*
Deborah Yashar   *Princeton University*

Rina Agarwala, *Informal Labor, Formal Politics, and Dignified Discontent in India*
Ronald Aminzade, *Race, Nation, and Citizenship in Post-Colonial Africa: The Case of Tanzania*
Ronald Aminzade et al., *Silence and Voice in the Study of Contentious Politics*
Javier Auyero, *Routine Politics and Violence in Argentina: The Gray Zone of State Power*
Phillip M. Ayoub, *When States Come Out: Europe's Sexual Minorities and the Politics of Visibility*
Amrita Basu, *Violent Conjunctures in Democratic India*
W. Lance Bennett and Alexandra Segerberg, *The Logic of Connective Action: Digital Media and the Personalization of Contentious Politics*
Nancy Bermeo and Deborah J. Yashar, *Parties, Movements, and Democracy in the Developing World*
Clifford Bob, *The Global Right Wing and the Clash of World Politics*
Clifford Bob, *The Marketing of Rebellion: Insurgents, Media, and International Activism*
Charles Brockett, *Political Movements and Violence in Central America*
Marisa von Bülow, *Building Transnational Networks: Civil Society and the Politics of Trade in the Americas*
Valerie Bunce and Sharon Wolchik, *Defeating Authoritarian Leaders in Postcommunist Countries*
Lars-Erik Cederman, *Kristian Skrede Gleditsch, and Halvard Buhaug, Inequality, Grievances, and Civil War*
Christian Davenport, *How Social Movements Die: Repression and Demobilization of the Republic of New Africa*
Christian Davenport, *Media Bias, Perspective, and State Repression*
Gerald F. Davis, Doug McAdam, W. Richard Scott, and Mayer N. Zald, *Social Movements and Organization Theory*
Donatella della Porta, *Clandestine Political Violence*

(continued after index)

Egypt in a Time of Revolution

Contentious Politics and the Arab Spring

NEIL KETCHLEY

King's College London

CAMBRIDGE
UNIVERSITY PRESS

CAMBRIDGE
UNIVERSITY PRESS

University Printing House, Cambridge CB2 8BS, United Kingdom

One Liberty Plaza, 20th Floor, New York, NY 10006, USA

477 Williamstown Road, Port Melbourne, VIC 3207, Australia

4843/24, 2nd Floor, Ansari Road, Daryaganj, Delhi – 110002, India

79 Anson Road, #06–04/06, Singapore 079906

Cambridge University Press is part of the University of Cambridge.

It furthers the University's mission by disseminating knowledge in the pursuit of education, learning, and research at the highest international levels of excellence.

www.cambridge.org
Information on this title: www.cambridge.org/9781107184978
DOI: 10.1017/9781316882702

© Neil Ketchley 2017

This publication is in copyright. Subject to statutory exception and to the provisions of relevant collective licensing agreements, no reproduction of any part may take place without the written permission of Cambridge University Press.

First published 2017

Printed in the United States of America by Sheridan Books, Inc.

A catalogue record for this publication is available from the British Library.

Library of Congress Cataloging-in-Publication Data
NAMES: Ketchley, Neil, author
TITLE: Egypt in a time of revolution : contentious politics and the Arab Spring / Neil Ketchley.
OTHER TITLES: Cambridge studies in contentious politics.
DESCRIPTION: Cambridge, United Kingdom : Cambridge University Press, 2017. |
Series: Cambridge studies in contentious politics | Includes bibliographical references.
IDENTIFIERS: LCCN 2016053990 | ISBN 9781107184978
SUBJECTS: LCSH: Arab Spring, 2010– | Egypt – Politics and government – 21st century.
| Revolutions – Egypt – History – 21st century. | Protest
movements – Egypt – History – 21st century.
CLASSIFICATION: LCC DT107.88 .K42 2017 | DDC 962.05/5–dc23
LC record available at https://lccn.loc.gov/2016053990

ISBN 978-1-107-18497-8 Hardback
ISBN 978-1-316-63622-0 Paperback

Cambridge University Press has no responsibility for the persistence or accuracy of URLs for external or third-party Internet Web sites referred to in this publication and does not guarantee that any content on such Web sites is, or will remain, accurate or appropriate.

For Lamiaa, Isobel, and Imogen

Contents

Figures

Tables

Preface and Acknowledgments

On 25 January 2011, several thousand Egyptians outmaneuvered Interior Ministry-controlled police to reach Midan al-Tahrir in downtown Cairo, setting the scene for eighteen days of rambunctious mass protests against the regime of Husni Mubarak. When I arrived in Egypt in May 2011, Mubarak had already left Cairo for self-imposed exile in Sharm El-Shaykh, but his security state remained intact. Meanwhile, Egyptians, many of whom hoped to deepen the gains of the Revolution, continued to stage daily protests across the country. With Midan al-Tahrir intermittently occupied and labor protests breaking out across the country, other parties and movements demobilized, choosing to pursue their claims through the ballot box. *Egypt in a Time of Revolution* tells that story: how Egyptians banded together against authoritarianism, how the revolutionary coalition that ousted Mubarak divided in the years that followed, and how elements within Mubarak's state conspired to defeat further challenges from below.

I never planned to write a book about contemporary Egyptian politics. I left Damascus for Cairo in the revolutionary spring of 2011 to begin researching three cases of "Islamist" mobilization in the interwar era. It did not initially occur to me to make the events of January–February 2011 the focus of my research. The Egyptian National Archives had other ideas. And so, while the authorities mulled over my application for a reader's pass, I began to collect newspapers and write down my conversations with protestors. This book is the result. To John Sidel, I owe a profound debt. His generosity, intellectual range, and guidance have all contributed immensely to this project, even as it evolved into a study of the diverse forms of contentious politics that I came to witness first-hand in Egypt. And if the title of the book recalls Benedict Anderson's (2006

[1972]) classic study of the Indonesian Revolution, it is thanks to the influence of John 'Ibn Anderson' Sidel, who has pushed me to think and to read comparatively, to the extent that it now seems only natural to locate this key episode from the Arab Spring beside other instances of mass mobilization and contentious politics found in Southeast Asia and beyond. Similarly, John Chalcraft was an essential source of help and guidance. He convinced me, in the autumn of 2013, to focus on Egypt and more contemporaneous street-level mobilization, thereby freeing me from my guilt about abandoning the interwar period.

Eitan Alimi, Morten S. Andersen, Walter Armbrust, Mark Beissinger, Dina Bishara, John Breuilly, Steven Brooke, Killian Clarke, Randall Collins, Brecht De Smet, Sarah ElMasry, Youssef El Chazli, Sarah ElMasry, Hannah ElSisi, Fawaz Gerges, Jeroen Gunning, Heather Hamill, Navid Hassanpour, Sune Haugbølle, Amy Austin Holmes, Ali Kadivar, Walid Kazziha, Laleh Khalili, George Lawson, Yasmine Laveille, Gauthier Marchais, Kevin Mazur, Nawal Mustafa, Patrick Präg, Lucie Ryzova, Atef Said, Hannah Scott Deuchar, Lamiaa Shehata, Kathryn Stapley, Richard Stewart, Andrea Teti, Felix Tropf, Elizabeth Trott, and Victor Willi gave feedback, suggestions, and encouragement on various aspects of the project. At Oxford, Michael Biggs was a superlative collaborator and mentor. It was Michael who first encouraged me to compile an event catalogue in the dark days of 2013 – and he has been a crucial source of advice and friendship ever since. Christopher Barrie and Michael Farquhar improved the manuscript immeasurably with their smart comments and salutary criticism. So too, Sidney Tarrow was unfailingly generous with his sage advice and critical feedback. At Cambridge, Lew Batemen, Robert Dreesen, Brianda Reyes, and Neil Ryan oversaw the journey from manuscript to publication. Llinos Edwards and Hannah Scott Deucher proofread various chapter drafts, and AElfwine Mischler oversaw the indexing.

I thank also my informants, several of whom read chapter drafts and offered detailed feedback and comments on the project. These brave and creative men and women, young Muslim Brothers and Muslim Sisters, lifelong activists and accidental revolutionaries, are the protagonists of this book, and I can only hope that they recognize themselves and their exploits in its pages. I am particularly grateful to Belal, Youssef, Esraa, and Abdullah for introducing me to members of the anti-coup movement, and to Muhammad for facilitating interviews with Tamarrod's leadership.

The book began life as a doctoral dissertation written in the Department of Government at the London School of Economics and Political Science (LSE). The research was funded by a Doctoral Training Centre Studentship from the Economic and Social Research Council. Janet Ketchley made all things possible. Paul Ketchley housed our small family while I wrote up my dissertation. Before I embarked on my doctoral studies, Richard and Judith Stewart supported me during a year spent studying Arabic at Damascus University in 2009. That study was also made possible by a Captain F. G. Boot language scholarship from the Culters' Guild. In 2010, the LSE Government Department paid for me to complete an intensive Arabic language summer school at Institut français du Proche-Orient (IFPO) Aleppo, while a Study Abroad Studentship from the Leverhulme Trust allowed me to spend the 2010–2011 academic year at IFPO in Damascus for language training and further study. The Leverhulme Trust also supported an eight-month Visiting Research Fellowship in the Department of Political Science at the American University in Cairo from May to December 2011. The book draws on data collected during fieldwork supported by the John Fell OUP Fund and the Project on Middle East Political Science. Sarah ElMasry and Christopher Barrie provided invaluable research assistance. The manuscript was completed while I was a Hulme Postdoctoral Research Fellow at Brasenose College, University of Oxford.

Chapter 3 was published as an article in *Comparative Studies in Society and History* (Ketchley 2014a). I gratefully acknowledge the managing editor David Akins and the anonymous reviewers for their comments. The manuscript has also benefited from comments and feedback received at the annual conferences of the American Political Science Association, the American Sociological Association, the British Society for Middle Eastern Studies, and the Middle East Studies Association, as well as at workshops and seminars held at the LSE and the University of Oxford.

This book was borne from my shared life and adventures with Lamiaa Shehata and Isobel Shehata-Ketchley. It is to them, and to my late sister Imogen Ketchley, that I dedicate all of the best ideas and none of the shortcomings.

A Note on Transliteration

I have used a simplified version of the *International Journal of Middle East Studies* transliteration system when rendering Arabic words into the Latin alphabet. Diacritics are used for the Arabic letters 'ayn (') and hamza ('), as well as the long vowels alif (ā), wāw (ū), and ya' (ī). When quoting chants or songs, I follow the Egyptian pronunciation and use g (gīm) instead of j (jīm) and ' (hamza) for q (qāf). Likewise, I give "el" rather than "al" for the definite article and elide short and long vowels where appropriate. I also use Anglicized variants of places and names, which are spelt according to convention.

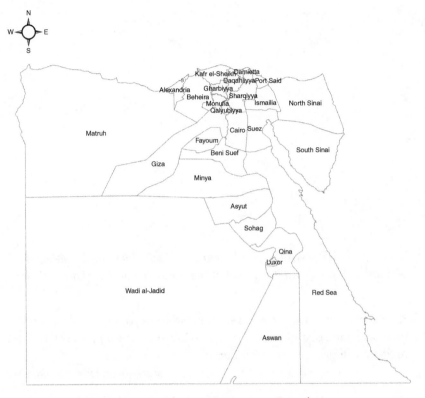

Map of Egypt with 2011 Governorate Boundaries.

Nasā'ih minna lil-yunāniyīn: Tubtak fī iydak, kimamtak 'ala wishak, khamirtak fī gibak wa illi yi'ūlak al-maglis al-'askarī hayehmi al-thawra, 'atta'u.

Advice from us to the Greeks: keep your stone in your hand, your scarf on your face and yeast in your pocket, and kill anyone who tells you that the military will protect the revolution.

Egyptian activist during Greek anti-austerity protests, 12 Feb. 2012

Introduction

Five Snapshots of Contention

- **25 January 2011.** Police in the Suez open fire on anti-Mubarak protestors as they leave Midan al-Isaaf and head for the governorate building. By the early evening, several protestors have been killed in violent clashes with security forces. The next day, local residents and the relatives of the martyrs hold a demonstration outside of the Arbayeen district police station in the Suez. As the crowd swells to several hundred, police officers fire tear gas and birdshot in an attempt to disperse the demonstrators. Young men respond by letting off fireworks and throwing Molotov cocktails. By nightfall, the police station is on fire.
- **2 February 2011.** A column of pro-Mubarak *baltigiyya* (approximately, thugs) approaches the Talaat Harb entrance to Midan al-Tahrir in downtown Cairo. An army officer confronts the thugs. Brandishing his pistol, he fires repeatedly in the air. When the thugs retreat, anti-Mubarak protestors rush to embrace the officer, chanting, "The army and the people are one hand." Weeks later, large posters and banners depicting the scene are erected outside military bases and army checkpoints across the country.
- **22 November 2011.** Protestors throw stones at a phalanx of soldiers, police, and Central Security Force (CSF) units stationed on Muhammad Mahmoud Street, a road leading from Midan al-Tahrir to the Interior Ministry. Security forces respond with volleys of tear gas and birdshot, while young men on motorcycles ferry wounded protestors to improvised field hospitals. Secular activists in the Midan

confront a senior Muslim Brother, whom they denounce for selling out the Revolution for electoral gain. Fearing for his safety, the Muslim Brother withdraws from Tahrir.

- **30 June 2013.** Uniformed police officers lead a protest march from outside of the Police Officers' Club in Giza to Midan al-Tahrir, calling on the military to remove Islamist president Muhammad Mursi. The crowd of ostensibly civilian protestors wave Egyptian flags and chant, "The police and the people are one hand." As large crowds continue to take to Tahrir, a retired Egyptian army general is interviewed on *CNN*, where he proclaims that 33 million Egyptians have taken to the streets to call for new presidential elections.
- **14 August 2013.** Egyptian army bulldozers and heavily armed police take up positions around a Muslim Brother protest occupation in Midan Raba'a al-Adawiyya, a public square in Eastern Cairo. In the hours that follow, police and military personnel launch a sustained assault on the forty-seven-day-old occupation, killing over 900 protestors in what Human Rights Watch (2013) describe as "the most serious incident of mass unlawful killings in modern Egyptian history."

These vignettes of collective violence, mass mobilization, and repression are taken from the key moments and episodes of contentious street politics witnessed in Egypt since 2011. When read together, these snapshots encapsulate the empirical focus and explanatory task of this book: how an authoritarian regime came under sustained attack from below only to violently resurrect itself, and what this process can teach us about the prospects and legacies of contentious politics in the Middle East and North Africa after the Arab Spring.

This restoration was not inevitable. When Husni Mubarak resigned on 11 February 2011, following eighteen days of unruly and boisterous mass protests in the streets and squares of Egypt's cities, many believed that a definitive rupture had occurred. Over subsequent months and years, however, a parlous and deeply flawed democratic transition, unfolding under the direction of the Supreme Council of the Armed Forces (SCAF), revealed a new set of problems and ambiguities for Egypt's self-styled "revolutionaries." With military powers and old regime prerogatives still intact, the rapidly convened coalition of forces that had come together in Midan al-Tahrir and elsewhere divided, as narrow partisanship trumped coalition building.

The eventual triumph of the Muslim Brothers' candidate Muhammad Mursi in the second round of presidential elections held in June 2012 seemed to presage a new institutional rubric in which the state apparatus would, at the very least, be brought under democratic control, but instead revived abiding anxieties and uncertainties about Islamist takeover and dictatorial intent. Two years after Mubarak's removal, a second round of mass protests, this time against Mursi's presidency, paved the way for a military coup that took place on 3 July 2013, precipitating an ongoing process of elite reconstitution that has since seen Abdel Fatah al-Sisi, a field marshal and former defense minister, installed as president in an elliptical return to Mubarak-style authoritarianism.

After a prolonged absence, the police fully redeployed to the streets of Egypt's cities, better armed and more numerous than before, charged with enforcing a new protest law that criminalizes opposition to the military-backed government. In the year following the 2013 coup, security forces killed over 3,000 protestors, while tens of thousands of regime opponents were detained. The arm of Egyptian State Security tasked with monitoring Egypt's Islamist movements and political dissidents, which was nominally disbanded following the 25th January Revolution, was formally reconstituted. A reinvigorated elite-level politics has not produced a model of governance responsive to protestors' original demands for "'aīsh, hurriyya, 'adāla igtimā'iyya" (bread, freedom, social justice). Meanwhile, human dignity (karāma insānjyya), which sometimes replaces social justice as the third demand, continues to be routinely violated through the state's use of torture and calibrated sexual violence against its opponents.

Against this backdrop of disappointments, reversals and retrenchments, the trajectories and legacies of the 25th January Revolution present important and interrelated puzzles for political sociologists and observers of the 2011 Arab Spring alike. How did Egyptians overthrow a seemingly well-fortified dictator of three decades in less than three weeks? How can we account for the position of the military during the eighteen days of mass mobilization? What explains the derailing of democratic transition in post-Mubarak Egypt? Why did the 25th January revolutionary coalition split? How did old regime forces engineer a return to authoritarian rule? How has repression shaped the possibilities for contentious collective action in post-coup Egypt? From a series of vantage points and seeking processual, agent-centered, and bottom-up explanations, this book shows that these puzzles, and the broader patterns of political change in post-Mubarak Egypt, can only be understood by paying close attention to the evolving dynamics of contentious politics witnessed in Egypt since 2011.

EGYPT IN A TIME OF REVOLUTION

Was the 25th January Revolution a revolution? The answer to this question has important analytical implications for how we account for the events of January–February 2011 and what followed. On the one hand, a significant number of Egyptians certainly referred to it as such. My informants frequently prefaced their recollection of events with *"fi ayām al-thawra..."* (in the days of the revolution) or *"fi wa't al-thawra ... "* (in the time of the revolution). Those who had joined the protests in Midan al-Tahrir and elsewhere were *"thuwār"* (revolutionaries).[1] Non-participants were members of *"hizb al-kanaba"* (the party of the sofa), while the revolution's opponents were *"al-nizām"* (the regime), and later *"al-filūl"* (literally, the remnants [of the regime]). Protestors killed during the mobilization were *"shuhadā' thawrat khamsa wa 'ishrīn yanāyir"* (martyrs of the 25th January Revolution). This "revolutionary idiom" (Sewell 1979), replete with a chorus of jokes, put-downs, and internet memes, infiltrated newspaper coverage, television chat shows, and even the press releases issued by the SCAF in the year following Mubarak's departure. Such a process of naming and narration was undeniably significant, not only in constituting the lived experiences of anti-Mubarak protestors (El Chazli 2015), but also in legitimizing and authenticating protestors' demands and expectations in light of the country's revolutionary heritage (Sabaseviciute 2011; Cole 2014; see also Selbin 2010).

On the other hand, it seems much harder to justify an analytical categorization of "revolution" when reflecting on the trajectory of post-Mubarak politics, even given that the scholarly definition of what constitutes a revolution has expanded considerably in the past few decades. A new literature on contemporary revolutions argues that the revolutions of the late twentieth century onwards differ in several important ways from those that preceded them. If the classic model of a "social revolution" (Skocpol 1979) involved protracted and frequently violent mobilizations to transform the social and economic order of semi-agrarian societies, today's "revolutions" are found to be "negotiated" (Lawson 2005), "electoral" (Bunce and Wolchik 2006), "non-violent" (Nepstad 2011), "unarmed" (Ritter 2014), and at least nominally, "democratic" (Thompson 2003)[2] in their ethos. Contemporary revolutions are more

---

[1] Later, to be a "revolutionary" narrowed considerably and came to be marked by a double rejection of the old regime and the Muslim Brothers.

[2] For a careful and thoughtful critique of "democratic revolutions," see Beissinger (2013).

urban and compact, lasting only weeks or months (Beissinger 2013; 2014), while the new measure of revolutionary "success" is increasingly the ousting of an incumbent authoritarian leader (Nepstad 2011: xiv). According to this definition, revolutions are, therefore, more a "mode of regime change" (Beissinger 2014), than a project of radical – political, social or economic – transformation (see Goldstone 1991; Goodwin 2001). As such, revolutions are increasingly seen as pathways to political liberalization, which strengthen rather than challenge the liberal international order (Lawson 2012: 12).

Scholars working in this vein have been quick to adopt the 25th January Revolution as evidence of this new modality of revolutionary action (Nepstad 2011: xv; Beissinger 2013: 574, 2014; Lawson 2015; Ritter 2014). But despite several tentative parallels that can be drawn with the 25th January repertoire of contention, political developments in Egypt in the three years and more since Mubarak's demise suggest that this designation was premature. Under the SCAF's guardianship, the Mubarak-era state was never upended, and it remains resolutely intact today. Nor, as I will go on to show, did the 2011–2012 parliamentary and 2012 presidential elections in Egypt result in civilians exercising meaningful democratic control over the state. Given all this, it seems clear that no democratic or political revolution, even in the expanded analytical sense, can be said to have occurred.

So, what do I mean by the 25th January Revolution? According to my analysis, the eighteen days of the 25th January Revolution are better captured by the concept of a "revolutionary situation" (Tilly 1978: ch.7, 2006: ch.7; El-Ghobashy 2011) in which an alternative claim to sovereignty in the name of "the people" (*al-sha'b*) formed the basis of a truly countrywide mobilization against the regime of Husni Mubarak. By revolutionary situation, I mean a conjunctural episode involving: "1) contenders or coalitions of contenders advancing exclusive competing claims to control of the state or some segment of it; 2) commitment to those claims by a significant segment of the citizenry; 3) incapacity or unwillingness of rulers to suppress the alternative coalition and/or commitment to its claims" (Tilly 2006: 159).[3] Egypt's revolutionary situation was brought about by anti-police violence, mass mobilization in the country's squares and main roads, and fraternization with the military – but it was never properly established and quickly subsided into

---

[3] For a useful discussion on the sociology of revolutionary situations, see Bennani-Chraïbi and Fillieule (2015).

a conventional democratic transition on 11 February 2011, following which constitutional and electoral forums came to structure a formal political process that unfolded under the direction of the military.[4]

Despite the initial revolutionary situation in Egypt being quickly averted, revolutionary expectations and the new dynamics of contentious politics arising from the eighteen days of mass protest continued to structure, shape, and energize political life. In what was for many a "time of revolution," Egyptians continued to mobilize. Figure 1.1 shows the frequency and size of contentious events in 2011. A massive strike wave by organized (and unorganized) labor, which began in the final days of the 25th January Revolution, was accompanied by local residents mobilizing across the governorates in a bid to achieve redress for their longstanding grievances (see Barrie and Ketchley 2016). There were even several episodes when the country appeared poised to return to a revolutionary situation: for instance, during the events of Muhammad Mahmoud Street in late November 2011, when protestors tried, unsuccessfully, to recreate the conditions of early 2011 and replace the SCAF with a civilian-led government.

These revolutionary aspirations were efficiently harnessed and redeployed on 30 June 2013, when both secular activists and old regime forces took to the streets in opposition to the divisive presidency of Muhammad Mursi. Egypt's democratic transition failed three days later, on 3 July 2013, following the military coup. In the subsequent period, the revolutionary idiom of 2011 was superseded by a discourse of *haybat al-dawla* (awe of the state), employed to justify several regime-orchestrated massacres of pro-Mursi supporters, the detention of many

---

[4] An alternative perspective argues that a "long-term revolutionary process" (Achcar 2013: 17; see also Abdelrahman 2014) is underway in Egypt that will continue so long as the underlying socio-economic grievances that gave rise to the Arab Spring remain unaddressed. Operating in a Marxian, historical materialist vein, the longue durée view cautions against prematurely calling time on whether the 25th January Revolution was or was not a revolution, deduced from short-term successes or failures. Unfortunately, it is difficult to see how this analysis survives the events of 3 July 2013 and the subsequent crackdown. Revolutions, as "second wave historical sociology" (Adams, Clemens, and Orloff 2005) has argued (Skocpol 1979; Goldstone 1991; Tilly 1993; Goodwin 2001; Foran 2005), do not simply flow from the objective contradictions of capitalism and class; rather, they unfold via particular pathways of state breakdown and require both coherent organizations capable of weathering sustained repression and innovative tactics to broker new alliances and mount effective challenges to the regime's apparatus of coercion. For these reasons, revolutionary outcomes, Tilly (1978: ch. 7) reminds us, remain extraordinary and exceptional events, precisely because most revolutionary situations and revolutionary forces are defeated by incumbent powers.

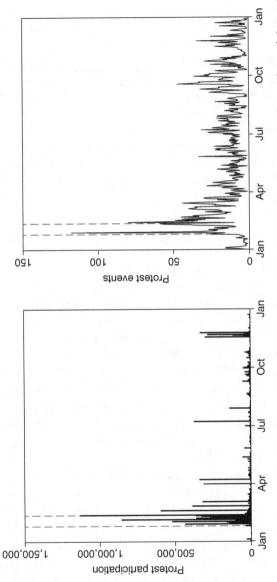

FIGURE 1.1 Protest participation and frequency, 2011–2012. Notes: The dashed lines mark the eighteen days of the 25th January Revolution.

7

of those who instigated the mobilization against Mubarak, and a new protest law. An anti-coup movement led by the Muslim Brothers launched daily street protests using a <u>repertoire of contention</u> evolving out of that employed in the 25th January Revolution. However, their efforts were quickly blunted by unprecedented repression, a fragmented political landscape (a consequence of the failed democratic transition), the anti-coup protestors' refusal to take up arms, <u>the tendency of Egypt's poorest to equate <u>protest with</u> socioeconomic threat</u> (Chalcraft 2014: 179), and international and regional support for the consolidation of the military-backed regime.

Against this backdrop, *thawrat khamsa wa 'ishrīn yanāyir* (the 25th of January Revolution) remains commonly accepted shorthand in Egypt for referring to the eighteen days of popular protest that began on 25 January and which ended with the resignation of Hosni Mubarak. It is in this sense that I use it.

CONTENTIOUS POLITICS

How can we place the 25th January Revolution, its trajectories and legacies within a broader scheme of social and political explanation? The heuristic adopted in this book is informed, most obviously, by the contentious politics literature associated with Doug McAdam, Sidney Tarrow, and Charles Tilly's (2001) *Dynamics of Contention* (DOC). That work sought to decompartmentalize the study of revolution, social movements, riots and other modes of transgressive collective action, and view them instead as belonging to a shared continuum of episodic, public and collective claim making. Under this common rubric, contentious politics is thus defined as "episodic, public, collective interaction among makers of claims and their objects when (a) at least one government is a claimant, an object of claims, or a party to the claims and (b) the claims would, if realized, affect the interests of at least one of the claimants" (Ibid.: 5).

Viewed in this mode, the 25th January Revolution, the post-Mubarak democratic transition and the anti-coup mobilization do not represent distinct processes or phenomena but can be understood by analyzing who is making claims, how those claims are made, the objects of those claims and regime responses to claim making. As Sidney Tarrow usefully sets out:

Within this arena, movements intersect with each other and with institutional actors in a dynamic process of move, countermove, adjustment and negotiation.

That process includes claim making, responses to the actions of elites – repressive, facilitative or both – and the intervention of third parties, who often take advantage of the opportunities created by these conflicts to advance their own claims. *The outcomes of these intersections, in turn, are how a polity evolves.*

(2012: 3; my emphasis added)

According to this perspective, the diverse ways in which Egyptians banded together to challenge the status quo are not simply manifestations of grievances to be explained, but were, in themselves, constitutive of the post-Mubarak political process. In this, to echo Dan Slater (2010: 5), to make sense of the patterns of political change in Egypt and the trajectory of the Arab Spring more broadly, we must account for "what contentious politics can explain in its own right."[5]

Here, my mode and manner of analysis is necessarily agentic and relational, treating "social interaction, social ties, communication and conversation not merely as expressions of structure, rationality, consciousness, or culture but as active sites of creation and change" (McAdam, Tarrow, and Tilly 2001: 22). As Tilly (2003: 5–8) notes, the conventional explanatory strategy pursued by social scientists has been to privilege either the *ideas* of participants, or their *behavior*. In contrast, "Relation people make transactions among persons and groups far more central than do idea and behavior people. They argue that humans develop their personalities and practices through interchanges with other humans, and that the interchanges themselves always involve a degree of negotiation and creativity" (Ibid.: 5–6).[6] In the empirical chapters that follow, I use this insight to develop a conjunctural and interactive account of the 25th January Revolution and the post-Mubarak political process, grounding my explanation in a series of relationships: between collective violence and nonviolent activism, protestors and security forces, elections and contentious collective action, elites and street protest movements, and repression and mass mobilization. In doing so, I show how a relational ontology can be employed to interrogate several key assumptions of the literature on civil resistance, emotions, democratization, authoritarian retrenchment, and repression.

Before then, a digression on one of the key analytical concepts that structures this book and its argument is germane. In the argot of the contentious politics literature, the ways in which Egyptians make claims is

---

[5] For two accounts of the formative history of contentious politics in making the MENA region, see Barrie (2016) and Chalcraft (2016).
[6] For the classic statement on relational sociology, see Emirbayer (1997).

constrained by the available "repertoire of contention." Tilly (1977) first introduced the "repertoire" metaphor to describe the evolving subset of protest tactics used in France between the seventeenth and twentieth centuries. This drew on one of his earliest and arguably most productive insights (1978: ch.6): that when people act collectively, they only do so in a limited number of ways. Expanding upon this in later works, Tilly argued that:

> Repertoires are learned cultural creations, but they do not descend from abstract philosophy or take shape as a result of political propaganda; they emerge from struggle. People learn to break windows in protest, attack pilloried prisoners, tear down dishonored houses, stage public marches, petition, hold formal meetings, organize special-interest associations. At any point in history, however, they learn only a rather small number of alternative ways to act collectively. The limits of that learning, plus the fact that potential collaborators and antagonists likewise have learned a relatively limited set of means, constrain the choices available for collective interaction. (1995: 41–42)

Michael Biggs (2013: 408–409) has reformulated Tilly's stance into two interrelated propositions: "repetition is far more likely than adoption; adoption is far more likely than invention." In Egypt, in the period between 2011 and 2014, the repertoire of contention was highly repetitive. This is well captured in Figure 1.2, which classifies protest events by their tactics during the eighteen days of the 25th January Revolution, the events of Muhammad Mahmoud Street, the 30 June protests, and the anti-coup mobilization. Four tactics – occupations, sit-ins, demonstrations, and marches – predominated, and were used in over 75 percent of protest events in each episode.

Just as the dynamics of mobilization in Egypt were constrained by the available modalities of claim making, they were also delimited by the spaces and ecologies of protest (see Sewell 2001; Tilly 2000). During the first days of the 25th January Revolution, a powerful and easily replicable model for mobilization emerged in Cairo that then diffused throughout Egypt and then other Arab Spring countries: protestors left designated mosques following prayer to join up with other protestors in public squares and main arterial roads. Mubarak's ousting on 11 February 2011 underlined the efficacy (and legitimacy) of this model, leading to its emulation by a multitude of other political actors in the years that followed, including old regime holdovers, Islamists, local residents, and workers in Egypt and beyond (e.g., Ketchley 2013; 2016). With time, security forces adapted to protestors' tactics and their use of space by targeting key nodes in the spaces of contention. How protestors responded to these countermeasures, and

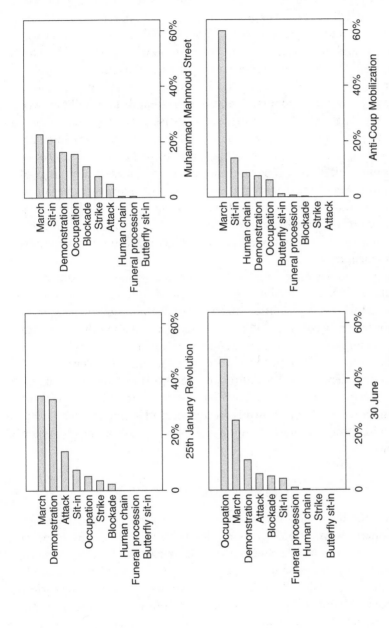

FIGURE 1.2 Major protest episodes by their tactics, 2011–2014.

the implications of regime learning for future episodes of mass mobilization in Egypt, will be a topic for later chapters.

Repertoires are, in turn, related to the broader political process. In line with Tilly's (2006) expectations, the Egyptian repertoire of contention delimited the possibilities of popular politics: this process was shaped by, and in turn shaped, the Egyptian political regime; especially the regime's degree of democratic participation and its capacity to police dissent. A powerful illustration of this approach is presented in Tilly's (1995; 1997) work on popular contention in Great Britain. Tilly showed that by the late eighteenth century the increasingly visible role of elections and parliament in organizing public life led to the "parliamentarization of contention," meaning that parliament became an object of contention. This shift was in turn inflected in the means and timings of contention. Marches, demonstrations, petitions, and rallies began to revolve around single issues and parliamentary debates. Short term objectives previously achieved by violent means were replaced by longer-term struggles and associational activities structured around the rhythms of parliamentary life.

In contemporary Egypt, we see an accelerated version of a process not dissimilar to that described here by Tilly. The demobilizing pressures of the post-Mubarak democratic transition saw certain movements pursue more routine, procedural politics as a consequence of a shift in the sites of claim making – from the contentious street to the chambers of a parliament – as the initial revolutionary situation folded into a more conventional democratic breakthrough (see also Robertson 2010: ch.6). Other movements and groups, however, continued to pursue their goals through the streets. Explaining this divergence, and its implications for the 25th January revolutionary coalition, will be a key task in the discussion to come.

METHODS AND DATA

To chart the dynamics of contentious politics that emerged from the 25th January Revolution, this book draws on over two years of field-work, involving multiple research trips, carried out in Egypt between 2011 and 2015. It marshals several different types of evidence, including event data, fatality data, informant testimony, newspaper articles, video footage, and still photography. In the following section, I briefly summarize my data collection methods, while considering several strategies for combining and triangulating different kinds of qualitative and quantitative data to study contentious collective action in Egypt and beyond.

Event Catalog

An event catalog is a "set of descriptions of multiple social interactions collected from a delimited set of sources according to relatively uniform procedures" (Tilly 2002: 249). Event catalogs have a long history in the study of contentious politics (e.g., Tilly, Tilly and Tilly 1975; Tilly 1995), with data usually drawn from newspapers, journals, and periodicals. The event catalog from which I draw contains detailed information on 8,454 protest events, and encompasses the 25th January Revolution, the first year of the post-Mubarak democratic transition, the anti-Mursi mobilization, and the first six months of the post-coup period. It primarily derives from protest reports published in four Egyptian national newspapers, *al-Masry al-Youm*, *al-Dostor*, *al-Shorouk*, and the Muslim Brothers' Freedom and Justice Party (FJP) newspaper, *al-Hurriyya wal-'Adala*. Drawing on multiple sources helps to address known problems of underreporting, fact-checking, and cross-referencing in event catalogs drawn from newspapers (e.g., Franzosi 1987; Maney and Oliver 2001; Earl et al. 2004). I also compared newspaper reports to videos of protests uploaded to social media, as well as human rights reporting of repression. Taken together, this data allows for the first systematic account of Mubarak's overthrow and what came afterwards. The source material, data verification, coding strategies, and variables for the event catalog are summarized in the appendix.

Interviews

As well as collecting comprehensive protest event data, I also conducted eighty semi-structured interviews in both Arabic and English. Since protestors are a relatively closed population, my primary method for selecting informants was snowball-based sampling. I aimed to conclude every interview by asking my informants whether they could introduce me to anyone who they thought could contribute to my research. I also conducted targeted interviews in which I approached individuals who had a public biography that made them of interest. I conducted follow-up interviews on several occasions. I have also drawn on interviews conducted through personal correspondence with protestors and activists who were not available for face-to-face interviews.

With regard to citing testimony and considerations of anonymity, I made it clear to informants that I would use only their first names. This was due to the risks informants face when speaking to foreign researchers on sensitive topics such as the police, the military, or the Muslim Brothers. Because of the frequency of certain names, I have used a single digit to distinguish between informants, e.g., Abdullah 1, Abdullah 2, and Abdullah 3. On several occasions when conducting interviews with established political figures, I gained consent to use the informant's full name. When informants asked to be quoted anonymously, I have referenced testimony by the informant's role, e.g., "interview with Muslim Brother" or "interview with Journalist."

Video and Photographs

Within hours of protestors reaching Midan al-Tahrir, on 25 January 2011, still photographs and video footage uploaded to social media sites had already come to constitute a searchable digital archive. The digitization of social processes and the ubiquity of camera-equipped mobile phones present new opportunities to study contentious politics. I assembled a photographic and video archive of protest events in Egypt from internet-based searches[7] and the personal "archives" that informants had saved on mobile phones, memory sticks, and hard drives. Video footage and still photographs uploaded to social media frequently had time stamps were uploaded shortly after the event that they captured, or included captions providing additional context,[8] while visual materials obtained from informants were accompanied by detailed commentaries of the events in question.

Of course, video footage and still photographs have limitations. Both show events in Egypt in real time, and thus one never sees the political process directly.[9] Instead, the macro is constructed through concepts and metaphors. This requires large amounts of data with snippets of contentious claim making sutured together to give a sense of the larger repertoire. With this kind of detective work, video footage and still photographs allow us to view dimensions of contentious episodes in Egypt that might

---

[7] I primarily searched YouTube, Bambuser, and Flickr – sites that support Arabic-language search terms and which are popular in Egypt.

[8] Most social media sites provide a function to contact the video uploader. For one video uploaded to YouTube, showing protestors attacking army vehicles as they deployed to Midan al-Tahrir on the night of 28 January, the video uploader went on to become a key informant who introduced me to other protestors present in Tahrir that night.

[9] I owe this point to Randall Collins (personal correspondence 9 Sept. 2013).

otherwise fall beneath the threshold of historical visibility. We also get a very different perspective on how protests unfolded. Captured in real time, contention appears unruly and emotional, with micro-interactions appearing to be formative in explaining situational outcomes (Collins 2008).

THE STRUCTURE OF THE BOOK

The chapters that make up this book consider both the causes and the consequences of Mubarak's removal at the hands of irrepressible "people power." In this, I follow a tripartite periodization of Egyptian politics, covering the eighteen days of mass mobilization, the democratic transition, and the post-coup period.

This introductory chapter is followed by a chapter that focuses on the first three days of the 25 January Revolution. When protestors outmaneuvered Interior Ministry-controlled CSF units to reach Midan al-Tahrir on 25 January 2011, they triggered protests in the streets and squares of Egyptian cities across the country. Scaling participation rates from the Arab Barometer's (2011) survey up to the total population suggests that over 6 million Egyptians took to the streets over this period (Beissinger, Jamal, and Mazur 2015: 23). Other scholarly studies, citing journalists' and informants' estimates, put that number even higher – between 15 and 20 million anti-Mubarak protestors (e.g., Gunning and Baron 2013: 164). This chapter questions these figures. Using the event catalog, it suggests that protest participation was probably considerably smaller than is currently assumed, and that the largest protests occurred over a week after the mobilization began. While this finding seems to confirm Lichbach's (1995) rule that no more than 5 percent of a national population mobilizes at any one time, it does problematize how protest scaled-up and overcame Mubarak's national security state. Chapter 2 takes up this puzzle, shedding light on a wave of anti-police violence that peaked on 28 January, and which led to the routing of a key wing of Mubarak's repressive apparatus, and thus helping to bring about a revolutionary situation. Here, the chapter problematizes accounts of the 25th January Revolution that stress the singular efficacy of nonviolent contention in bringing about Mubarak's overthrow, pointing instead to a dynamic interplay between collective violence and nonviolent contention during the critical early phase of the mobilization.

With a view to explaining the military's role during the 25th January Revolution, Chapter 3 picks up events on the early evening of 28 January.

Using video evidence, still photographs, Egyptian newspaper reports, and informant testimony, it develops a focused account of the micro-interactive dimensions of protestor-soldier relations that developed in and around Midan al-Tahrir. The practices that came out of these encounters, this chapter shows, were situational and should be understood vis-à-vis an improvised fraternization repertoire that made immediate, emotional claims on the loyalty of regime forces. Fraternization contained military opposition to the mobilization and the possibilities for protestor-soldier violence through the forging of a precarious solidarity, which was later appropriated by the SCAF to legitimize its assumption of executive powers in the post-Mubarak democratic transition.

Turning to the post-Mubarak democratic transition, Chapter 4 draws on interviews with Muslim Brothers, the movement's publications, and the event catalog. It begins by considering the part played by the Muslim Brothers in the 25th January Revolution and the nature of the revolutionary coalition that emerged in Egypt's streets and squares. It then spotlights the Brothers' demobilization and privileging of electoral and constitutional forums in the first eighteen months of the transition. The chapter explores how the Brothers' decision to sit out further protests to focus on elections facilitated the breakup of the revolutionary coalition that had ousted Mubarak and insulated the SCAF from street-level mobilization, leaving bad legacies for Mursi's year in office.

Chapter 5 considers the events leading up to the 3 July 2013 coup. On 30 June 2013, massive protests were held in Midan al-Tahrir and outside the presidential palace calling for early presidential elections and the resignation of elected Islamist president Muhammad Mursi. Smaller protests were held in the governorates. Drawing on informant testimony, video footage, newspaper accounts, and event data, this chapter finds the 30 June protests to be problematically rule-bound, with security forces dictating the sites and targets of protest. Here, the chapter shows how the army and the police, in ways reminiscent of "elite-orchestrated" protest in other contexts, facilitated and then co-opted the 30 June protests that would pave the way for Mursi's removal and a full blown return to military rule.

The final substantive chapter maps the patterns of mobilization and demobilization after the 3 July 2013 coup. Chapter 6 begins by examining the Muslim Brothers' decision to counter-mobilize in the weeks before the coup. Drawing on interviews with leading Muslim Brothers and anti-coup activists, it traces the origins of the anti-coup movement to a decision in December 2012 by the Muslim Brothers to establish a street presence to defend Mursi's presidency, and considers the events leading up to the 3 July coup, the Brothers' strategy of occupying public squares, and the formation of new "against the coup" movements. Using event data and informant testimony, the chapter then charts how the repertoire, sites, and timings of anti-coup contention were transformed by repression following the killing of over a thousand anti-coup protestors of 14 August 2014.

A concluding chapter summarizes the book's findings and considers several unresolved questions and silences in the study of contentious politics, the 25th January Egyptian Revolution, and the Arab Spring.

2

Collective Violence

Khalās al- sha'b rakab kida (It's over, the people are in control now)

Police officer in Alexandria, 28 Jan. 2011

On 25 January 2011, Egyptian police shot and killed Mustafa Ragab Mahmoud, a nineteen-year-old high school dropout, in the Arbayeen district of the Suez.[1] Mahmoud, one of several thousand anti-Mubarak protesters who had taken to the streets that day, was the first martyr of the 25th January Revolution. By the evening of 25 January and following violent clashes with the police, three more protestors had died in the Suez, and over a hundred were wounded. In response to the killings, local residents and the relatives of the martyrs laid siege to the Arbayeen district police station. Armed with Molotov cocktails and other improvised weapons, the protestors skirmished with police units, before setting fire to the police station and a number of police vehicles.[2] Several police checkpoints, as well as the headquarters of Mubarak's National Democratic Party, were also attacked.

---

[1] Mustafa Ragab Mahmoud lived with his widowed mother and four sisters in the neighboring district of al-Ganayen, where he worked in a fertilizer plant. Interestingly, he does not appear to have been politically active prior to the outbreak of protest on 25 January. Though still a relatively unknown figure both inside and outside Egypt, several Arabic-language documentaries have chronicled Mahmoud's life and death. See, e.g., YouTube video (3 Jan. 2012) "*Qisat shahīd - Mustafa Ragab Mahmoud | Misr25tv#*" https://youtu .be/FVueG-xGZRs and (22 May 2011) "*Al-midān Gihan Mansour taqrīr 'an awal shahīd lil-thawra min al-Suez wa musabī al-thawra min madinat al-Suez halaqa 20 05 2011 00*" https://youtu.be/XNbI3g_RXsA.

[2] For video footage of the attack and its aftermath, see, e.g., YouTube video (31 Jan. 2011) "*Hujūm 'ala qism shurta wa tahrīr al-mawqufīn thawrat al-ghadab*" https://youtu.be/9Y UJTa5-39Q.

By the afternoon of 28 January, police commanders, stunned by the outbreak of violence, had ordered their forces to fall back to the outskirts of the city, leaving upwards of 50,000 anti-regime protestors to march on the governorate building. Meanwhile, amid rumors of looting, Suez's residents formed impromptu neighborhood popular committees (*ligān sha'biyya*) and descended onto the streets to protect their property.

As police forces in the Suez beat a hasty retreat, comparable scenes of collective violence,[3] mass mobilization and civic associationalism were being repeated throughout Egypt. Figure 2.1 shows the frequency and size of anti-Mubarak protests between 23 January and 11 February, using the event catalog. What is immediately striking about the scale of anti-regime contention during this period is the relatively modest number of protestors taking to the streets between 25 and 27 January; that is, when Mubarak's national security state remained resolutely intact. The mobilization would only reach its apogee on 11 February, when over a million protestors took to the streets. So how did a mobilization that began with such a small number of participants bring about a revolutionary situation that toppled a seemingly well-fortified dictator of thirty years?

This chapter addresses this puzzle. In doing so, it takes as its locus a wave of attacks on police stations and state security offices, which began in the Suez on the night of 26 January and then proliferated nationwide on 28 January. An analysis of these incidents, and their significance for the unfolding trajectory of the 25th January Revolution, reveals the limits of an emerging conventional wisdom which holds that Egyptians were able to overthrow Mubarak without resorting to violence (see e.g., Bassiouni 2016; Chenoweth and Cunningham 2013; Nepstad 2011, 2013; Ritter 2014; Lawson 2015; Zunes 2011). Studies that draw this conclusion do so by truncating their empirical purview to scenes of activists mobilizing in public squares under the banner of *silmiyya* (peaceful) protest. The reality, however, was more complex: protestors' ability to sustain and intensify street-level mobilization during the critical early phase of the 25th January Revolution was inextricably entwined with anti-regime violence.

---

[3] I follow Charles Tilly (2003: 3) in defining collective violence as an "episodic social interaction that immediately inflicts physical damage on persons and/or objects ('damage' includes forcible seizure of persons or objects over restraint or resistance); involves at least two perpetrators of damage; and results at least in part from coordination among persons who perform the damaging acts."

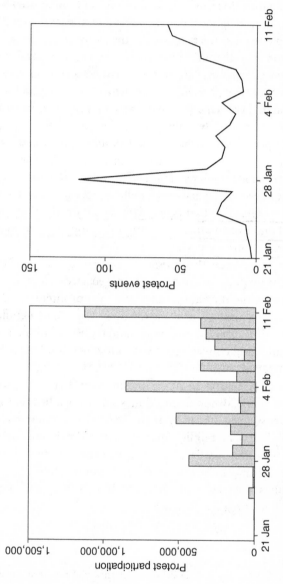

FIGURE 2.1 Protest participation and frequency, 21 Jan.–11 Feb. 2011. Notes: Includes labor protests and attacks on police stations, but excludes pro-Mubarak protests.

Attacks on district police stations provide a clear illustration of this dynamic.[4] These episodes of collective violence, carried out by local residents in retaliation for police killing protestors from their district, served to shield anti-Mubarak marches from repression by diverting police and CSF units away from frontline protest policing duties. As the frequency and ferocity of these assaults grew in several of Egypt's largest cities, police forces either melted away or were burnt out of their stations. The combined effect of this onslaught was to degrade the regime's coercive capacity across whole swathes of urban space, crippling the Interior Ministry's ability to regroup, and thus enabling other kinds of contentious politics and associational activities to break out and scale up. In many districts, police control was superseded and replaced by civilian-led popular committees.[5] Viewed from this perspective, episodes of anti-regime violence and street protest during the first days of the 25th January Revolution appear both synergetic and complementary, forming a continuum of contentious collective action that paved the way for Mubarak's ousting.

VIOLENCE

In the new literature on revolutions, violence is typically portrayed as outdated and counterproductive. Smart modern revolutionaries, it is argued, increasingly embrace nonviolent methods (e.g., Nepstad 2011, 2015; Ritter 2014).[6] This claim receives empirical support from an influential study carried out by Erica Chenoweth and Maria Stephan (2011), which finds that mobilizations employing nonviolent civil resistance – as opposed to violent insurgency – tend to be more successful at overthrowing autocracy.[7]

The key factor here is the extent of mobilization (Chenoweth and Stephan 2011: 10–11; Schock 2013: 283). Civil resistance scholars

---

[4] Here, the chapter builds on several valuable studies of anti-police violence during the 25th January Revolution (e.g., Abul-Magd 2012; Ismail 2012, 2013; El-Mahdi 2011). Those works tend to focus on the class backgrounds and grievances of attackers. I expand on these analyses by exploring the interrelationship between anti-police violence and street level mobilization.

[5] On the formation and role of popular committees during the 25th January Revolution, see Lughod (2012) and Hassan (2015).

[6] By nonviolent methods, I mean an "activity in the collective pursuit of social or political objectives ... [that] does not involve physical force or the threat of physical force against human beings" (Schock 2003: 705). I use nonviolent methods, nonviolent contention, and nonviolent civil resistance interchangeably.

[7] Although a recent review article by Fabrice Lehoucq (2016: 277–279) suggests that this inference may not hold when omitted cases are accounted for.

argue that potential participants view nonviolent contention as more legitimate and less dangerous. This broadens the popular appeal of protest and raises the cost of state repression. According to this argument, revolutionary mobilizations that adhere to nonviolence are more likely to succeed because they bring more people out onto the streets, while simultaneously denying authoritarian regimes their comparative advantage in the realm of force (see especially Nepstad 2011: ch.1; Chenoweth and Stephan 2011: ch.1).

A convergent claim is that violent and nonviolent contention are almost always antithetical, because violent groups will tend to scotch the efforts of contemporaneously mobilizing nonviolent actors. According to this argument, violence carried out in the name of the revolution legitimizes state repression and increases the risks associated with protesting, which acts as a disincentive for mass nonviolent protest (Chenoweth and Schock 2015; Schock 2013: 281–283).[8] This scenario is sometimes referred to in the social movements literature as a "negative radical flank effect" (Haines 1988: 3–11; see also Haines 1984).[9]

An alternative perspective suggests that violent and nonviolent contention are subject to a more complex and intertwined relationship than many civil resistance scholars would allow. In apartheid South Africa, for example, the struggle against racial oppression saw numerous attacks on state security forces carried out by the armed wing of the African National Congress. These attacks are in turn credited with inspiring nonviolent contention in the country's townships and trade union movement (see Seidman 2001; Schock 2005: 158–160). Similarly, the anti-Assad mobilization in Syria, which is typically understood by civil resistance scholars to have begun life as a nonviolent mobilization (e.g., Chenoweth 2011), only began to accelerate and spread after residents in Daraa burnt down the local headquarters of the Ba'ath party (see Leenders 2012: 421; Tripp 2013: 1–2). In Serbia, during the "Bulldozer Revolution," protestors set fire to the federal parliament and armed paramilitaries took over key government buildings. Justifying these actions, the mobilization's architect proclaimed that "opposition forces must clearly show that they are ready to use violence to fight back in case

---

[8] In a recent multivariate study, Tompkins (2015) found that while the co-presence of a violent actor increases the likelihood of repression and decreases popular participation, this was not necessarily detrimental to a mobilization's success.

[9] A "flank effect" encompasses both a mobilization's goals (e.g., reform versus revolution) and its tactics (e.g., violent versus nonviolent contention). I am primarily interested in the realm of tactics, and so confine attention to "violent flank effects."

of repression [...] security forces must realize that they cannot resort to violence without risks" (cited in Way 2008: 58). These examples suggest that episodes of collective violence can facilitate, inspire and protect nonviolent mobilization and so help to bring about a revolutionary situation (see also Isaac, McDonald and Lukasik 2006).

The co-presence of violent actors can also enhance the bargaining power of nonviolent civil resisters. In the Philippines, for instance, armed communist and Islamist insurgencies in the countryside boosted the position of soft-liners within the Marcos regime and increased the leverage of the liberal democratic opposition when they took to the streets during the anti-Marcos "People power" revolution (see Bermeo 1997: 313; Hedman 2006; Thompson 2003). Similarly, the emergence of militant black power groups in the United States is understood to have made the federal government more receptive to the demands of the mainstream civil rights movement (see Haines 1984, 1988). Thus, a "positive radical flank effect" (Haines 1988: 3–11; Schock 2005: 157–162) occurs when a violent group creates opportunities for another movement, often by making the latter's tactics and demands appear as the least worst option to those in power.[10]

Still, as Kurt Schock (2013) notes, the relationship between violent and nonviolent contention remains understudied and analytically underspecified. This is, in part, because the extant literature accords much less attention to the interaction between violence and nonviolence during the life course of a mobilization than it does to political effects and negotiated outcomes.[11] A close examination of the Egyptian case can help to illuminate the ways in which episodes of collective violence can combine with, and enable, other modalities of protest to create a revolutionary situation.

POLICE LINES

The tendency to overlook the interplay between mass mobilization and collective violence during the 25th January Revolution most likely derives from the disciplined and highly visible adherence by some activists to nonviolent methods during the first days of protest. When protestors in Greater Cairo took to the streets on 25 January, rather than attacking police and security forces, they instead sought to outmaneuver and evade them. This

---

[10] An alternative reading of this dynamic is that nonviolent civil resisters subvert potentially more radical political change (see Chabot and Sharifi 2013).

[11] For notable exceptions see Alimi, Bosi, and Demetriou (2015), della Porta and Tarrow (1986), McAdam, Tarrow, and Tilly (2001), Tarrow (1989), and Tilly (2003).

strategy began to take shape in the days beforehand, when the "April 6" youth movement announced that protest marches on 25 January would set off at 2 p.m. from four districts in Greater Cairo and conclude at 5 p.m. outside of the Interior Ministry (cited in *al-Masry al-Youm* 24 Jan. 2011: 1, 6).[12] The departure points – Gameat al-Duwal al-Arabiyya in Muhandiseen, al-Dawaran in Shubra, Midan al-Matariyya in north east Cairo, and outside Cairo University in Giza – were well-known landmarks, and so easily monitored and defended by Mubarak's security forces. Participants, the April 6 Movement declared, would protest peacefully and chant for a national minimum wage, the cancellation of the emergency law that had ruled the country since the assassination of Anwar Sadat in 1981, and the resignation of Mubarak's Interior Minister Habib al-Adly.[13] Meanwhile, Mohamed el-Beltagy, a prominent Muslim Brother and former parliamentarian, announced that he and members of the National Association for Change would hold a sit-in on the steps of the Judges' Club in downtown Cairo (*al-Masry al-Youm* 24 Jan. 2011: 6).

The Interior Ministry took the bait. On 25 January, twelve "boxes" – the distinctively-shaped paddy wagons used by the Interior Ministry – were lying in wait for protestors on Gameat al-Duwal al-Arabiyya. A further eighteen were stationed outside Cairo University (El-Ghobashy 2011: 6). Police were also deployed along the Nile's Corniche, while the streets around the Interior Ministry were sealed off (Ibid.: 6). Two hours before the scheduled start time, activists gathered in side streets and residential areas several kilometers away from the heavily policed advertised departure points. As police commanders quickly realized that their forces had been deployed, a game of cat and mouse was played through Cairo's backstreets and popular quarters.[14] The police struggled to detect and intercept columns of anti-regime protestors converging on Midan al-Tahrir from several different directions while the protestors sought to evade their pursuers (*al-Shorouk* 26 Jan. 2011: 1, 3–5; see also El-Ghobashy 2011: 6–9; Trombetta 2013: 140–141).

---

[12] Marches were also called for in Alexandria, Asyut, Damietta, Daqahlia, Gharbia, Ismailia, Kafr el-Sheikh, and Port Said. Activists from the Nile Delta governorates of Sharqia, Qalyubiyya, and Menoufiyya were directed to join protestors in Greater Cairo, while protestors from Qina, Sohag, and Minya were advised to protest in Asyut (*al-Masry al-Youm* 24 Jan. 2011: 6).

[13] For an account of April 6's involvement in the mobilization, and their experience with nonviolent methods, see Gunning and Baron (2013: 165–169).

[14] We see a similar dynamic in Alexandria, see e.g., El Chazli (2016).

The following timeline of events, based on protest reports published in the Egyptian newspaper *al-Masry al-Youm* (27 Jan. 2011: 7), provides a useful overview of the day's developments in downtown Cairo:[15]

12 p.m.	Protestors gather on the steps of the Judges' Club and are surrounded by black-uniformed CSF units. A second group of protestors suddenly emerges from a side street. Amid rising tensions, Mohamed el-Beltagy tries to calm the crowd and calls on the protestors to remain in front of the Judges' Club. The protestors ignore el-Beltagy and break through the police cordon to reach Galaa Street.
1 p.m.	Protestors march down Galaa Street towards Midan Abd al-Moneim Riyyad chanting, "Freedom, Freedom." They break through a second police line to reach Midan al-Tahrir. Some protestors attempt to march on the Interior Ministry, but are repelled by police who fire tear gas. The crowd of protestors has reached several thousand. Upon reaching Midan al-Tahrir the crowd splits, with simultaneous demonstrations being held outside the NDP headquarters, the state television broadcaster housed at Maspero and outside the Foreign Ministry.
3 p.m.	Another column of protestors arrives in downtown Cairo having set off from another part of the city. These protestors break through a police cordon to reach Midan al-Tahrir. The protestors chant for bread, freedom, and social justice.
4 p.m.	Some protestors begin to throw stones at CSF units, but are restrained by other protestors who chant "peaceful, peaceful." Police forces gather at the intersection between Kasr al-Aini Street and the American University in Cairo and begin to fire volleys of tear gas into Midan al-Tahrir.
5.30 p.m.	Marches that began in Giza and Imbaba arrive in downtown Cairo. The protestors chant, "This is it, this is it, this is it, the Egyptian people are here."
8 p.m.	Protestors in Midan al-Tahrir hold an ad hoc meeting in the center of the square to decide on the next course of action.
9 p.m.	Protestors circulate a statement among the crowd. Food and water are also distributed. A division of labor emerges; one

---

[15] Many of these scenes were captured on video and archived for posterity by the same newspaper. See e.g., YouTube video (24 Jan 2016) *"Film «al-thawra..khabar»* https://yo utu.be/9YIW6kFYER0. I am grateful to Sarah ElMasry for sharing this with me. A similarly detailed timeline, including interviews with participants, is given in *al-Shorouk* (27 Jan. 2011: 7).

	group of protestors maintains a line in front of the police cordon, while the others rest in the center of the Midan.
10 p.m.	A protestor climbs one of the green lampposts that ring the edge of Midan al-Tahrir and unfurls an Egyptian flag – an iconic picture carried by news media around the world.
1 a.m.	More police units arrive at downtown Cairo and police lines are heavily reinforced. Shortly afterwards, over a hundred canisters of tear gas are fired into Tahrir in the space of just a few minutes. Protestors begin to disperse, with many running down side streets to avoid the gas.
2 a.m.	CSF units clear Midan al-Tahrir. Small groups of protestors continue to move through the streets of downtown Cairo.

The relative ease with which protestors broke through police lines during this and other episodes of anti-Mubarak contention on 25 January is especially noteworthy. In interviews with activists, the protestors' ability to overwhelm security forces at key moments during the day is attributed to the demonstrators' fast-moving tactics (see Gunning and Baron 2013: 168–178). We should also acknowledge the extraordinary *élan* and resolve of the protestors themselves.

Another, less explored, factor relates to the number of officers assigned by the Interior Ministry to police the 25 January protests (see El-Ghobashy 2011: 6). Speaking in the run-up to the protests, Interior Ministry officials announced that 4,000 police officers were being deployed to secure downtown Cairo on 25 January (cited in *al-Shorouk* 25 Jan. 2011: 1, 5). It was subsequently reported that 30,000 police officers and CSF troopers were called up nationwide to contain the protests (*al-Masry al-Youm* 26 Jan. 2011: 5).

If these figures are accurate, they represent only a small fraction of the manpower available to the Interior Ministry. By way of comparison, during nationally coordinated days of protest during the post-Mubarak transition (discussed in Chapter 5), the Interior Ministry deployed up to ten times that number of officers, often with the expressed desire of avoiding a repeat of the events of 25 January.

These figures might suggest that the Mubarak regime initially underestimated the scale of opposition in the capital. As a result, police commanders found themselves ill-equipped and unprepared to hold back large and determined crowds. Revealingly, by the evening of 25 January, the Interior Minister Habib al-Adly had been forced to order a dramatic increase in the number of police deployed to downtown Cairo. A reported

13,000 additional officers had to be called up to clear Midan al-Tahrir of protestors (cited in *al-Masry al-Youm* 27 Jan. 2011: 1).

FRIDAY OF ANGER

From this perspective, the symbolic breakthrough on 25 January owed much to the protestors' guile and the Interior Ministry's lack of planning. These factors explain the authorities' inability to contain and repress the protests, rather than the Ministry's unwillingness to use force against nonviolent civil resisters. This point is reinforced in the days that followed, when anti-regime protestors continued to take to the streets, albeit in smaller numbers. Several dozen smaller marches, demonstrations and sit-ins were held on 26–27 January, and were met with harsh repression that led to the temporary demobilization and ostensible containment of anti-regime opposition. (see e.g., *al-Masry al-Youm* 27 Jan. 2011: 1, 4; *al-Masry al-Youm* 28 Jan. 2011: 1, 4–7; *al-Shorouk* 27 Jan. 2011: 1).

The Suez was the exception to this trend. Here, activists and residents continued to mobilize and escalate their demands, and their role in inspiring anti-regime protest elsewhere in Egypt in the days following 25 January was crucial. On the afternoon of 25 January, police fired live ammunition at anti-Mubarak protestors as they left Midan al-Isaaf and headed for the governorate building (see *al-Shorouk* 27 Jan. 2011: 6, 9; *al-Masry al-Youm* 28 Jan. 2011: 7). In the days that followed, against a backdrop of escalating anti-police violence and the use of harsh repression, several thousand anti-Mubarak protestors continued to take to Midan al-Arbayeen and Sharia al-Geish in defiance of a governorate-wide crackdown (see *al-Masry al-Youm* 27 Jan. 2011: 4; *al-Masry al-Youm* 28 Jan. 2011: 1; *al-Shorouk* 28 Jan. 2011: 5; *al-Shorouk* 31 Jan. 2011: 10).

So vital were these continuing protests that journalists and activists alike referred to the Suez as Egypt's "Sidi Bouzid" (see e.g., *al-Shorouk* 27 Jan. 2011: 9), invoking the Tunisian city where Mohammed Bouazizi's self-immolation had triggered the first protests of the 2011 Arab Spring.[16]

As Egyptians followed, and took courage from, events in the Suez (see Nunns and Idle 2011; Chalcraft 2014), the anti-Mubarak mobilization elsewhere continued to gain momentum. After the police in Cairo retook Midan al-Tahrir in the early hours of 26 January, Egyptian activist

---

[16] On the figure of Mohammed Bouazizi, the framing of his death, and its significance for the Tunisian Revolution, see Hmed (2015).

groups, including April 6, the Revolutionary Socialists and the National Association for Change, as well as anti-regime social media pages, called for a second national day of protest, dubbed the "Friday of Anger."[17]

Marches were planned to follow the conclusion of Friday prayer on 28 January, from mosques in central urban areas converging on the main roads and public squares of the capital. In a major blow to the regime, and despite the concerted efforts of Mubarak's internal security apparatus to demobilize Egypt's main opposition movements, the Muslim Brothers, the Wafd, and several Nasserist parties all declared that their members would participate (see Chapter 4).[18]

With the security situation in the Suez deteriorating and wider protest seemingly inevitable, the Interior Ministry called up police and CSF troopers across the governorates in a bid to lockdown central urban areas. Police positions outside central and local government buildings were reinforced, and checkpoints were established in public squares and on roads leading to major cities (*al-Masry al-Youm* 27 Jan. 2011: 4; *al-Shorouk* 27 Jan. 2011: 2). In the capital, police and CSF units were stationed on roads leading to Midan al-Tahrir, while 2,000 plainclothes officers were dispatched to downtown Cairo to monitor signs of dissent and arrest potential troublemakers (*al-Masry al-Youm* 27 Jan. 2011: 1; *al-Shorouk* 27 Jan. 2011: 1, 6). Metro stations in the downtown area were closed. The Ministry of Endowments declared that the Amr Makram mosque, which sits on the edge of Midan al-Tahrir, would be closed for Friday prayer (*al-Masry al-Youm* 26 Jan. 2011: 6; *al-Masry al-Youm* 29 Jan. 2011: 7).

Within 24 hours of the first protests occurring, Interior Ministry officials and human rights monitors reported that up to 1,000 protestors, activists and political figures had been arrested across Egypt (*al-Masry al-Youm* 27 Jan. 2011: 1; *al-Shorouk* 27 Jan. 2011: 3). The regime's countermeasures culminated on the night of 27 January. The Interior Ministry, looking to disrupt activists' ability to publicize and coordinate the protests, ordered internet service providers to cut access to the internet (see Hassanpour 2014). The Ministry also took the unprecedented step of shutting down the country's mobile phone network.

---

[17] Also referred to at the time as the "Friday of the Martyrs and the Arrested" – an attempt by activists to draw attention to intensifying regime repression (see *al-Masry al-Youm* 28 Jan. 2011: 5; *al-Shorouk* 28 Jan. 2011: 4).

[18] For a discussion of the role of established movements in brokering anti-regime activism during this period, see Clarke (2014).

DISTRICT POLICE STATIONS

If the size and agility of the protests on 25 January caught the Mubarak regime by surprise, the authorities were well prepared for the Friday of Anger. As tens of thousands of protestors spilled out of mosques in cities across the country on 28 January, many found themselves speedily confronted by security forces units firing tear gas and birdshot (see accounts in Holmes 2012; Trombetta 2013).[19] However, Interior Ministry officials and police commanders had not anticipated in their pre-protest planning that their officers would soon be defending police stations and state security offices from widespread attacks.

In Egypt, routine police activities and operations are organized and coordinated at the district level. In January 2011, there were 342 districts located in 27 governorates. Each district had its own police station (*qism al-shurta*), as well as manned checkpoints (*nuqtat al-shurta*) located at key intersections and roads. In addition, each governorate had a security directorate (*mudiriyyat al-amn*) located in the governorate's administrative center, along with an array of courts, CSF barracks and state security offices.

Beginning in the Arbayeen district of the Suez, Egyptians attacked at least eighty-four district police stations throughout Egypt during the 25th January Revolution. This figure, which is derived from Egyptian newspaper reports and analysis of video footage, represents nearly a quarter of the police stations in the country, and is almost certainly an underestimate.[20] We should also take account of the numerous police checkpoints, courts and state security offices that were attacked, as well as the 4,000 police vehicles that were destroyed during this period (see Ashour 2012: 9).[21]

[19] According to one estimate, security forces in Cairo fired 20,000 tear gas rounds on 28 January in a bid to stop protestors from reaching Midan al-Tahrir (*al-Shorouk* 30 Jan. 2011: 5).

[20] Other studies and sources put that number significantly higher. Mona El-Ghobashy (2011: 12) and Salwa Ismail (2013: 872), for example, have reported that ninety-nine police stations were burnt down during the eighteen days of protest – equivalent to a third of the police stations in Egypt. Meanwhile, a police commander, speaking to journalists on 30 January 2011, announced that 90 percent of the police stations in Greater Cairo had been set on fire in the five days since protestors first reached Midan al-Tahrir (cited in *al-Masry al-Youm* 31 Jan. 2011: 3). Later, a senior Interior Ministry official would claim that 150 police stations had been torched by the time Mubarak was ousted on 11 February (cited in *al-Shorouk* 4 Nov. 2011: 3). I found it impossible to verify these figures and so have retained my more conservative figure.

[21] The symbols and infrastructure of Mubarak's National Democratic Party were also singled out for destruction, with party headquarters attacked in Alexandria, Beni Suef, Cairo,

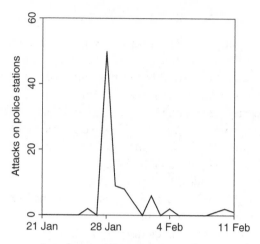

FIGURE 2.2 Attacks on police stations, 21 Jan.–11 Feb. 2011.

As Figure 2.2 shows, the vast majority of these attacks occurred on the afternoon of 28 January, as protestors in the streets were engaged in pitched battles with police and CSF units. Anti-police violence was particularly intense in Greater Cairo, where over 50 percent of the police stations in Giza and Cairo were attacked. Meanwhile, in Alexandria, Egypt's second city, over 60 percent of the police stations were targeted.

These acts of collective violence, which typically involved several hundred attackers armed with Molotov cocktails, and in virtually all cases ended with the looting and arson of the abandoned police station, provide the backdrop to the bloodiest phase of the 25th January Revolution.[22] This is most obviously reflected in the fatality rate amongst protestors and police officers, which peaked on the Friday of Anger, only to fall precipitously in the days and weeks that followed (see Figure 2.3).

Participants and bystanders captured video footage of these attacks on their mobile phones, which was then uploaded to social media

Damietta, Daqahliyya, Gharbiyya, Minya, and the Red Sea (see *al-Dostor* 30 Jan. 2011: 3–8; *al-Masry al-Youm* 29 Jan. 2011: 1, 5; *al-Masry al-Youm* 31 Jan. 2011: 4, 9; *al-Masry al-Youm* 6 Feb. 2011: 4). Government offices, including governorate buildings and city councils, were also sacked in Alexandria, Gharbiyya, Giza, Kafr el-Sheikh, Luxor, Monufia, and Port Said (see *al-Masry al-Youm* 29 Jan. 2011: 1; *al-Dostor* 30 Jan. 2011: 5; *al-Masry al-Youm* 31 Jan. 2011: 4; Said 2014: 202–203; *al-Shorouk* 30 Jan. 2011: 9).

[22] The exception was in Shaykh Zayad in North Sinai, where armed gunmen took part in a series of assaults on the district police station (see *al-Masry al-Youm* 29 Jan. 2011: 5; *al-Shorouk* 28 Jan. 2011: 6)

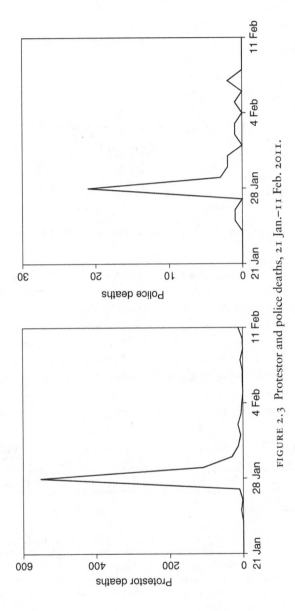

FIGURE 2.3 Protestor and police deaths, 21 Jan.–11 Feb. 2011.

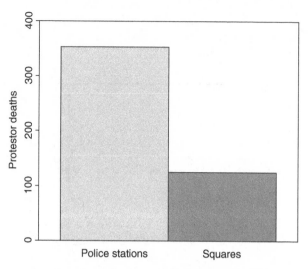

FIGURE 2.4 Locations of protestor deaths, 25 Jan.–11 Feb. 2011.

sites.[23] Despite the abundance of such recordings, and the column inches devoted to anti-police violence in Egyptian news media (see e.g., *al-Dostor* 30 Jan. 2011: 2, 4–5; *al-Masry al-Youm* 29 Jan. 2011: 1, 10–11; *al-Masry al-Youm* 31 Jan. 2011: 4, 9; *al-Shorouk* 30 Jan. 2011: 5–9), these violent episodes are almost entirely absent from the scholarly literature on the anti-Mubarak mobilization.[24]

This lacuna is puzzling. Numerous academic accounts cite police violence, both before and during the 25th January Revolution, as a powerful grievance motivating protestors to join occupations in Midan al-Tahrir and elsewhere (e.g,. Halverson, Ruston and Trethewey 2013; Khamis and Vaughn 2012; Olesen 2013; Jumet 2015: 203–205).[25] Yet, during the eighteen days of protest, police forces killed far more Egyptians during attacks on police stations than they did peaceful protestors occupying public squares (see Figure 2.4).

[23] See video footage, e.g., YouTube video (2 May 2011) "*Harīq qism al-khalifa wa-iqtihamu*" https://youtu.be/umQOyhz2hFs; (2 Feb 2011) "*Harīq qism al-ʿatārīn*" https://youtu.be/tij WfDP9KkU; (9 Jul 2011) "*Harīq qism al-basātīn*" https://youtu.be/Dvzr6l2wtmQ; (28 Feb 2011) "*Jumʿat al-ghadab wa maqtal al-shahīd Tariq*" https://youtu.be/LxgI1XnloSQ.

[24] For several notable exceptions, see Abdul-Magd (2012), Ismail (2012, 2013), and El-Mahdi (2011).

[25] Such accounts invariably begin with the figure of Khaled Saed, whose violent death at the hands of police in 2010 spawned an influential Facebook group (*kullina khalid said*) that publicized the first anti-regime protests (see Ghoneim 2012).

THE OTHER EARLY RISERS

That a significant number of Egyptians took matters into their own hands and attacked their local police station should come as no surprise to civil resistance scholars, who maintain that a cohesive opposition movement with clearly defined authority structures is a necessary condition for sustaining nonviolent action (see especially Chenoweth and Stephan 2011; Pearlman 2011). With the possible exception of the Muslim Brothers, no such movement existed in Egypt in early 2011. Still, we are left with the puzzle of who the assailants were, and why some police stations were attacked during the 25th January Revolution and not others. By excavating the dynamics underlying this anti-police violence, we can, in turn, begin to see more clearly the interactive and reciprocal relationship between violent and nonviolent forms of contention during the anti-Mubarak mobilization.

In Egypt, attacking and setting fire to police stations is an established part of the repertoire of contention (see Ismail 2012). Beginning in the 1990s, there are reports of local residents burning down several police stations following incidents of police violence. These often involve the deaths of residents in police custody, or the killing of local protestors (see e.g., Ismail 2006: 162–163). Mona El-Ghobashy (2011: 6) notes that, as recently as 10 January 2011, residents from the working class neighborhood of Warraq in Giza attacked the district's police station, after a rumor spread that a neighbor had died inside (see also *al-Shorouk* 12 Jan. 2011: 1).

The targeting of district police stations was widely popularized in the years leading up to the 25th January Revolution. The final scenes of the Egyptian blockbuster *Hiyya Fawda?* (This is Chaos?) (2007) depict local residents storming a district police station in northern Cairo in retaliation for a corrupt police captain detaining and torturing the district's inhabitants.

Qualitative accounts note that there was a similarly interdependent, district-level relationship between the killing of local protestors and violent reprisals during the 25th January Revolution. In Alexandria, for example, residents in Dekheila burnt down the police station and the court house and incinerated four police trucks, after police forces killed four anti-Mubarak protestors (including at least two locals – we lack biographical details on the other two fatalities) as they marched through the district (see Schielke 2015: 181; WikiThawra 2013). Residents are recorded as having burnt down the Sayyida Zaynab police station in Cairo after police opened fire on anti-Mubarak protestors, killing several locals (Ismail 2013: 872; see also WikiThawra 2013).

Salwa Ismail (2012; 2013) has also argued that anti-police violence was more likely to occur in Egypt's poorer districts: in particular, in Cairo's urban popular quarters, where residents' everyday interactions with the security forces are often characterized by police violence (see also Ismail 2006). In these areas, Ismail (2012) suggests, the 25th January Revolution should be understood as a "Revolution against the police."

We can examine this contention using regression analysis. As a binary variable, an attack is naturally modeled using logistic regression. The unit of analysis is the police station located in its census district. The event catalog inventories the police stations that were attacked and provides a measure of anti-Mubarak protest in each district before an attack occurred. WikiThawra (2013) provides statistics on the number of protestors killed from a district prior to an attack.[26] This allows us to account for the role of local social networks in responding to police violence. From the census of 2006 (the most recent Egyptian census), we can measure two socioeconomic variables: the percentage of the labor force employed in agriculture (a proxy for rural areas) and the percentage of the population with a university education. Since geographical location affects the scale of protest and the degree of repression by the state, a control variable is entered to measure a district's distance (km) from Cairo transformed to the square root.[27]

Table 2.1 presents the results with coefficients expressed as odds ratios. Three contextual variables are significant. As expected, districts with large numbers of workers employed in agriculture were less likely to experience an attack. A similar pattern is observed when taking into account the number of university graduates in a district (see Figure 2.5). Setting all other variables at their median value, increasing the percentage of the population (aged ten years and over) employed in agriculture from 1 percent to 54 percent (from the 10th to the 90th percentile) reduces the probability of a district police station being attacked from .40 to .08.[28] Likewise, the predicted probability of an attack decreases

---

[26] Note that this does not include protestors killed while attacking police stations. Protest participation and protestor deaths are analyzed as unbounded counts. Transformations to the square root provide substantively similar results.

[27] Distance is as the crow flies (great-circle) and is calculated using the Stata program, *geodist*.

[28] Effect sizes were calculated using *genatmedian*, a user-written command for Stata created by Michael Biggs.

TABLE 2.1 *Predicting the Probability of an Attack on a District Police Station.*

Independent Variable	Full Model		
	or	*se*	*p*
Percentage of agriculture workers in district	.96	.01	.00***
Percentage of university educated in district	.92	.03	.00**
District's distance from Cairo, sq root	.91	.03	.00***
Number of protestors in district	.99	2.90	.97
Number of protestors killed from district	1.55	.22	.00**
Constant		1.98	.01*
Number of districts		333	
Number of attacks		84	

Logistic regression; or: odds ratios; se: standard error; p: p-value (two-tailed), *** p<0.001, ** p<0.01, * p<0.05

by more than half from .30 in districts in which 3 percent of the population hold a university degree (the 10th percentile) to .08 in districts where 23 percent of the population are university graduates (the 90th percentile). The likelihood of an attack similarly decreases with distance from Cairo.

The killing of anti-regime protestors is a substantive and significant predictor of an attack. Controlling for the number of protestors in a district, the killing of a protestor increases the odds of a police station being attacked by 55 percent in the protestor's home district, compared to districts from which no protestors were killed. This finding suggests that anti-police violence during the 25th January Revolution followed the established pattern: residents, upon learning of the death of a neighbor or relative on a protest, attacked their local police station to avenge the killing.

The biographies of the attackers supplement the quantitative findings. Detailed information is available for 210 Egyptians killed during attacks on police stations (WikiThawra 2013). The majority of these deaths occurred on 28 January (87 percent). Those killed were almost exclusively male and in their mid-twenties.[29] Of these, 80 percent

[29] On the role of young, poor males in contentious street politics in Egypt, see especially Ryzova (2011; 2015).

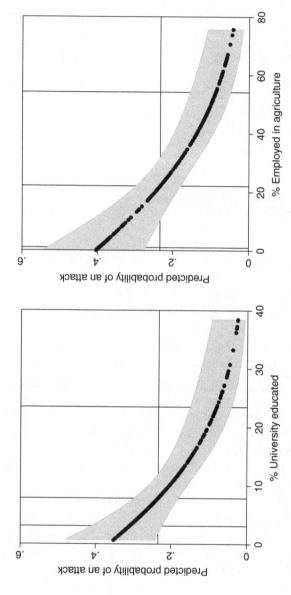

FIGURE 2.5 How attacks varied by university educated and agricultural workers in a district. Notes: The horizontal lines mark the 10th, 50th, and 90th percentiles.

lived in the district where they were killed. That proportion rises to 90 percent if we include fatalities from immediately neighboring districts.

This contrasts with anti-Mubarak protestors killed in and around Midan al-Tahrir during the 25th January Revolution. Of the 140 protestor deaths that occurred in downtown Cairo during this period, and for whom sufficiently detailed biographical information is available, none lived in the Kasr el-Nil district that is home to Tahrir.[30]

This indicates that there were, in fact, two groups of "early risers" (Tarrow 2011) during the first days of the mobilization. The first (and more familiar) group comprised of often highly networked activists (Beissinger, Jamal, and Mazur 2015: 11; Gunning and Baron 2013: 165–166), and who often had to travel, at a minimum, several miles from their homes to reach their protest destination. By contrast, the second group of early risers – those who attacked police stations – came from poor urban districts, and acted locally to where they lived.

"SECURE THE POLICE STATIONS!"

While there is little evidence to indicate that protestors and local residents were coordinating their activities, it is impossible to fully understand the dynamics of the 25th January Revolution if we look at the actions of either group in isolation. At this early stage of the mobilization, contention was at one time and place nonviolent and, at another, profoundly and openly violent. This dynamic was to play a crucial role in determining the Interior Ministry's ability to police anti-regime protests on the afternoon of 28 January.

As police stations came under attack in several key governorates, Interior Ministry officials and police field commanders rushed to protect their bases of operation. Police and CSF units, who had until that point been charged with containing and repressing protest marches, were withdrawn from frontline protest policing duties and redeployed to defend police stations (see especially Gunning and Baron 2013: 200; El-Ghobashy 2011: 12).

This dynamic is particularly well evidenced in Alexandria, where large protest marches and demonstrations had set off on 28 January from mosques in al-Atarein, al-Manshiyya, al-Raml, and Muharram Bey. Each march commanded over 10,000 participants, with the

---

[30] Only one protestor killed in Midan al-Tahrir came from a district bordering Kasr el-Nil.

largest demonstration departing from the Qaid Ibrahim mosque in the center of the city (*al-Masry al-Youm* 29 Jan. 2011: 11). As the crowds swelled, police fired birdshot, tear gas, and live ammunition in an attempt to disperse the protests. Over sixty protestors were killed (WikiThawra 2013).

In response to the killings, local residents turned their ire on their district's police force. A transcript of police radio chatter from Alexandria on the afternoon of 28 January offers an unparalleled insight into the confusion and panic precipitated by such attacks among police commanders in the city, as they struggled to hold back large and unruly protest marches:[31]

Police officer: This is the last time ... the residents have come in and set fire to a CSF vehicle ... the situation is worse than you think ... I repeat, Sir, the situation is worse than you think.

Police officer: The people have taken over now.

Brigadier General Essam Gad Allah: If Major Mohamed Metwalli doesn't move his cars, something similar will happen to them. I need help to hold [the protestors] from left and right. We are trying to deal with them. As soon as we ran out of gas, they came in and set fire to the CSF vehicle. The situation is worse than you think.

Police officer: Let him move the cars.

Gad Allah: We're doing that now. Let the [CSF] formation reach you first then God will help us.

Gad Allah: Sameh El Laqqani, what's the situation where you are?

Major General Sameh El Laqqani: Essam, the situation is very dangerous. The situation is dangerous, Essam. Send me someone.

Gad Allah: Mohammed Hatem and Gamal Maqrahi, leave the troops and come to me. Gamal Maqrahi, leave whatever you're dealing with. Don't deal with it and go protect Montaza al-Awal [a police station in eastern Alexandria].

Gamal Maqrahi: We are surrounded by people from all directions, Essam. We're trying to deal with it. Let Tarek Abdo go to him.

---

[31] This transcript was originally published in *al-Masry al-Youm* (15 Mar. 2011). Its provenance most likely traces to one of several raids launched by activists on state security offices in March 2011. Many of the documents recovered during these attacks, detailing the Mubarak regime's apparatus of surveillance, detention, and torture, were serialized in Egyptian newspapers, as well as being uploaded to social media sites, see e.g., https://www.facebook.com/AmnElDawlaLeaks/.

Gad Allah: Brigadier General Tarek Abdo.

Maqrahi: Essam, I can't leave the place here. The situation is serious and we're trying to deal with it.

Gad Allah: That's fine, Gamal. That's fine.

Gad Allah: Unit 4, what's your location? Where is 303? Mahmoud, go ahead.

Mahmoud: The CSF have entered the police station. It's now under control, thank God. There were some clashes in front of the police station, and a CSF officer was shot in the heart.

Hossam Al Sagheer: If you have a [CSF] formation in Mandara, send them to Montaza al-Awal police station. Mohamed, stay where you are and deal with what you have and we will deal with what we have. God help us all.

Gad Allah: 5 M, Lieutenant, 5 M. Go ahead.

Lieutenant Sayyid Nasr: Essam, there are 15,000 people marching in front of Mostafa Kamel buildings.

Gad Allah: If you don't have the capacity to deal with them, don't engage.

Nasr: OK. It's impossible to deal with them. The situation here is very tense.

Gad Allah: Gather your forces, and I will be in touch.

Gad Allah: D4, where is the [CSF] formation? Where is your formation?

Police Commander D4: On a side street near Midan al-Saa'a.

Police Commander D4: Essam, it's going to become unsafe in the police station very soon.

Gad Allah: D4, where are you?

Police Commander D4: We are on a side street near Midan al-Saa'a.

High-ranking Interior Ministry official: The most important thing now is to secure the police stations! If anyone is being faced with a march that they cannot deal with, disengage so long as they're peaceful. If they're peaceful, let them march while we secure the police stations and return to our positions.

Gad Allah: Copy, sir. We will send all formations back to police stations to secure them.

High-ranking Interior Ministry official: That's right. Secure the forces, the troops and the police stations and if the rally is peaceful let it be.

With police units falling back from frontline protest policing duties across Egypt, protestors were suddenly left free to establish and reinforce occupations in main roads and public squares. This moment features prominently in testimony and reporting from the afternoon of the Friday of Anger, with many participants and observers remarking on the sudden and oftentimes inexplicable retreat of police and CSF troopers – forces who had for hours held back protestors from reaching main roads and public squares suddenly melted away (see e.g., Holmes 2012: 404; Schielke 2015: 181; Trombetta 2013: 142). In many districts, the police would not return to the streets for weeks.

As attacks on police stations and state security assets continued, the Interior Ministry quickly lost its ability to regroup and demobilize further protest in key areas of the country. This is well illustrated in Figure 2.6, which maps the extent of police control in Greater Cairo and Alexandria in the days following the Friday of Anger. In districts where the police station was still functioning, police commanders ordered their officers to bunker down inside (see *al-Masry al-Youm* 31 Jan. 2011: 12; *al-Shorouk* 31 Jan. 2011: 2). Yet in many cases, police officers are reported to have disobeyed this order, opting instead to change into civilian clothes and return home, too discouraged to continue. Speaking to journalists in the days after 28 January, one Interior Ministry official admitted that police officers in Greater Cairo were refusing to turn up for work, even in districts where the police station had been spared, because they were "scared of being attacked by local residents" (cited in *al-Shorouk* 2 Feb. 2011: 10). Such was the psychological impact of anti-police violence on officers' morale that an Egyptian politician, following discussions with senior Interior Ministry officials, would later describe the police as "a broken army. More or less like the Egyptian army after the defeat of 1967" (cited in Ashour 2012: 9).

This points to a very different dynamic from that found in studies stressing the prepotent efficacy of nonviolent contention. According to that literature, it was pressure from Western governments on senior Mubarak regime officials that precluded the use of harsh repression against members of "civil society," thereby neutering the Interior Ministry's ability to demobilize protest by force (e.g., Ritter 2014: 168). In contrast, the explanation offered here suggests that the freedom of members of "civil society" to demonstrate relatively safely and peacefully in the period after police forces withdrew from the streets on 28 January owes a considerable debt to the violent attacks on police stations carried out by elements of "uncivil society" (Kopecký and Mudde 2002).[32] This is well illustrated in Figure 2.7, which shows the dramatic fall in the number of protest events being repressed after the Friday of Anger (see Figure 2.7).

This reading of events is reproduced in the analyses of Egyptian protestors and state security officials (see e.g., Chalcraft 2013; Gunning and Baron 2013; Ismail 2012). "The power of the Revolution," concludes one activist, "came from these *harāfīsh* [poor young men] burning police stations and from the collapse of the Interior Ministry ... Without this confrontation, the revolution wouldn't have been possible" (cited in *Egypt Independent* 24 Jan. 2012).[33] Another activist asks, rhetorically:

Do you seriously think that the Revolution could have succeeded without first cutting off the arm of the security apparatus and the police? Would the police, whose officers prospered under this regime, have stood idly, in their police stations and offices, as Mubarak's reign crumbled, without killing or arresting more people?" (*al-Masry al-Youm* 4 Mar. 2012)

Significantly, in governorates where the Interior Ministry's repressive apparatus remained intact, police forces continued to detain protestors and repress protests in the days and weeks following the Friday of Anger. In Sohag, for example, a combination of police, NDP members and pro-regime thugs launched a series of attacks on an anti-regime protest march as it left Sharia al-Muhata and headed towards the governorate on 1 February (see *al-Shorouk* 2 Feb. 2011: 6). The following day, police in Aswan arrested three activists and violently dispersed a protest march organized by members of April 6, the Muslim Brothers, and the National Association for Change (*al-Shorouk* 3 Feb. 2011: 5). Similarly, in Kafr el-Sheikh, dozens of activists were arrested after police broke up an anti-Mubarak demonstration on 5 February (*al-Dostor* 6 Feb. 2011: 7). These episodes of repression, in turn, provoked further episodes of anti-police violence. Sixty protestors were wounded in al-Kharija, the capital of Wadi al-Jadid governorate, after police forces opened fire on an anti-Mubarak

---

[32] As several scholars have argued, a failure to acknowledge the formative contribution of the urban poor during the 25th January Revolution amounts to a kind of "classwashing," in which a sterilized narrative of the anti-Mubarak mobilization privileges the contribution of peace-loving and tech-savvy middle-class youth activists (see Armbrust 2013a; Ismail 2012, 2013; Mellor 2014).

[33] The role of anti-police violence during the 25 January Revolution was revisited during the post-Mubarak transition, as activists campaigned to have local residents killed during these attacks officially recognized as martyrs thus making their families eligible for state compensation. I am grateful to Walter Armbrust for this point.

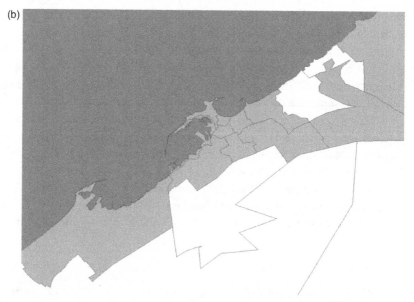

FIGURE 2.6 Police control in Greater Cairo (a) and Alexandria (b), 2 Feb. 2011.
Notes: Shaded areas indicate districts where the police station was attacked.

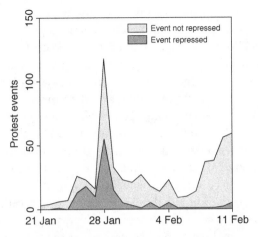

FIGURE 2.7 Proportion of protest events repressed, 21 Jan.–11 Feb. 2011.

march departing from Midan Basatayn on 7 February (*al-Masry al-Youm* 9 Feb. 2011: 6). In response, anti-Mubarak protestors and local residents burnt down the district police station, leading to the complete withdrawal of police forces from the city (*al-Masry al-Youm* 10 Feb. 2011: 12).

CONCLUSIONS

It would be misleading to attribute Mubarak's downfall entirely to the effects of anti-police violence in the early days of the 25th January Revolution. Yet to gloss over instances of anti-regime violence, or to portray these episodes as incidental to the trajectory of the mobilization, is to obscure and distort the process by which Egyptians were able to bring about a revolutionary situation. Of course, the freedom of Egyptians to organize without police interference must be weighed against the potential support that anti-police violence alienated (see Schock 2005: 159–161). Here, and contrary to the expectations of the civil resistance literature, participation in anti-Mubarak protests actually intensified *after* the Friday of Anger. At the same time, the proportion of protest events being repressed and the number of protest-related deaths fell rapidly during the same period. Viewed from this perspective, it seems reasonable to conclude that any demobilizing effects of anti-police violence were not only short-lived, but that the weakening of the police as a repressive actor served to protect protestors and activists mobilizing in Egypt's public squares and main roads.

This has important implications for how we understand the fate of subsequent episodes of transgressive contentious politics. After all, the "Tahrir model" of massing peaceful protestors in central urban spaces is credited with inspiring a "movement of the squares" (Gerbaudo 2014). The first emulation of the Tahrir repertoire came in Bahrain with the occupation of the Pearl Roundabout, and the formative influence of the Tahrir model can be seen in the Occupy Movement in the United States and Europe (see Kerton 2012). However, unlike in the Egyptian case, those protest movements failed to make serious inroads, or otherwise proved ephemeral. This is particularly true in the Middle East and North Africa, where every subsequent attempt to oust an incumbent authoritarian regime during the Arab Spring by peacefully occupying central urban spaces was brutally repressed by the regime's security forces, leading to the demobilization of protestors, or to a process of escalating radicalization and civil war.

One may be tempted to conclude that Egyptians taking to the streets during the 25th January Revolution might have suffered a similar fate were it not for the fact that protestors in Midan al-Tahrir and elsewhere never faced the full repressive apparatus of Mubarak's police state. There were two principal reasons for this: first, the Interior Ministry-controlled police initially underestimated the intensity and scale of street protest on 25 January, leaving security forces unable to hold back roving columns of protestors; second, in the days that followed, attacks on police stations and other security installations averted a crackdown on anti-regime opposition, and in the process fatally undermined the Interior Ministry's coercive reach. As Mubarak's infrastructure of repression was being dismantled from the bottom-up, police forces in key cities and governorates either evaporated, or were withdrawn from frontline duties by commanders fearful of sustaining further losses.

In the resulting security vacuum, Egyptian activists and revolutionaries were free to coordinate, organize, and build on the momentum generated by their initial breakthroughs. At the same time, civilian-led popular committees erected checkpoints and barricades at the entrances of their neighborhoods, further undermining and disrupting regime control over the streets. This process brought Egyptians out of their homes and made ordinary citizens responsible for managing the affairs of their district (see Lughod 2012; Hassan 2015). In many cases, civilian-manned checkpoints barred security officials from entering residential areas, and disarmed police units who they suspected of sowing chaos as a means to discredit the anti-Mubarak mobilization.

With a key pillar of Egypt's national security state crumbling, military units had to be called up and deployed across the country on the evening of 28 January to preserve some order. How protestors came to terms with the military's unexpected arrival will be the subject of the next chapter.

3

Fraternization

el-geysh we-l-sha'b iyd wāhda! (The army and the people are one hand!)
Chant first heard in Cairo, 28 Jan. 2011

At 5.00 p.m. on the afternoon of Friday, 28 January 2011, the Egyptian army was deployed onto the streets following three days of escalating protests. The order to leave barracks coincided with an unprecedented wave of attacks on district police stations, and the withdrawal from Alexandria, Cairo, and the Suez of the Interior Ministry's Central Security Forces (CSF), the shock troops of President Hosni Mubarak's regime, along with all other branches of Egyptian police, including prison guards and traffic police. Hours earlier, columns of protestors from Cairo's different neighborhoods and popular quarters had clashed with CSF units as they struggled to converge at Midan al-Tahrir, the locus of the previous days' protests. A pitched battle was fought on the Kasr el-Nil Bridge as CSF troops blocked protestors advancing from Giza to downtown Cairo and the road to Tahrir. As elsewhere, the battle for Kasr el-Nil lasted most of the afternoon and culminated in the bottom-up defeat of the CSF, but only after protestors endured armored vans plowing indiscriminately into their ranks and seemingly endless volleys of tear gas, water cannon, and shotgun pellets. By early evening, increasing numbers, bloodied from the afternoon's fighting, began arriving in the Midan. Approaching Tahrir, many of them, in some cases still pursuing vestiges of the CSF, would encounter newly arriving armored units of the Egyptian army.

In the previous chapter we saw how anti-police violence degraded the coercive reach of the Interior Ministry's forces during the critical early days of the mobilization, allowing protestors to take to the streets unopposed in areas where regime control had collapsed. In this chapter, I turn to the position of the military. How protestors came to terms with the army's deployment amidst anti-police violence and an unprecedented mobilization against Mubarak's dictatorship has hitherto received little to no attention in the academic literature on the 25th January Revolution.[1] This chapter addresses this lacuna by recounting fragmentary micro-histories of protestor-soldier encounters, from the first rush to surround newly arriving Egyptian army armored personnel carriers (APCs) to sustained interactions over the course of the fifteen days from the army's initial deployment to Hosni Mubarak's resignation. Drawing on these largely occluded interactions, the chapter asks: how did protestors try to co-opt and neutralize the threat posed by a military assumed to be loyal to a regime that was determined to end protest?

With that puzzle in mind, the chapter adopts a microanalytical lens to explain the prevalence of protestors chanting in the name of the army, graffitiing, and climbing aboard military vehicles, sleeping in tank tracks, and physically embracing and posing for photographs with soldiers, in and around Midan al-Tahrir. It brings these together by excavating a category of action common to histories and handbooks of contentious politics: fraternization.

FRATERNIZATION REPERTOIRE

Fraternization is an intuitively familiar idiom of contentious street politics that dates back to at least the eighteenth century. Then, insurgent Europeans would mount barricades and call out to those regime forces sent to put down their insurrection, entreating them to listen to their demands, hoping that, "face-to-face contact and a frank sharing of

---

[1] One important exception is Atef Said (2012: 405–11), who draws on informant testimony detailing protestors' reactions to the army's arrival. Another relevant study is that published by Jeffrey Alexander, who has called the 25th January the "performative revolution" (2011). While I am receptive to Alexander's stress on performance, his list of sacred and profane objects in protestor performances omits the Egyptian army entirely, despite the vast array of performances, many of which I will discuss here, that include or reference the army (Ibid.: 18). Alexander's omission can seem justified if one accepts his claim that to those in Tahrir, "by the evening of 29 January, the side that the army was taking had become manifest and clear" (Ibid.: 79). In contrast, I aver that the army was prominent in protestors' performances precisely because their position vis-à-vis the struggle to oust Mubarak was, to many protestors, *manifestly unclear*, and these performances figured as kinds of claim making.

perspectives would forge an indissoluble bond capable of overcoming any initial antagonism" (Traugott 2010: 209). The effects of fraternization on army discipline during the 1848 French Revolution were so disastrous that army officers would later order that any approaching fraternizer be shot, lest their soldiers succumb (Ibid.: 211).

Leon Trotsky (2003 [1932]: 136–44) became perhaps the most famous proponent of fraternization, when, in his history of the Russian Revolution, he encouraged future revolutionaries to get physically close so that they might provoke that "psychological moment" when soldiers could contemplate to which side they belonged.[2] Such was the association between fraternization and revolutionary socialism that it was first formally studied by an English aristocrat, Katherine Chorley, who, in her bid to combat the "Militant Left," warned military officers of its dangers: "An important method for tampering with the morale of troops ... used where the soldiers are dispersed in relatively small numbers in such a way that there can be personal contact between them and the insurgent population ... [fraternization] implies any method of winning sympathy, from direct argument and persuasion to the generation by one means or another of that subtle emotional sense of an underlying community of sentiment and interests between troops and people" (1973 [1943]: 158–59). Fraternization continues to be prescribed by such luminaries of protest as Gene Sharp (1980: 250; 2005 [1973]: 146–47), doyen of non-violent direct action and compiler of "how-to" protest manuals, as a tactic to usurp the grip of an occupying military power

In Egypt, fraternization was a repertoire of contentious performances that made immediate, situational claims on the loyalty of regime security forces. "People," Tilly noted, "make claims with words such as condemn, oppose, resist, demand, beseech, support, and reward. They also make claims with actions such as attacking, expelling, defacing, cursing, cheering, throwing flowers, singing songs, and carrying heroes on their

[2] Lenin (1964 [1917]: 318–20) also conceived a role for fraternizing in the trenches of the eastern front. In practice, fraternization between Bolsheviks and Austrian conscripts, as described by Red Navy leader F. F. Raskolinikov (1982 [1918]), often meant adhering to what Tony Ashworth (1968; 2000 [1980]) described as a "live and let live" system. Soldiers from all sides would seek to restrict the scope for violence by aiming to miss or by not taking the initiative to open fire. When fire was exchanged, its volume, timing and deliberate ineffectiveness often revealed it to be ritualistic. Perfunctory and routine firing served to sate the demand for aggression by military commanders, while communicating a message of non-aggressive intent to the soldiers on the opposing side. The reciprocal and micro-interactive aspects of live and let live has led to its being invoked as a prisoner dilemma in game theory (see Axelrod 1984).

shoulders" (2008: 6). During the 25th January Revolution, fraternization performances initially emerged as improvised techniques of micro-conflict avoidance. This occurred first with CSF troops during protests on 28 January, and continued later in and around Midan al-Tahrir after protestors attacked newly arriving tanks and APCs. During other episodes, fraternizing protestors made claims on army units to guarantee their security, especially when threatened by other pro-Mubarak forces. Thanks to these and other performances, protestors and soldiers developed a polyvalent repertoire that came to ritualistically structure protestor-soldier interactions by producing visceral, if often contingent feelings and symbols of protestor-soldier solidarity. Here, I explore fraternizing and the "generative power of the practices of protest" (Dzenovska and Arenas 2012: 675) in constructing a precarious "internal frontier" (Laclau 2007), which balanced protestors' desires for security with their demands to bifurcate Mubarak's governmental apparatus from what would become a reaggregated claim to sovereignty in the name of the army and the people.[3] Here, fraternization performances made claims on regime agents through stimulating feelings of solidarity, and came to figure as interaction rituals – "a mechanism of mutually focused emotion and attention producing a momentarily shared reality, which thereby generates solidarity and symbols of group membership" (Collins 2004: 7).

HOW TO PROTEST SMARTLY

During the 25th January Revolution, fraternization performances were not limited to coping with the army's unexpected arrival. Protestors also fraternized with police and black-uniformed CSF troops, although this occurred only sporadically and involved a much narrower range of performances. Spectacular video footage exists, for example, of protestors fraternizing with a CSF unit in Alexandria on 28 January.[4] As protestors approached a line of truncheon and shield-wielding CSF, there was no clash: rather, protestors moved to kiss, hug, and embrace individual soldiers, all the while disrupting their formation. While individual troopers

---

[3] Parenthetically, it is important to note that I refer, rather conveniently, to "protestors" to signify a mobilized bloc interacting with the army. This might appear unsatisfactory given that in Arabic-language accounts from the 25th January Revolution, this bloc is usually referred to in the plural as *mutathāhirūn* (demonstrators) and only on occasion as *muhtajjūn* (protestors). I use the latter for stylistic purposes.

[4] See footage: YouTube video (26 Apr 2012) "Protestors in Alexandria fraternise CSF troops, 28th January, 2011" http://youtu.be/NLTh3HaAEc4.

FIGURE 3.1   A woman kisses a member of the CSF, Cairo, 28 Jan. 2011 (Lefteris Pikarakis/AP/Press Association Images).

attempted to maintain their distance, others were physically encircled, remonstrated, and pleaded with. In the video, the effects of these interactions are profound: both protestors and soldiers visibly moved to tears.

In and around Tahrir, it is important to note, women were often in the vanguard of would-be fraternizers; this suggests that fraternization as contentious performance belies the masculine, exclusivist solidarity implied by the word's etymology. In Cairo on the same day, for instance, the image of a woman kissing the cheek of a CSF trooper featured in both local and international news coverage (see Figure 3.1).[5] In that photograph, the trooper continues to stare straight ahead, seemingly unaffected by the kiss; a clue to his emotional detachment? The riot helmets of his colleagues are visible over his shoulder, perhaps suggesting a unit whose internal discipline and solidarity remains intact. Later that afternoon, near the famous Groppi restaurant in downtown Cairo, further incidents of

---

[5] Likewise, this photograph's popularity recalls a set of fraternization performances familiar to contemporary histories of contentious politics in which both male and female protestors hand out flowers, kiss members of security forces, or place flowers in rifle barrels as happened variously during anti-Vietnam protests in the United States, the Portuguese "Carnation Revolution" of 1974, and the Filipino People Power Revolution.

fraternization occurred when advancing protestors isolated twenty CSF troopers. That unit had exhausted its ammunition and found itself cut off from the main CSF lines barring protestors' advance to Midan al-Tahrir. Surrounded, protestors moved to embrace them, chanting, "These are poor men following orders." They then formed a cordon around the riot police and escorted them to safety, while the protestors were soon subjected to fresh attacks from CSF units stationed further down the road who fired tear gas at them (el-Refai 2011).

These instances of fraternizing with the CSF were exceptional, and most CSF interactions with protestors were characterized by violence. Informants frequently attributed this to an irreconcilable hatred for the CSF, who are frequently brutal in their policing of street politics, although as the examples above indicate this does not rule out fraternization entirely. Alternatively, we might observe that the CSF were trained in crowd control and equipped with ranged weapons including water cannon, shotguns, rubber bullets, live ammunition, and tear gas. The tactics they employed leading up to the army's deployment made liberal use of these weapons, the emphasis being on controlling space and maintaining distance between the two sides, which made fraternization impossible in most cases. Even when protestors encountered units of riot police in non-conflict situations, the CSF engaged in techniques of intimidation. One observer, during the prelude to the march on Kasr el-Nil, recalled, "When the first protestors appeared . . . the policemen closed ranks. They began to stamp the heels of their boots rhythmically on the tarmac, and to let out low, guttural sounds. It was meant to be a scary warning. And it worked" (Trombetta, 2013: 142).

This question of distance remains key in many respects. The relative absence of fraternization with police and CSF troops equipped with ranged weapons is broadly consistent with micro-sociological studies (Collins 2008), which suggest that the frequency and intensity of violence is situationally affected by distance and shared emotional moods.[6] By intimidating protestors, maintaining distance, and attacking with ranged weapons, the CSF increased both the fear of further confrontations

---

[6] For further evidence of this dynamic, Khalid Fahmy (2013) details how, on 28 January, after setting off on a march from Giza to Tahrir his group unexpectedly encountered a CSF trooper wielding a tear gas gun. As the distance between the two sides narrowed and amid salvoes of teargas, Khalid recounts, "He shouted at us, 'Don't come any closer' and we responded, 'So don't shoot at us.' He shook his head and said in a clear Upper Egyptian accent, 'This is wrong. There's something wrong here.' He lowered his gun and collapsed weeping."

and the situational tension experienced by CSF troops and protestors alike, all the while negating the possibility of interactional solidarity and making further violence more likely.[7] As the examples above suggest, and as we will encounter later, fraternization performances were initially used by protestors to transform these emotional moods, to try to inculcate feelings of solidarity between fraternizer and fraternized in ways that limited the opportunities for violence to break out.

Fraternizing with the CSF, and later the army, has been claimed as a tactic by the "April 6" Movement, who conducted activist training focused on protest tactics prior to 25 January. They taught chants and embodied actions similar to those that I will identify in the fraternization

FIGURE 3.2 "The police and the people together against oppression. Long live Egypt!" (*Kayfa Tathūr bi-Hadā'a: Ma'lūmāt wa Taktikāt Hāmma* 2011: 22).

---

[7] Collins (2008: ch. 2) suggests this is why snipers, fighter pilots, and drone operators tend to inflict the highest casualty rates, since distance from those deemed hostile, coupled with greater technical competence and ranged weaponry, allows for the overcoming of confrontational tension and fear.

repertoire.[8] Similarly, an anonymously authored Arabic-language protest handbook entitled, "How to protest smartly" and illustrated by women physically embracing and posing for photographs with CSF soldiers (see Figure 3.2), circulated in Cairo days before 28 January, urging activists to, "try to bring individual policemen and soldiers to the side of the people" (*Kayfa Tathūr bi-Hadā'a* 2011: 3). I largely discount the relevance of both of these sources due to my repeated inability to locate graduates of protest workshops, or readers of such manuals, during the formative moments when protestors began to fraternize. Instead, fraternization appears to have emerged, not under the direction of trained activists, or from learned manoeuvres outlined in handbooks, but rather through improvisation and innovation, in ways that appear quite independent of any orchestrating hand or radical leadership.[9] Protestors arriving to Midan al-Tahrir responded to the introduction of a new force in Egyptian street politics by fraternizing with soldiers. These performances, in turn, would establish the "norms of co-mingling" (Goffman 1971: xi) between protestors and soldiers, ineluctably drawing those army units to the revolution's side.

FRATERNIZING THE EGYPTIAN ARMY

At the end of a busy news day, international news media on 28 January showed nighttime Cairo, army vehicles passing through the streets. That evening's Associated Press (2011) package was typical of the coverage: it showed footage of protestors ostensibly welcoming tanks and APCs, before reporting that the headquarters of Mubarak's NDP party were ablaze, Egyptian Internet service providers had cut access, and mobile phone coverage had been similarly disrupted, and then concluding with scenes from the monumental battle for the Kasr el-Nil bridge.

In and around Midan al-Tahrir the situation was manifestly more complicated. As far as I have been able to establish, the first documented encounter between protestors and soldiers occurred around 5.20 p.m.:

---

[8] We find here a link with Gene Sharp's writings on non-violent action. Members of "April 6" have known connections with Serbia's Otpor movement, which was partially inspired by Sharp's work. Arabic-language versions of his *The Politics of Nonviolent Action* circulated in Egypt prior to 25 January (Rosenberg 2011). Still, I tend to concur with As'ad AbuKhalil (2011), who argues that Sharp's influence has been overstated, mostly to sate the desire among commentators to locate a Western "guiding hand" behind the 25th January Revolution.

[9] For a discussion on the "leaderful" (as opposed to "leaderless") character of the 25th January Revolution, see Chalcraft 2012.

tanks and APCs were reported entering downtown Cairo and heading for the state radio and television stations at Maspero, not far from the National Museum's entrance to Midan al-Tahrir.[10] The arrival of a lone, Soviet-era, Egyptian Army APC near the 6 October bridge was captured by *Al-Jazeera English Live*.[11] In this footage, daylight is giving way to dusk as the 5.30 p.m. *maghrib* (sunset) prayer approaches. A crowd of some thirty protestors sights the vehicle and immediately surrounds it, gesticulating, beckoning others to join. Young men quickly begin to haul themselves aboard. The crowd around the APC increases to eighty or a hundred as more protestors arrive. The soldiers atop are largely left undisturbed. Within a few seconds, the APC begins to reverse away. Those who had successfully climbed aboard the APC jump free. A small number give chase as the vehicle backs away.

That same, lone APC was caught on camera shortly afterward by *Al Jazeera Arabic Live*, only a few hundred meters from where the first, fleeting interaction took place.[12] Dusk has not yet arrived, suggesting that little time has passed. The APC has broken down and is being pushed by soldiers. In a fifty-second clip, seven pedestrians walk past the vehicle, paying it no attention. Two young men sit on the Nile's bank looking out away from the stricken APC. Traffic continues to move around it.[13] The camera pans out to the 6th October Bridge above. Protestors cross the bridge from the Giza side, heading toward Maspero and Tahrir, passing abandoned cars, the remnants of the afternoon's traffic.

[10] *Al-Dostor's* live blog of the day's events, updated despite limited Internet access in the country, gives a good account of the army's movement as they left barracks and moved into the city (*al-Dostor* 2011a).

[11] See footage: YouTube video (24 Apr 2012) "First sighting of the Egyptian army" http://youtu.be/CVQceo1d6EU.

[12] See footage: YouTube video (24 Apr 2012) "Broken down Egyptian APC" http://youtu.be/SWBkJflJd7Y.

[13] This apparent obliviousness to events is a reminder, omitted from breathless accounts of the 25th January Revolution, that Cairo did not simply stop functioning with the occupation of Midan al-Tahrir. For the eighteen days of the revolution, outside of protest hotspots (including pro-Mubarak counter-demonstrations), life for the vast majority of the city's residents continued at varying degrees of normality. The main disruption was the withdrawal of police; popular committees were established in residential areas that maintained their own patrols and often constructed checkpoints limiting the flow of traffic. The city's unmobilized residents would form a competing frontier that spoke in the name of "the people," the so-called *hizb al-kanaba* (party of the sofa), a term adopted by Egyptian chat shows, newspapers, and social media to signify the millions of seemingly apathetic Egyptians who followed the 25th January Revolution on television.

It is here we begin to see the incipient contours of the fraternization repertoire.[14] From that first rush to surround the soon-to-be-broken-down APC, we find a fraternization performance that amounts to a ritualized trespassing. The juxtaposition above is particularly useful in tracing the emergence of trespassing as a particularly important example of fraternization. This dynamic is rendered all the clearer by understanding the ubiquity of the military and its boundaries in Egypt. Any Egyptian taxi driver picking up fares in Cairo or one of Egypt's other cities, either prior to or after the 25th January Revolution, would as a matter of routine encounter the army in everyday life. Traveling from the outskirts to the center of Cairo, our imaginary taxi driver will drive by numerous barracks, administrative buildings, army hotels, and officers' clubs, army-specific bank branches, pharmacies, and sports clubs, and other elements of a literal military-industrial complex, which as a percentage of the national economy is "too vast and dispersed to estimate with any confidence" (Marshall and Stacher 2012: 12). Around sensitive military installations or presidential buildings, or when crossing into a different governorate or approaching the Suez Canal, our driver must pass through manned military checkpoints.

In this partial cityscape, military space is well organized and respected, with clearly defined borders.[15] Military installations often have high walls and watchtowers, and it is common to see signs around them written in Arabic and English announcing that photography is forbidden. As I discovered while researching this book, photographing army vehicles, be the photographer a northern European male or his Egyptian brother-in-law, is only possible if done surreptitiously. People passing through military checkpoints tend to go to extraordinary lengths to observe the boundary markers soldiers place around their territory. On my daily walk from Dokki in Giza, I passed through two military checkpoints to access a shortcut via the Pakistani and Yemeni embassies and arrive at the metro station. Soldiers stationed there had placed crowd-control barriers on the corners of both entrances, partially blocking the pavement. Pedestrians, I observed, would seldom sidestep the barrier, manned by a soldier who was frequently bored; they preferred instead to step down into the road, continue there for twenty

---

[14] Here the suggestion is that fraternization began as individual performances that coalesced into a repertoire as the days passed. I am grateful to Sidney Tarrow for encouraging me to consider this point.

[15] On the micro-interactive aspect of borders, markers, and territories, see Goffman (1971: 40–44).

meters until they passed the second checkpoint, cross another small road, and remount the pavement. The pavement on my shortcut had effectively become military territory.

During the fifteen days between the army's initial deployment and Mubarak's resignation, there emerged a set of performances which through their emulation and recursion challenged this "right of separateness" (Goffman 1972: 69) enjoyed by the army, and came to figure as interaction rituals. The response by protestors at first sighting army vehicles was to trespass, first by surrounding the vehicle and then by hauling themselves aboard. Pedestrians passing the stricken APC otherwise respected the established boundaries of military space. In shaping micro-interactions, the mounting of Egyptian army vehicles asserted a right to physical co-presence that allowed for other kinds of fraternization later. One cannot overstate the importance of trespassing and the demand to share military space in literally setting the stage for other fraternization performances. Goffman explains, "It is apparent that a precondition for the performance of ... rituals is that the giver and the receiver be in contact, whether face-to-face or mediated. No contact, no interpersonal ritual" (1971: 71). One of my key arguments here is that as physical distance between protestors and security forces decreases, we should find an attending increase in ritualized interaction and a decrease in sociological distance; that is to say, the embodied representation that "the army and the people are one hand" is a plausible performance. If fraternization requires physical co-presence, it is equally apparent that accessing police, soldiers, or other arms of a state's apparatus of violence is often difficult: security forces jealously guard the boundaries of their territories and their right to organize that space.

Egyptian soldiers did not simply surrender their vehicles in this regard. In the first encounter with protestors, the APC reversed away when it seemed about to be enveloped by the crowd. As protestors continued along the Nile Corniche, still clashing with the rearguard of retreating CSF units, they encountered further APCs on the road to Maspero.[16] Initially, when approaching the first such army vehicle, protestors took shelter behind it from CSF tear gas and rubber bullets. Many more stood off the vehicle's sheltering flank to arc stones at the

---

[16] See footage: YouTube video (6 Sep 2012) "Protestors pursuing CSF units encounter an Egyptian army APC. Corniche el-Nile, January 28th, 2011." http://youtu.be/mYYgTohq_YY.

CSF; the APC marked the new frontline of the protestors' offensive. After the CSF troops retreated, numbers remained with the APC. No longer gathered on just one side, they corralled the vehicle with their bodies, the most enterprising pulling themselves on board. Informants reported soldiers manning the vehicles initially trying to stop this, often demanding that the crowd open up so as to allow the vehicle free movement. Indeed, this was a common scene in footage from 28 January and into the next morning, as soldiers attempted to assert control over their vehicles.[17] As will become apparent, though, protestors could not be deterred in their trespassing, and they made continual claims to access military vehicles and their personnel, all indicative of a crowd that accepted no boundaries aside from those of its own making, especially boundaries that might allow soldiers to remain neutral bystanders in the struggle against Mubarak.

THE ARMY AND THE PEOPLE ARE ONE HAND!

As night fell, protestors gathered outside Maspero, near the National Museum entrance to Midan al-Tahrir. The situation was in flux, and running battles between CSF units and protestors on the road leading to Maspero had been replaced by an uneasy calm. Newly arrived Egyptian army units in APCs and battle tanks, some identifiable by their claret and blue insignia as belonging to the Republican Guard, had taken position outside Maspero. Armed soldiers wearing gas masks – necessary given the volume of tear gas fired by the recently departed CSF – manned the windows and entrances to the large, convex building.

In video footage recorded by the Egyptian newspaper *al-Masry al-Youm*, protestors can be seen climbing atop stationed army vehicles, many waving flags and cheering on their comrades.[18] It is outside Maspero that we hear for the first time protestors chanting, "The people

---

[17] See footage: YouTube video (6 Sep 2012) "Soldier tries to stop protestors climbing on APC. Corniche el-Nile, 29th January, 2011." http://youtu.be/WA55CKbqBo4. This Associated Press video, filmed on the morning of 29 January on the road to Tahrir from Maspero, shows a soldier trying to push a protestor off his APC. Protestors below hold an Egyptian flag penned with the slogan, "Down with Mubarak" as they chant, "The army and the people will complete the task." After passing the flag to their comrade above, he tries to hand it to the soldier and when he refuses to take it, attempts to wrap him in it. Clearly exasperated by the persistence of the protestor, the soldier gives up and moves on to remove the next trespasser.

[18] See footage: YouTube video (25 Mar 2012) "The people and the army are one hand!" http://youtu.be/FXQzq_y2SDU.

and the army are one hand."[19] The footage continues with a Republican Guard officer using his signal flag to hit a protestor trying to board an APC. In informant testimony, the interactions with the army have been described as a negotiation, in which a shared emotional mood of victory after having defeated the hated CSF was tempered by fear of the Guards attacking (interview Youssef 1 13 Aug. 2011; interview Abdullah 1 13 Oct. 2011).[20] One informant, Khalid, told me that ad hoc meetings were held between protestors and army officers to try and establish what the army's role was to be in the unfolding events (interview Khalid 13 Oct. 2011). From his own ethnographic data, Atef Said speaks of the army's presence as a "black box" – an unknown element that provoked "anxiety and uncertainty" (2012: 408). While elated by the unprecedented defeat of the CSF, nobody was sure what would happen next.

The army had only twice before been deployed onto Egyptian streets: once in 1977 during the Bread Uprising (*Intifādat al-Khubz*; alternatively *Thawrat al-Harāmiyya*, "the Thieves' Revolution"), and again in 1986 to put down a revolt by CSF officers. On the evening of 28 January, these previous interventions were referenced to highlight the potential threat of soldiers attacking protestors. One activist who arrived in Midan al-Tahrir after setting off on a march from a populous district in eastern Cairo recounts:

Rumours ran in Tahrir that Mubarak ordered the army to descend in the streets. How did the protesters feel towards the army? On several occasions since I joined the march in Nasr City, and till we reached Tahrir, some protesters were calling on the army to intervene and "protect them from the police" like what happened in Tunisia. And when tanks showed up in Tahrir speeding towards Garden City to protect the U.S. and U.K. embassies, many protesters cheered their arrival. But at the same time, I also witnessed several occasions where the protesters intervened with anger against those who were chanting for the army, shouting: "Well, hasn't the army been ruling now since 1952? Aren't they responsible for the Egypt we have today? Didn't they kill protesters in 1977? Who gave them the orders to intervene, Mubarak, right?" All those were questions and arguments that broke out on several occasions. (el-Hamalawy 2011)

---

[19] Here the chant takes the form "The people and the army are one hand," as opposed to "The army and the people are one hand." I came across both instances regularly and interchangeably, both on that night and during the 25th January Revolution generally. However, in the formulation adopted by the military post-revolution, the army always precedes the people.

[20] The protestors had good reason to suspect the Republican Guard. Egyptian press would report their facilitating pro-Mubarak rallies outside the presidential palace, and even distributing posters of the President to his supporters (*al-Masry al-Youm*, 3 Feb. 2011: 6).

There is no sense that such historical episodes provided any interaction rituals or repertoire of contention for protestors to draw on when dealing with the army; these had to be improvised.[21] Outside of Maspero, nobody, least of all the newly deployed soldiers, seemed to know what part the army was to play in events. In response to the ambiguity of the situation, the crowd began to chant anew, demanding that Mubarak issue a statement.

At 10.50 p.m., a column of battle tanks and APCs departed from Maspero and approached Tahrir. Meanwhile, some remaining units of the CSF continued to fire tear gas and live ammunition into Tahrir from roads leading to the Interior Ministry. A rumor quickly spread that the army were coming to reinforce the CSF. As the column of army vehicles entered the Midan in single file, protestors chanted, "Are you with us, or are you with them?" Hazem, a veteran of the pitched battles fought that day on Kasr el-Nil bridge, describes the protestors' reaction to the army's arrival: "In general, as the army came into the square that night there was a very mixed mood – not just between protesters, but within them. It was a mix of fear and joy – as in 'Yay, the army is here boys,' to 'Shit, they're sending the army to attack us.' I myself felt a lot like this. Rumors were erupting constantly. On the one hand, there was an initial belief that the army was here to take on the remaining police units guarding the Ministry of Interior. Then there was the rumor that they came to join forces with the police and would begin to attack us once they took hold of the square" (interview Hazem 9 Nov. 2011). To expand briefly on the content of the rumors: earlier in the afternoon during the battle for Kasr el-Nil, military police jeeps were reportedly seen resupplying CSF units with tear gas and live ammunition as a military helicopter hovered over Tahrir. After the protestors had broken through CSF lines, a lone APC entered the Midan at speed, heading for the remnants of the CSF near the Interior Ministry. Protestors threw stones at it with little effect before it sped off.

Whether the rumors of the military rearming the CSF were true is not so important as that they sowed fear of further confrontations and situational tension in Tahrir when the army arrived. About thirty minutes after the column of army vehicles began to enter Tahrir a tank sat isolated in front of the Egyptian National Museum, some 400 meters

---

[21] For an historical overview of the Egyptian army in state-society relations see, variously, Fahmy (1997); Ramadan (1977); Springborg (1987); Kandil (2012).

from the center of Tahrir, its path blocked by protestors.[22]
The remaining vehicles continue on. A crowd of about a hundred people
surrounded the tank and five young men climbed onto the turret to douse
the tank with petrol before setting it alight. Stones were thrown at the
vehicle, their ricochets audible in the video footage recorded by protestors. When the petrol proved ineffective, the young men poured it on
rags, set them alight, and posted them in the tank's vents. The vehicle
"smoked-out," the soldiers scrambled free, only to be attacked by
members of the crowd.

Closer to the epicenter of Tahrir, more army vehicles were being
attacked. One dramatic video captured on a mobile phone shows an
APC entering the Midan and skirting the western edge of Tahrir.[23]
Approximately twenty protestors run towards the APC, throwing stones.
A second APC approaches, roof ablaze. The protestors who had been
throwing stones stop and watch the vehicle. The second APC then wheels
towards the protestors, mounting the pavement and scattering the stone
throwers. The APC stops. Stone throwing reaches a new intensity as
protestors surge towards the army vehicle chanting, "God is Great!"
The number of protestors swells to about fifty. The fire on top of the
APC goes out. Since the first APC's appearance, less than a minute has
elapsed: the second APC sits motionless. A voice (the cameraman?)
shouts, "Set it on fire, set it on fire!" and the crowd takes up this chant.
The stone throwing intensifies, and another voice shouts, "Stop, stop!"
and now this chant is taken up, seemingly by the same voice previously
calling for the fire. The crowd swells further. A man shouts, "Stop hitting
them." An element of the crowd begins to chant for the soldiers to
surrender and this continues and develops in intensity as more voices
join. A small group of protestors climbs on top of the APC, a fire is lit at
the back of the vehicle. Somebody, possibly one of the fire lighters,
exclaims, "There's somebody inside, get him out!" The crowd around
the burning APC thins out, and the protestors come to resemble
spectators.[24]

Aside from some surviving photographs (see Figure 3.3), this episode of
protestors attacking army units in Tahrir is completely absent from any

[22] See footage: YouTube video (25 Mar 2012) "Protesters attack an Egyptian Ramses II
Battle Tank, 28th January, 2011 (2)" http://youtu.be/pjx_oYXs_Hw.
[23] See footage: YouTube video (7 May 2012) "Protesters attack Egyptian army units in
Tahrir, 28th January, 2011 (1 extended)" http://youtu.be/nyi5lxLu7TE.
[24] Alisdare, who arrived minutes after the initial attack, recalled metal poles being placed in
the APC's tracks to immobilize it (personal correspondence Alisdare 13 Jun. 2013).

FIGURE 3.3 An Egyptian army APC on fire in Midan al-Tahrir, 28 Jan. 2011 (Goran Tomasevic/Reuters).

journalistic account of the 25th January Revolution.[25] While I will not sustain this detailed narrative to cover the full period for which soldiers and protestors shared Tahrir, these few hours on the night of 28 January seem especially important. Here, the action appears "eventful" (Sewell 2005) rather than following any structural, cultural, or ideological logics linked to the historical position of the Egyptian army in society, or to the fact that, it being a conscript army, most households have a male relative completing or having completed military service. Informants like Khalid, who had completed military service and, outside of the situation at hand, held a positive view of the Egyptian military, told me they felt threatened by the army's presence during this and many of the other episodes I will discuss here. This is not to overstate or stylize the argument – several informants were equally insistent that Egyptian soldiers were irrevocably on the side of protestors, and celebrated their arrival. Here, an understanding rooted in the situational dynamics in which soldiers and protestors found themselves interacting explains these contradictory positions.

[25] I have been otherwise unable to establish the fate of those soldiers attacked; the Egyptian military has, however, acknowledged the deaths and injury of soldiers during the 25th January Revolution (*al-Dostor* 2011c).

While the available chronology of events is partial, what we do know happened before, during, and after the attack maps well onto Randall Collins's ideal-type of a "forward panic":

A forward panic starts with tension and fear in a conflict situation. This is the normal condition of violent conflict, but here the tension is prolonged and built up; it has a dramatic shape of increasing tension, striving towards a climax. ... There is a shift from relatively passive – waiting, holding back until one is in a position to bring a conflict to a head – to be fully active. When the opportunity finally arrives, the tension/fear comes out in an emotional rush .... Running forward or backward, in either case they are in an overpowering emotional rhythm, carrying them on to actions that they would normally not approve of in calm, reflective moments. (2008: 85)

Upon the army's arrival in Midan al-Tahrir a similar emotional release is observed, and then swiftly reined in. In the second attack, a voice is heard encouraging protestors to set the APC on fire, which is then echoed by other protestors who rush to attack the vehicle. Almost immediately the same voice calls for restraint. These contradictions, or reassessments, Collins argues, accompany the building up and release of emotional energy. In this sequence of events, what appears formative are the features of the situation – the buildup of tension, the existing situation of violence and continued presence of the CSF, the role played by rumors, and the point at which tension spilled over into a forward panic. For my discussion, what is key are the next moves that protestors make after exiting the emotional tunnel of attack.

Returning to the Midan, a military truck had followed the column of tanks and APCs and was similarly surrounded by protestors. The soldiers in the cab were pulled out and attacked, and informants reported ransacking of the truck's cargo and the discovery of food rations. Soldiers manning nearby tanks then moved to intervene and a protestor was pushed to the ground. While this drama unfolded, protestors commandeered the smoked-out tank, and even managed to pilot it forward a few meters (Shalaby 2011). A search of the tank discovered boxes of ammunition, tear gas canisters and grenades and, like the food, these were distributed to protestors in the Midan. Other army vehicles and soldiers were likewise attacked with two smoldering military jeeps littering Tahrir the next morning. One had been stopped and commandeered earlier in the evening as it entered Tahrir and found to contain live ammunition before being set ablaze (El-Hamalawy 2011).

When it appeared the situation would deteriorate further, informants recall, a group of protestors crowded round the remaining parked tanks chanting, "The army and the people are one hand" (interview Abdullah 2 21 Jul. 2011). In an act of micro-conflict avoidance, I would suggest, protestors chanted for the army as a means to dissipate fear of further confrontations and bring under control the situational anxiety felt by both sides.[26] Fraternization techniques superseded any prolonging of attacks on soldiers, despite protestors being armed with weapons seized from the army, weapons many suspected had been intended for the CSF. That protestors did not, in effect, militarize the revolution, speaks to the constraints of the broader 25th January repertoire of contention, which cautioned against militarization through the chanting of *silmiyya* (peaceful) protest.

Significantly, it is here and elsewhere that we find the nascent formation of a new frontier in the struggle against Mubarak through the articulation of the collective subject of "the people." Particularly cogent is Ernesto Laclau's (2007) argument that the emergence of "the people" as a collective actor exists not as an a priori category, but proceeds instead through the formation of an antagonistic internal frontier, differentiating "the people" from power via the naming of demands. One chant from the broader 25th January repertoire that we will encounter below illustrates this well: *al-sha'b yurīd isqāt al-nizām* (the people want the overthrow of the regime). In chanting "The army and the people are one hand" protestors would extend this frontier to include newly deployed soldiers, with the Mubarak regime present as the silent Other: the army and the people were one hand in their struggle to overthrow the regime.

To grasp how a political frontier forms we must, as Dzenovska and Arenas (2012: 645) have insisted, account for the concrete political practices that made it possible. One protestor, Alia, describes the chant's emergence: "'The army and people are one hand' was certainly a strategy for nonviolence in the beginning – it wasn't a statement – we weren't welcoming the army. For some it was more like 'You, we have nothing against' [or] 'You we won't attack,' and for others it was 'Let's be one

---

[26] It has been suggested to me that the chant, "The army and the people are one hand" owes its origins to the slogan, "Muslims and Christians are one hand" (alternatively, "The people of the Book are one hand"). Just weeks before 28 January, this version of the "one hand" metaphor was invoked by activists looking to rally inter-communal support following the much publicized bombing of the Two Saints Church in Alexandria on 1 January (Colla 2012: 12). If this was indeed the origin of the chant, protestors chanting, "The army and the people are one hand" adhered to Tilly's contentious claim making model by innovating on a publicly available, shared script to signal a nonsectarian solidarity.

hand,' [but] it certainly wasn't an announcement of the status" (personal correspondence Alia 27 Sept. 2011). Accordingly, this was, then, a precarious and incomplete solidarity, an act of micro-conflict avoidance, rather than the formation of a new collective actor.

When explaining the de-escalation, informants also attest to a protracted lull in fighting with the CSF on the eastern side of Tahrir, which contributed to a temporary abatement of the shared mood of impending violence. Protestors, for their part, immediately sought to establish face-to-face contact with soldiers. One informant spoke of protestors – who had minutes before been throwing stones – embracing soldiers whose tanks were by then parked in the Midan. Protestors posed for photographs with soldiers; others hugged them, shook their hands, and kissed their cheeks.

Recounts Hazem, "Eventually … once the tanks had all parked, protesters began to join them on top of the tanks and talk to them …. Conversation and laughter soon broke out and protestors began taking pictures with their phones standing next to military personnel and their tank. Food was shared between protester and soldier" (interview Hazem 9 Nov. 2011). Above all, in the wider context of the army's deployment, this episode provides an important backdrop to explaining the confrontational fear and tension that surrounded the army's presence and the mechanisms that protestors adopted to avoid the outbreak of further violence.

While some protestors attacked newly arriving army vehicles, others set about establishing their own system of markers on them. Graffiti on tanks and APCs represented a new way to contest the army's claim to organize its own territory. The graffiti tended to draw on chants and slogans from the larger 25th January repertoire: often variations on a theme of "The people want the overthrow of the regime" and "Leave, Mubarak." What Mona el-Ghobashy (2011: 13) has described as the "branding of public goods" is illustrative of how fraternizing protestors could enact a symbolic trespassing that broke down the distinction between a military space and a public space claimed by the protestors. Army vehicles became canvases, encoded with the protestors' contestation announcing the protestors' shared focus of occupying Tahrir until Mubarak was deposed.

The graffiti itself was almost completely anti-Mubarak in content. From my review of photographs, I found no explicitly pro-army slogans graffitied on vehicles. When graffiti did mention the army it tended to highlight its ties to the Mubarak regime, while drawing it into the wider symbolic field of protestors' contention. The graffiti on one APC read, "This is Egypt's army, not Mubarak's army."[27] Another piece of graffiti from the same vehicle proclaimed: "We were betting on the Egyptian army, that it would not sell its children; but we found out the truth, that it had sold the Egyptian people for its president." As a fraternization performance, graffitiing tanks and APCs further challenged the army's claims to ownership of that space, in turn placing those vehicles on the side of the protestors. Protestors arriving in the Midan over the following days would report feeling reassured by the graffiti, emboldening them to approach the vehicles, a logic related by one informant, Ahmad, as, "If the army has let us [the protestors] do this, they must be on our side" (interview Ahmad 10 Jul. 2011).

ONE, TWO, WHERE IS THE EGYPTIAN ARMY?

I have suggested that the chant, "The army and the people are one hand" was a contentious performance that protestors employed situationally when they felt threatened by the army units in their midst, or when trying to de-escalate protestor-soldier violence. This was almost always face-to-face action, which through its recursion became an interaction ritual invoked, if not always successfully, in situations when protestor-soldier coexistence was threatened. Even in response to threatening actions by military units some distance away (including episodes of fighter jets over-flying the Midan, unsettling protestors with their sonic booms), or the presence of a military helicopter hovering overhead, protestors directed their chants at army units closer at hand.[28]

A second use of chanting occurred when protestors were, while in the presence of army units, either threatened or under attack by remnants of the CSF or pro-regime loyalists. The first instance of this that I have been able to identify comes on the morning of 29 January. Video shows three APCs maneuvering their vehicles between protestors and shotgun-wielding CSF units on a road leading to the Interior Ministry.[29] The intervention is not

---

[27] I am grateful to Mariam Aboelezz for sharing this photograph with me.

[28] In episodes of low-flying F-16s on 30 January, informants reported a mood of impending attack, to which they responded with chants of, "The army and the people are one hand." This is captured on footage: YouTube video (7 May 2012) "Protestors chant, "The army and the people are one hand" as F-16s fly over Midan-Al Tahrir (1)" http://youtu.be/FQh y3c3cRNo and (7 May 2012) "Protestors chant, "The army and the people are one hand" as F-16s fly over Midan al-Tahrir (2)" http://youtu.be/UQWVMyBTPLA. Atef Said (2012: 408) corroborates this fear of attack, reporting that his informants considered such episodes "an attempt to terrorize protesters and disperse them."

[29] See footage: YouTube video (29 Apr 2012) "One, two, where are the Egyptian army chant" http://youtu.be/AwPUJnymqVM.

totally on the side of the protestors. As protestors threw stones at CSF troops, individual soldiers tried to restrain them, and minor scuffling broke out. Nevertheless, the protestors persisted. A gunshot then rang out, fired from the CSF side. The crowd started to chant, "One, two, where is the Egyptian army?" The footage cuts to the APCs aligned on the street, offering maximum shielding to the protestors who continue their skirmish with the CSF.

Another example is that of Captain Maged Boules, or the "Lion of Tahrir." Boules became a hero to those occupying Tahrir after he confronted pro-regime thugs approaching the Midan from the Talaat Harb entrance on 2 February (*al-Shorouk* 2011: 5; *al-Ahram* 6 Oct. 2011). In video footage, we see Boules confronting the approaching thugs before retreating towards his APC at the entrance to Tahrir.[30] Brandishing his pistol, Boules repeatedly fires in the air. As the column continues to advance, more soldiers appear, heading to collect their weapons from the hatch of the APC. As one soldier kneels to load his rifle, protestors begin to chant, "The people and the army are one hand." The chant quickly spreads. The footage ends with protestors jumping up and down, the column of advancing thugs halted, protestors and soldiers buzzing with the emotional energy of averting attack. A weeping Boules is then embraced by protestors after mounting the APC to be cheered by the crowd and proclaimed with further chants of, "The people and the army are one hand" (see Figure 3.4).

Chanting at the army took on particular significance during the Battle of the Camel on 2 February, so-called after pro-regime elements, thugs, and plainclothes police attacked Tahrir, many riding horses or camels. This was another consequence of anti-police violence discussed in the previous chapter. Faced with a serious deterioration in the regime's capacity to overcome dissent, Mubarak was forced to mobilize irregular forces. For a brief period, members of Mubarak's National Democratic Party, along with hired thugs, violently attacked anti-regime protestors under cover of pro-Mubarak marches.[31] This synthetic mobilization reached its crescendo on 2 February when NDP members and local bosses

---

[30] See footage: YouTube video (29 Apr 2012) "The Lion of Tahrir and The Army and the People are One Hand Chant" http://youtu.be/Av4gwKjjgSc.

[31] In the days leading up to the 25 January, senior NDP officials had promised that up to 500,000 party youth members would take to the streets in a "day of loyalty" to show popular support for Hosni Mubarak (*al-Masry al-Youm* 24 Jan. 2011: 1; *al-Shorouk* 24 Jan. 2011: 1). The youth never materialized. Instead, the first pro-Mubarak protest is reported to have taken place on 28 January, when several dozen NDP members staged a demonstration in Damietta (*al-Masry al-Youm* 29 Jan. 2011: 10).

FIGURE 3.4 A protestor embraces Maged Boules after he confronts a column of approaching regime thugs, Midan al-Tahrir, 2 Feb. 2011 (Lefteris Pitarakis/AP/ Press Association Images).

launched a sustained attack on protestors in Midan al-Tahrir. For a full day and night, the two sides exchanged stones and Molotov cocktails. During lulls in the fighting, protestors approached army units, entreating them to intervene, chanting, "Where is the Egyptian army?" During one episode when a tank at the National Museum entrance did intervene, with soldiers firing guns above the heads of regime thugs and driving their vehicle forwards, protestors chanted, "The army and the people are one hand." Meanwhile, according to one informant, Ahmad, those in the center of the Midan misunderstood the situational context and panicked, thinking the army had opened fire on protestors (interview Ahmad 10 Jul. 2011).

The Battle of the Camel was doubly important not only as the last serious attempt by the Mubarak regime to displace the occupation of Tahrir, but also for reminding protestors of the ambiguous position of the army. This is borne out through the situational analyses protestors themselves developed through their interactions with soldiers. Informants frequently identified army units positioned at both the Kasr el-Nil and National Museum entrances to Tahrir as actively collaborating with the Mubarak regime. It was at Kasr el-Nil that regime elements successfully entered the Midan and it was outside the National Museum that the fiercest fighting continued into the next day. Informants explicitly accused those soldiers of being complicit in the attack or of not intervening to protect the protestors when asked. This was a view shared by military personnel, too. One soldier, who had been deployed days earlier, remembers:

One of my friends in Tahrir called. He was hysterical, crying and screaming: 'Where is the army, where were you? Nobody intervened, they left us.' ... It was one of the most difficult moments of my life. It was clear that the army was complicit one way or another: either it was indirectly supporting what was happening, or refusing to intervene, which is the same. (*Ahram Online* 2013)

When implored to intercede to stop the advance of regime supporters after fighting initially broke out in front of the National Museum, soldiers refused, insisting their duty was simply to secure the area (*al-Masry al-Youm*, 3 Feb. 2011: 5). Later, as regime thugs broke onto the roofs of buildings opposite the National Museum to rain Molotov cocktails down onto protestors sheltering behind impromptu barricades below, the army again ignored calls to step in (*Egypt Gazette* 2011b: 2). As the battle raged, one eyewitness described how "Egyptian soldiers looked on, lined up motionless in their armored vehicles in the middle of the two opposing sides" (Trombetta 2013: 143).

After the Battle of the Camel a series of confrontations broke out between units of the Egyptian army and protestors. These centered on burnt-out trucks improvised into barricades outside the National Museum. The following morning tanks attempted to tow these away and protestors, fearing the loss of their fortifications, immediately moved to block the army, physically surrounding their vehicles. In several instances scuffles broke out between protestors and soldiers only to be defused, with protestors physically restraining their comrades and chanting pro-army slogans (interview Ahmad 10 Jul. 2011; interview Alaa 13 Nov. 2011). In this and other instances, we find small numbers of violent protestors brought under control by members of their own side via fraternization performances. These confrontations, informants feared, were provoked by regime *agents provocateurs* whose goal was to draw the army into attacking the protestors. Fraternizing was thus utilized on two fronts: first, to constrain the behavior of the violent minority by setting an alternative mode of interaction with soldiers, and second, to signal to army units a pacific intent by returning to now familiar interaction rituals signaling protestor-soldier solidarity. The barricades were otherwise left untouched.

A further point of contention arose from the handing over to the army of tens of thugs and undercover policemen detained by protestors after the attack. These detention practices continued until Mubarak's resignation, with suspected *agents provocateurs* kept in the "people's prison" – the stairway to the closed Sadat metro station that services the Midan *(al-Shorouk* 2011: 5; *al-Masry al-Youm,* 7 Feb. 2011: 5). Many believed that, once handed over, these pro-regime elements were simply set free by the army so they could again terrorize the protestors.

Despite their sharing the Midan for nearly a week, the actions of the army remained for many a constant source of distrust and suspected malfeasance. The army would declare on 31 January, three days after their initial deployment, that they would not use force to put down the mobilizations, but not until 3 February, after the Battle of the Camel had been lost by the regime, did the military offer to guarantee the security of protestors in the Midan, and it was all the while calling on them to demobilize and vacate Tahrir *(al-Masry al-Youm,* 3 Feb. 2011: 7). This commitment soon took the form of stop and search checkpoints at the Midan's entrances *(al-Masry al-Youm,* 5 Feb. 2011: 6). Informants, however, complained of soldiers stopping the flow of food and medicine, and protestors continued to maintain their own cordon around the Midan, checking identity cards, and searching newcomers. When explaining this duplication to me, Alaa, who had manned a checkpoint, insisted the protestors' cordon was there both to assert their control of the Midan and because, "We didn't trust the army" (interview Alaa 13 Nov. 2011).

WHAT IS THE LOVE STORY WITH THE TANKS?

What is the love story with the tanks? So reads the title of an *al-Masry al-Youm* article of 2 February 2011 (p. 12), seemingly one of the few Egyptian journalistic accounts published during the revolution that focused specifically on protestor-soldier interactions. The title echoed a question posed by an Egyptian army officer stationed in Tahrir whose tank was surrounded by men and women taking photographs of their friends atop the vehicle. In Tahrir, the article noted, tanks had been transformed into sites for taking photographs. Those being pictured often made victory signs and waved Egyptian flags. Soldiers had tried to stop the climbing on the tanks, but were overrun by the large number of photograph hunters. "Please cooperate with us and stay away" the army officer implores, "and make our job easier."

Posing for photographs was one of a set of fraternization performances that involved trespassing upon army vehicles in nonviolent situations, performances we first encountered on the night of 28 January and which quickly became an emergent symbol of army-protestor solidarity, to be emulated as long as protestors and soldiers were physically co-present. So synonymous did this act become with being in Tahrir during the 25th January Revolution that it gave rise to the popular (and characteristically sarcastic) Egyptian Facebook meme, "I didn't take a photograph next to the tank" (*ana matsawartish ganb al-dabāba*). Walking through Midan al-Tahrir in the summer of 2011, it was commonplace to see visitors to the Midan recreate such images, suggesting that to do so had come to be seen as a politically contentious act. I have already cataloged how, in fighting the CSF, protestors used newly deployed APCs as physical cover. In other instances, tanks at the Kasr el-Nil entrance to Midan al-Tahrir were literally incorporated into protestors' barricades. All these performances made immediate claims on the soldiers manning those vehicles to give security to the protestors, or to neutralize any future threat those units posed. Posing for photographs underlines a further dimension to the fraternizing of soldiers in Midan al-Tahrir comparable to what Dzenovska and Arenas (2012) have called a, "barricade sociality." In this, posing for photographs was one of many embodied fraternization performances that both reflected and made possible a protestor-soldier solidarity. These interpersonal rituals, designated by Goffman (1971: 194–99) as "tie-signs" – hugging, kissing, shaking hands, a protestor's arms around the shoulders of a soldiers, a soldier hoisted on the shoulders of protestors – all enacted a political frontier: the army and the people together in occupied Tahrir in the face of regime oppression. These tie-signs took on a particular consequentiality, for instance with the "Lion of Tahrir," after soldiers committed to intervene on behalf of protestors, or when protestors attempted to diminish the risk of protestor-soldier violence as occurred on the night of 28 January, and, indeed, on the few occasions protestors fraternized with the CSF.

Tie-signs were key to sustaining this frontier: they communicated information regarding intentions and the nature of relationships, both to those interacting and to wider audiences. If every day tie-signs inform third parties as to the nature of the relationship, these tend to map to degrees of familiarity. Fraternization tie-signs are in this sense exceptional, since the usual rules of embodied action are suspended. In a successful fraternization performance protestors and security forces, people almost always unconnected outside of the situation at hand, sign highly intimate relations that collapse everyday social heterogeneity, such as gender, class, or other group membership.

The ritualistic mounting of army vehicles was not exclusively the domain of protestors. Army officers used tanks and APCs as platforms from which to address those occupying the Midan. Upon the army's deployment on 28 January, officers commanding army units in the Midan delivering such speeches would be interrupted and interrogated, with questions shouted at them demanding to know whether they were with or against Mubarak. In el-Amrani's (2011) account of a speech by a general in Tahrir on 29 January, he describes:

an amazing moment when a charismatic one-star general addressed the public. . . . People kept shouting, are you with or against Mubarak? He answered that his mission is making sure the looting stops, and that the issue of who governs is the people's decision, not the army's, and that government should be civilian. Of course there is mounting tension and uncertainty about where the army stands. There are so few tanks (maybe twenty to thirty) and personnel around Midan Tahrir that I feel they could easily be overwhelmed.

Speeches took a somewhat different form after 4 February when senior military officers, surrounded by bodyguards, began to take tours of Tahrir. These included Field Marshal Tantawi, Mubarak's then Minister of Defense and head of the Supreme Council of the Armed Forces (SCAF), who visited the Midan to be greeted by chants of, "O Field Marshal, O Field Marshal, we are your children in Tahrir" (*al-Masry al-Youm*, 5 Feb. 2011: 5). These addresses were received with a greater degree of reverence, and when assurances were offered as to the army's loyalty to the protestors' cause, rewarded with chants of, "The army and the people are one hand." Still, despite the invoked paternalism of protestors' chants and the frequency of these speeches, informants who were present later reported officers who walked through the Midan being accosted by protestors demanding to know if the army would attack them (interview Khalid 13 Oct. 2011).

This was symptomatic of the lingering uncertainty and anxiety many retained concerning the army's presence, a point well illustrated by a further addition to the fraternization repertoire: sleeping in the tracks of tanks and APCs. The first instance of this was reported on 5 February after tanks stationed in Tahrir started their engines (*Egyptian Gazette* 2011a: 1).[32] Just as in the earlier, 28 January episode in which protestors

---

[32] An earlier version of this performance came on 30 January as eight tanks entered Tahrir. Journalists reported protestors rushing up to the tanks shouting, "God is great!" before

attacked newly arriving army units, a rumor preceded this action, this time suggesting the tanks planned to withdraw from the Midan in anticipation of a renewed attack by regime loyalists. Records of the rumor are unclear as to whether the army was supposed to be participating in the attack, or else complicit in coordinating it.[33] In response to the tanks' engines starting, protestors quickly surrounded tanks and APCs in Tahrir. The logic of this performance was seemingly that, following the corporeal surrounding of army vehicles individual units could be isolated and made responsible for the protestors' security. If graffiti made military vehicles in Tahrir symbolically compromised, the sleeping in vehicle tracks made them operationally so. Physically encircled and unable to move, the Egyptian army had effectively lost these vehicles and their crews by 6 February, along with any semblance of a military order organizing a contiguous territory. Protestors would remain encamped there until Mubarak's resignation on 11 February, as physical and symbolic forms of defense against the predations of the Mubarak regime.

CONCLUSIONS

To mark the first anniversary of the 25th January Revolution, a convoy of Egyptian army APCs drove through central Cairo. Each vehicle flew a national flag and had emblazoned on its side, "The army and the people are one hand." Commercial billboards on Cairo's main thoroughfares were rented, proclaiming, "The 25th January Revolution – the army protected it. The army and the people ... are one hand," accompanied by images of children posing for photographs on tanks stationed in Midan al-Tahrir. Similar posters appeared outside the many army barracks and military administration buildings located in and around the city (see Figure 3.5).

In the post-Mubarak transition, the Supreme Council of the Armed Forces used the residual symbols of fraternization performances as

---

lying in their path. Their advance blocked, soldiers and protestors engaged in a tense standoff lasting several hours. Eventually, an army officer mounted one of the tanks and addressed the crowd, assuring them that the tanks would not encroach any further into the Midan (*Star* 2011; *Guardian* 2011).

[33] This fear of attack may have been exacerbated by the visit on 5 February of army general Hassan Ruweini. Flanked by soldiers, he approached the protestor's fortifications, which led protestors to link arms to block his entry into the Midan. Journalists present reported protestors preparing for an attack after Ruweini's bodyguard partially dismantled a barricade, prompting protestors to chant "We will die here!" While no attack materialized, protestors voiced their suspicions of the army to journalists present (*Atlantic* 2011).

FIGURE 3.5 "The army and the people are one hand." Poster outside Egyptian military checkpoint on Suez Road, Cairo. Feb. 2012 (author's photo).

a source of political capital, employed to legitimate their assuming executive control after Mubarak's departure. Those symbols of fraternization, the storage vessels for the ephemeral feelings of protestor-soldier solidarity, were quickly detached from the wider symbolic universe of revolutionary Tahrir and put to work elsewhere.[34] In SCAF's narrative, the

---

[34] See Collins (2004: 81–101) on the way symbols act as containers for the emotions produced by interaction rituals.

army's role during those fifteen days was to be fêted as one intended to safeguard peaceful protest against the Mubarak regime. Nowhere is this more evident than in the "messages" through which SCAF communicated with the Egyptian citizenry, and specifically its 2011 messages, many of which invoked SCAF's claims to a stake in the post-Mubarak order on the basis of defending the 25th January Revolution and not using force against protestors.[35] That the SCAF was able to plausibly draw on these symbols of fraternization speaks to the deep reimagination of politics that fraternizing protestors and their contentious performances made possible in reaggregating a claim to sovereignty in the name of "the people" in opposition to the increasingly desperate and violent actions undertaken by the Mubarak regime. This bifurcation of governance from sovereignty was not missed by the regime, as epitomized by its announcement on 7 February, and later relayed via a Greater Cairo-wide SMS message, that the police force would be returning to the streets under its pre-Mubarak motto, "The police are in the service of the people" (*al-Dostor* 2011b: 6; *al-Masry al-Youm*, 10 Feb. 2011: 3).[36] This was followed, shortly after Mubarak's resignation, with posters plastered around the city declaring, "For Egypt: The army, the police and the people are one hand," dubiously signed off by the "Youth of Egypt" (see Figure 3.6).

As this chapter has argued, and contrary to SCAF's posturing, it is wrong to assume that protestors singularly embraced the army's new role in street politics, or that protestor-solider solidarity was unequivocal. The argument presented here has suggested instead that protestors surrounding and hauling themselves aboard army vehicles, chanting for the army, graffitiing tanks and APCs, and tie-signing with soldiers, constituted instances of claim making. These protestor-soldier interactions were in themselves sites of action, sites at which protestors and soldiers forged a new political frontier through their performances. Theoretically, this has involved a conception of contentious performance that captures ritualistic claim making at the micro-interactive level. Exploring the micro-interactive dimensions to one episode of contention reveals a good degree of improvisation and innovation on scripted performances in response to situational dynamics. Key here is taking seriously the capacity for claims

[35] The messages were made available at: https://www.facebook.com/Egyptian.Armed .Forces.
[36] Under Mubarak, the motto had been changed to, "The police and the people in the service of the nation."

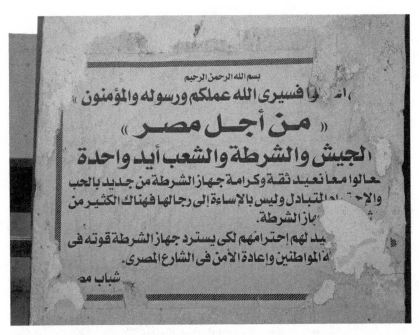

FIGURE 3.6 "For Egypt: The army, the police and the people are one hand."
Poster on wall in downtown Cairo. May 2011 (author's photo).

made on the agents of regime power to decide situational outcomes,
primarily by affecting emotional moods and stimulating feelings of solidarity. In Tahrir, that solidarity was at once fragile and contingent, having
constantly to be remade as protestors fraternized with army units stationed in their midst in an attempt to both neutralize any potential threat
they posed and sway their loyalty by forging common bonds and a shared
political horizon. This dissonance and an attending polyvalence in performances was acknowledged by protestors themselves, one of whom
described a "mix of feelings/actions toward the army ... on the one
hand we have chanted the people and the army are one hand, and on the
other, protestors decided to sleep under tanks and block them from
encroaching on the square or dispersing the Tahrir sit-in" (quoted in
Said 2012: 409). As a political frontier born of the practices of street
politics, this frontier was for many protestors only ever actualized situationally, by what became ritualized fraternization performances, and by
interventions by brave soldiers such as Maged Boules, or the sixteen army
officers who reportedly came to the Midan to declare solidarity with the

protestors (Reuters 2011). Many of them were later prosecuted in military courts for this.[37]

Meanwhile, preliminary comparative studies of the 2011 Arab Spring have tended to reproduce SCAF's narrative, taking as their point of departure the decision by Egypt's generals not to intervene as having decided the course of the 25th January Revolution (e.g., Barany 2011; Nepstad 2013). This, even though the military leadership only cut Mubarak loose on 10 February, which triggered his resignation the following day. In the absence of reliable accounts from Egypt's military command concerning the fifteen days the army were deployed, we can only speculate on the formativeness of fraternization in shaping the trajectory of the revolution. Certainly, army officers, speaking to Egyptian journalists in Midan al-Tahrir in the last week of the mobilization, report receiving orders to stop protestors from entering Midan al-Tahrir, an order they refused to carry out (see *al-Shorouk* 5 Feb. 2011: 5). The question remains whether an order for the army to attack protestors was ever issued. The SCAF themselves have released a series of contradictory statements, claiming they refused an order to fire on protestors in Tahrir, only to later retract the claim (*Egypt Independent* 2011). The trial of Mubarak and others implicated in the killing of protestors has otherwise failed to resolve this question with testimony given by Field Marshal Tantawi and Sami Anan (then army chief of staff), heard *in camera*. While we do not have an official court transcript of these exchanges, it is commonly understood that Tantawi denied receiving an order to fire. This is contradicted by video footage that shows a soldier in the Midan telling protestors that his unit had disobeyed an order to attack on 7 February, although I could not otherwise corroborate this.[38]

There is a counterfactual argument to be made that hangs on the reliability of army units in Tahrir to follow orders, as perceived by their officers. In Tahrir at least, there was a breakdown of all semblance of a separate military discipline and authority structure standing apart from protestors' claims to control the Midan. In response, red-bereted military police were later drafted into Tahrir in an attempt to bolster the discipline of the army units stationed there. In issuing any order to attack those

---

[37] See the case of Major Ahmad Shuman who appeared in the Midan wearing a uniform to call for Mubarak's dismissal. Despite being initially pardoned, Shuman was later rearrested and sentenced to six years in prison by a military court (*al-Shorouk* 2012).

[38] See footage at: YouTube video (25 Apr 2012) "Soldier tells of order to attack protestors in Midan al-Tahrir 7th February, 2011." http://youtu.be/hRHnX6CcbAw.

occupying the Midan, senior army officers would have been forced to question the reliability of troops in Tahrir and their solidarity with those who had for days been embracing them, posing for photographs atop their vehicles, and chanting in their name.

If fraternization succeeded in separating the army units in Tahrir from military command and control structures, the Egyptian military soon developed countermeasures. On 9 March 2011, with the democratic transition underway, the army attempted to "clear" Tahrir, prompting protestors to hastily link arms and chant to a column of approaching soldiers, "The people and the army are one hand."[39] Others attempted to tie-sign with soldiers, all the while imploring them not to destroy the protestors' encampment. Faced with overwhelming odds and the threat of violence, these protestors fell back on a fraternization repertoire that communicated their solidarity with the army. But here their performances fell flat – the column, marshaled at a distance by military police and kept in tight discipline at a running pace, followed orders. The tents in the Midan were dismantled and protestors beaten by gangs of thugs.

After this and other episodes of contentious street politics during the post-Mubarak democratic transition – the subject of the next chapter – new performances quickly supplanted fraternization when interacting with the army. Peaceful protestors were killed by soldiers at Maspero in October 2011, and then on Muhammad Mahmoud Street in late November 2011 and outside the Defense Ministry in Abbasiyya in May 2012. These events occurred alongside allegations of torture, forced virginity testing, and the army's repressive policing of street politics and labor agitation as the revolutionary coalition that had ousted Mubarak and temporarily neutralized the military fragmented. By the revolution's first anniversary, new chants had innovated on the old: "The people and the people are one hand!" and "The army and the police are one dirty hand!"

---

[39] See footage at: YouTube video (7 May 2012) "Protestors chant, 'The army and the people are one hand' as the army 'clears' Tahrir March 9th, 2011" http://youtu.be/JY2mU-Drmx8.

4

Democratic Transition

al-intikhābāt hiyya al-hall! (Elections are the solution!)
al-Hurriyya wa-l-'Adala, 22 Nov. 2011

On 22 November 2012, Egyptian President Muhammad Mursi issued a constitutional declaration retroactively placing his presidential decrees beyond the purview of Egypt's courts. The declaration came just weeks before the country's Supreme Constitutional Court was due to rule on the legitimacy of Egypt's latest constituent assembly, which had been tasked by Mursi with drafting a new constitution. In April, the Higher Administrative Court had dissolved the assembly's first incarnation, citing membership irregularities. This was followed in June by an expedited ruling from Egypt's infamously dilatory Supreme Constitutional Court, annulling the election results for parliament's lower house – the first freely elected parliament since the Free Officers seized power in 1952 – on a technicality. Mursi and his supporters insisted that these judicial interventions amounted to a conspiracy between Egypt's judges and Mubarak-era regime figures known as *filūl* (literally, remnants) to eviscerate the institutions newly elected after the 25th January Revolution. Judicial oversight could therefore only return when a new constitution was passed by a national referendum. In a sound bite that featured prominently in both domestic and international news coverage, liberal politician Mohammad ElBaradei denounced Mursi, accusing him of acting like "Egypt's new pharaoh" (cited in *BBC* 22 Nov. 2012).

While Mursi's ostensible power grab persuaded an already ambivalent international audience that he and his movement, the Muslim Brothers, had only a weak commitment to the constitutional niceties required for a successful transition away from authoritarian rule, the Brothers' high-minded, dismissive attitude to the objections of Egypt's largely secular opposition triggered a new cycle of protests demanding Mursi's resignation. Organized under the banner of the National Salvation Front and galvanized by the Tamarrod (rebellion) petition campaign, these protests reached their apogee outside of the Presidential Palace and in the streets of downtown Cairo on 30 June 2013. On 3 July 2013, the military seized upon these protests to stage a coup.

How can we explain the derailing of democratic transition in Egypt following the 25th January Revolution? If the modal outcome of post-Cold War democratic transitions is to produce "hybrid regimes" (Diamond 2002; Schedler 2002; Levitsky and Way 2010) in which military powers and former regime prerogatives largely remain intact while newly elected civilian authorities consolidate only a limited degree of democratic authority, then the full-blown return to military rule in Egypt in less than three years presents a puzzle.

In the previous chapter I adopted a microanalytical lens to problematize the military's role in the 25th January Revolution. I suggested that the military, far from siding with the Revolution, instead came to question the fealty of key armored units stationed in Egypt's streets and squares as a result of fraternization with protestors. This chapter zooms out of the micro-interactions of contentious street politics and adopts a more wide-angled lens to focus on the role played by elections and protests in contributing to the failure of the post-Mubarak democratic transition. More specifically, it examines the consequences of the Muslim Brothers' demobilization following the 25th January Revolution and the movement's decision to put its faith in the transition administered by the Supreme Council of the Armed Forces' (SCAF), electoral mechanisms and the authority of a new parliament and president. In doing so, the argument departs from an emerging conventional wisdom according to which Mursi's autocoup (Brownlee 2013), the Muslim Brothers' organizational introversion (El-Sherif 2014), and the movement's Islamist identity (Lust, Soltan, and Wichman n.d.) fatally, and all too predictably, undermined the democratic transition. Such a singular focus on movement attributes and the indubitable failures of Mursi's tenure in office, neglects broader processual dynamics related to the nature of the revolutionary coalition that ousted Husni Mubarak, the traditions and legacies of Mubarak-era machine politics, and concerted efforts by entrenched powers and old regime holdovers to subvert attempts to open up the state to democratic control.

Though the chapter's empirical terrain is focused on the eighteen months following Mubarak's ousting, the argument has broader implications for how we understand the trajectory of Mursi's brief tenure in office and the cycle of protest that led to his downfall (discussed in the subsequent chapter), as well as how we account for the relationship between elections and protests during episodes of democratic transition away from authoritarian rule in late Third Wave democratization. Here, contrary to extant theories of democratic transition, we might very well conclude that contentious politics in transgressive mode plays a meaningful role in late Third Wave democratization, both in keeping together rapidly convened negative coalitions and in deepening the democratization process.

ELECTIONS AND PROTEST

Demobilization and "mere electioneering" are typically seen as unproblematic, if not desirable, in extant theories of democratic transition. Such is the legacy of a "top down" transitology approach that views mobilization and popular politics as exogenous to the unfolding of a successful transition (Huntington 1991; Przeworski 1991; for overviews and critique see Collier 1999: ch.1; Bermeo 2003: ch.1). Social movements and mass protest, this literature acknowledges, are frequently harbingers of democratization and key elements in bringing about democratic breakthroughs (O'Donnell and Schmitter 1986: 53–54; Linz and Stepan 1996: ch.4). However, once a regime has been toppled, the tactical imperative for a successful democratic transition, if it is to avoid alienating the middle classes, business elite, military, and reformist factions within authoritarian regimes, must be to moderate and institutionalize the "threat from below" (Bermeo 1997), pushing for social justice and other forms of redress. Accordingly, a transition is most likely to succeed if it is guided into a sequence of elite-level strategic interactions involving regime reformers and the leaders of a centrist opposition (O'Donnell and Schmitter 1986). Even studies that emphasize the positive role played by "civil society" in democratization processes have argued that for transitions to be successful – that is, for democracy to be consolidated – civil society, and by implication transgressive contention, must quickly be subordinated to the norms, procedures, and institutions of "political society" (Linz and Stepan 1996: 10).

This conclusion finds support in scholarly accounts of democratization in Eastern Europe, Southern Europe, Central America, Latin America, and Southeast Asia, which have found that transitions away from authoritarian rule frequently coincide with the demobilization of social movements and a decline in transgressive contentious politics – even if many of those same scholars lament the passing of popular forces capable of deepening the democratization process (Canel 1992; Oxhorn 1994; 1996; Hipsher 1996, 1998; Sandoval 1998; Pickvance 1999; Tarrow 1995; Sidel 2014; Trejo 2014).[1] Accounting for the demobilizing pressures of democratization, these studies stress developments in the political process: as polities transition away from authoritarian rule following democratic breakthroughs, movements demobilize, shifting their focus from the street to securing a foothold in formerly closed state institutions via elections. Anticipated electoral success further incentivizes demobilization, with movement leaders looking to pursue their agendas in the chambers of parliaments and in the corridors of executive power (Kadivar 2013; Robertson 2010: ch.5). Benedict Anderson (1998: 266) calls this the "Janus-face of electoralism": the promise of electoral authority and access to state power and patronage also commands the domestication and pacification of more popular modes of politics.

In the subsequent discussion, we will find that the Muslim Brothers' demobilization following the 25th January Revolution confirms the political process thesis outlined above. However, rather than produce the kind of conservative and constrained consolidation typical of post-Cold War democratization, the Brothers' attempts to electoralize contention and restrict a democratic transition to a process of negotiation, transaction, and electioneering actually worked against the post-Mubarak democratic project. Here, the Muslim Brothers "uncoordinated demobilization" (Tarrow 1995), a product of their strategic reading of the transition and relentless electoralism, undermined the efficacy of protest in deepening the democratization process, while facilitating the division of the revolutionary coalition along unequal electoral lines. In this, to echo Adrienne LeBas (2011: 7), democratization in Egypt proved to be "considerably more contentious than the transitions that have served as the empirical base for the transitology theory of past decades."

---

[1] This is not to suggest a deterministic relationship. As Ekiert and Kubik (1999) have chronicled, democratic transitions in Poland, Hungary, East Germany, and Slovakia saw increased protest resulting from the ineffectiveness of political parties and the paucity of official channels for participation. Nancy Bermeo (1997) has also shown that mobilization continued throughout transition periods in Spain and Portugal in ways that actually strengthened democratization efforts.

NEGATIVE REVOLUTIONARY COALITION

As Lucan Way (2011: 24) noted just after Mubarak's downfall, an absence of international support for democratization in Egypt – Jason Brownlee (2012) subsequently described US policy regarding Egypt as amounting to "democracy prevention"[2] – meant that the transition's success hinged "almost entirely on ... [the] domestic balance of power between pro-and anti-democratic forces."[3] The coalition that cohered in Midan al-Tahrir and elsewhere during the 25th January Revolution enjoyed few natural advantages in this regard. The years before Mubarak's ousting had seen new connections made between the Muslim Brothers, liberals in the form of ElBaradei's National Association for Change and Ayman Nour's al-Ghad party, leftists and Nasserites (El-Hamalawy 2007; Abdelrahman 2009; Hamid 2014: 144–145). These followed several protest initiatives and petitions in which the Brothers joined with the anti-war (and later anti-Mubarak) Kifaya movement, the Revolutionary Socialists, and several others to coordinate protest activities (Gunning and Baron 2013: chs.1–3). But these intersections – while marking an important departure from the mutual suspicion and antagonism of previous decades – were tentative and never properly institutionalized. The Brothers' youth members were usually the leading edge in brokering these relationships, with the Brothers' leadership, which saw the parliament, not the street, as "the engine for political reform in Egypt" (Shehata and Stacher 2012: 162), acting as a brake on deeper collaborations.

Against this backdrop, the Muslim Brothers' failure to fully mobilize on the first day of protests of the 25th January Revolution irrevocably undermined Mursi and the Brothers' claims later to exercise their

---

[2] We should also consider the implacable opposition to democratization in Egypt from Saudi Arabia and members of the Gulf Cooperation Council. After leading a military intervention into Bahrain in early 2011 to crush a pro-democracy uprising, Saudi Arabia went on to play a key role in propping up Egypt's economy, providing aid in the form of financial deposits and petroleum products totaling several billion dollars following the 3 July coup. Following the massacre of anti-coup protestors at two protest camps on 14 August 2013, the Saudi government even committed to meeting any financial shortfall should Western governments cancel aid in protest at the military-backed government's brutal tactics (*Washington Post* 19 Aug. 2013).

[3] Instances of demobilization during successful democratic transitions in Southeast Asia, Latin America, Eastern Europe and elsewhere might even appear over-determined given that demobilization in those cases was offset by strong regional and international support for democratization, which significantly raised the costs of backsliding by old regime holdovers (see Levitsky and Way 2010).

democratic authority in the name of the revolution. Both scholarly and journalistic accounts of the revolution frequently reference this failure to commit to 25 January as evidence that the Muslim Brothers were opportunistic latecomers, or even as entirely absent from the action (for a review, see Mellor 2014; Hellyer 2014). According to the Brothers, the decision not to fully mobilize can be traced back to an extraordinary meeting held on 24 January between the movement's leadership in Cairo and Egyptian State Security, who threatened to suppress the movement if it called its members out into the streets (*al-Hurriyya wa-l-'Adala*, 17 Nov. 2011: 10). Speaking to Egyptian news media, members of the Guidance Bureau reported that branch heads across the governorates had been called in by State Security to receive the ultimatum (*al-Shorouk* 24 Jan. 2011: 1; *al-Masry al-Youm* 24 Jan 2011: 1). The Brothers' leadership, reluctant to risk the movement's sizeable social welfare infrastructure on a protest that could claim only indeterminable support, heeded the warning.[4] Still, a handful of the Brothers' branches did mobilize on 25 January, as did large numbers of the movement's youth, many of whom had helped plan the protests in coordination with the April 6 youth movement, elements from the National Association for Change, and the Democratic Front Party (*al-Masry al-Youm* 24 Jan. 2011: 1; see also Wickham 2013: ch.7; Gunning and Baron 2013: 168–175).

The decision to allow youth members to participate on 25 January seems to have been taken as early as 22 January, during a secret meeting of the Guidance Bureau (*al-Shorouk* 25 Jan. 2011: 1). As a precondition of their participation and in a bid to limit any backlash should the protests flop, the Brothers' leaders demanded that members not chant Brothers slogans like "Islam is the Solution" while protesting, and forbade them from self-identifying as movement members if speaking to news media (interview Sara 14 Mar. 2014). Justifying this decision hours before the first protest was scheduled to begin, Essam el-Erian, a member of the Guidance Bureau, insisted, "We [the Brothers' leadership] will only participate symbolically, but we cannot ban our youth from joining, it is their duty and their right" (*al-Masry al-Youm* 24 Jan. 2011: 6). Meanwhile, as we saw in Chapter 2, Mohamed el-Beltagy, the head of the Brothers' parliamentary bloc, along with a handful of senior Brothers, staged

---

[4] The Muslim Brothers were not alone in making this calculation. The leftist Tagammu party likewise only partially mobilized, leaving the decision to participate to individual members (*al-Shorouk* 25 Jan. 2011: 5), as did the largest Nasserite party who closed their HQ out of respect for Police Day (*al-Masry al-Youm* 25 Jan. 2011: 1).

a demonstration on the steps of the Courthouse in downtown Cairo, in coordination with members of the National Association for Change (*al-Masry al-Youm* 27 Jan. 2011: 7).

On 27 January, demonstrators having reached Midan al-Tahrir on 25 January and well-attended protests having been held in Alexandria, Asyut, Gharbiyya, Ismailia, Qalyubiyya, and Suez, the Brothers' leadership abandoned its initial hesitancy and instructed its branches to mobilize for the "Friday of Anger" protests planned for the next day (interview Mona 30 Apr. 2014; interview Hend 17 Dec. 2014). In an attempt to decapitate the movement and force it to demobilize, State Security made good on its earlier threat, detaining 500 leading Brothers in Cairo on the morning of 28 January (*al-Masry al-Youm* 29 Jan. 2011: 3; *al-Hurriyya wa-l-ʿAdala* 17 Nov. 2011: 10).[5] The move failed. According to one estimate produced shortly after Mubarak's ousting, up to one hundred thousand Brothers took to the streets on 28 January (*al-Ahram Weekly Online* 2011a).[6] More concretely, WikiThawra (2013) records that seven Muslim Brothers were killed on protests in Cairo and Alexandria on the Friday of Anger. For many Brothers this was their first opportunity to strike back against a security state at whose hands they had suffered decades of arbitrary detention and harassment. By way of illustration, when I conducted interviews in the Suez Canal city of Ismailia in the autumn of 2011, local Brothers proudly showed off the gutted State Security office as evidence of their part in inflicting a defeat on the Interior Ministry-controlled security forces.

With Midan al-Tahrir occupied and anti-regime protests breaking out across the country, the Brothers were playing an as yet largely unacknowledged role in sustaining the mobilization. During the critical early days of the mobilization, the event catalog records Muslim Brothers as being present on over fifty protests in sixteen governorates. In Tahrir, their presence was co-ordinated by Osama Yassin (*al-Hurriyya wa-l-ʿAdala* 10

---

[5] Those arrests led to a now infamous episode in which Muhammad Mursi, along with members of the Guidance Bureau, was imprisoned in the Nile Delta city of Wadi al-Natrun, only to escape on 29 January when the Interior Ministry opened Egypt's prisons in a bid to destabilize the country (*al-Hurriyya wa-l-ʿAdala* 26 Jun. 2013: 5). The circumstances of Mursi's escape went on to form the basis of a conspiracy theory (and later a court case) promulgated in Egyptian media in the year before the coup that he had been freed by Hamas, the Gaza-based offshoot of the Muslim Brothers – a narrative that attempts to discredit the 25th January Revolution as a foreign plot to weaken Egypt (see *Ahram Online* 12 May 2013).

[6] Both Carrie Wickham (2013: 162) and Gunning and Baron (2013: 175) have previously cited this number as a credible estimate.

Nov. 2011: 10), who would go on to become Youth Minister in Mursi's cabinet. In interviews with Egypt's secular activists, the Brothers' efforts, marshalled through their superior organizational structure, are credited with sourcing many of the supplies vital to maintaining the occupation during its early days (cited in Gunning and Baron 2013: 179–180; see also Cambanis 2015: 56). The Brothers likewise played a pivotal role in defending Tahrir against attack, including during the "Camel Battle" of 2 February, when pro-regime thugs threatened to overrun the protestors' barricades at the National Museum entrance to the Midan (interview Abdullah 3 20 Aug. 2011). Four Muslim Brothers were killed during that episode (WikiThawra 2013). "They [the Muslim Brothers] were at the forefront," reported one Coptic protestor, "They defended all of us. This is a fact" (cited in *al-Ahram Weekly Online* 2011b).

That the principal actors of Egypt's democratic breakthrough are frequently portrayed as having emerged from outside Egypt's defined oppositional hierarchies is partly due to the Muslim Brothers, wary of overshadowing the secular face of the protests and so provoking an "American veto" fearful of an Islamist revolution (Hamid 2014: 140–141; Wickham 2013: 169), did not publicize their presence in Midan al-Tahrir and elsewhere. The Brothers instead deferred to the "horizontalist" (Chalcraft 2012) spirit that characterized the mobilization, taking a back seat to a broader conception of "the People" opposing the regime. Of course, this was also a matter of expediency: the Brothers were impressed by the scale and success of the mobilization, and fully aware that "Egyptians were not protesting for the Muslim Brothers. If it had been just us [the Brothers] taking to the streets, then there wouldn't have been a revolution" (interview Mona 30 Apr. 2014).

ELECTORAL ALLIANCES

After Mubarak's resignation on 11 February, the SCAF looked to foreclose this emergent revolutionary situation by calling on Egyptians to abandon protest, while seeking a political dialogue with Egypt's Mubarak-era opposition in general and the Muslim Brothers in particular.[7] In its early embrace of the Brothers, the SCAF invited the

---

[7] Hazem Kandil (2014: 15) has suggested that leading Brothers Mursi and Saad al-Katatni met with head of Egyptian General Intelligence Omar Suleiman on 1 February 2011 to "enter into secret negotiations ... for a larger share of power in return for stopping the revolt." Pro-SCAF news websites have made similar claims of a meeting on 1 February in

movement to play a leading role in a democratic transition. The first actualization of this commitment came on 15 February, when the SCAF appointed an eight-member committee to propose constitutional amendments to the 1971 constitution in preparation for fresh parliamentary and presidential elections. Subhi Salih, a Muslim Brother and former Member of Parliament, was the committee's sole representative of Egypt's Mubarak-era opposition movements.

Two weeks after Mubarak's ousting, the Muslim Brothers announced the formation of the Freedom and Justice Party to compete in future elections (*Al-Masry Al-Youm* 22 Feb. 2011). The Muslim Brothers had long cultivated electoral ambitions. In 1942, Brothers founder Hassan al-Banna and several of the movement's candidates were forced to withdraw from the parliamentary elections under threat of internment (Lia 1998: 256–268; Heyworth-Dunne 1950: 39–40). The Wafd's rigging of the elections in 1945 denied the Brothers access to parliamentary representation for a second time, leading to a split in the movement's leadership and the rise of the Special Section, an underground paramilitary unit that brought the Brothers into violent confrontation with successive governments (Lia 1998: 270–271). These confrontations culminated in the movement's suppression by the Palace in 1948 and again in 1954 by Gamal Abdel Nasser (Mitchell [1969] 1993). Following the Brothers' partial rehabilitation by Anwar al-Sadat in the 1970s, the movement renounced violence and turned instead to Egypt's parliament and syndicates to advance its religiously inspired social reform agenda (Wickham 2002). Later, in the 1980s, the Brothers' candidates began running on electoral lists with the Wafd and later the Labor party and in spite of routine electoral fraud formed the main opposition to the NDP in parliament (El-Ghobashy 2005; Shehata and Stacher 2012).

The Brothers' parliamentary activities were abruptly curtailed in late 2010 when a nakedly fraudulent election contrived to wipe out the Brothers' representation once and for all. With Mubarak gone, the

which Suleiman offered to release imprisoned senior Brothers in return for the movement vacating Tahrir, but note that the Brothers refused any deal. Speaking on *al-Jazeera* on 3 February, Mursi denied that the movement had met with Suleiman (see YouTube video (27 Jul 2012) "*Mohamed Mursi i'tirād 'ala ma jā'a bi-kalimat Omar Suleiman al-yawm 3 2 2011*" http://youtu.be/xW6d9-2pJBE). What is clear is that Suleiman publicly called for a dialogue with the Brothers on 5 February, following which the movement attended a meeting along with fifty other representatives of the Tahrir occupation (*Al-Masry Al-Youm* 5 Feb. 2011: 1). Whatever the inducements to demobilize offered were, they clearly failed: the Brothers left the meeting publicly committing to continue the protests until Mubarak was removed (*New York Times* 6 Feb. 2011).

Brothers' embeddedness in Islamic associational life, along with its national network of branches, charities, and grassroots activities, ensured that the movement possessed the experience and the infrastructure to perform well in elections (see Blaydes 2011: ch.8; Masoud 2014).[8] Conscious that no other party or actor from the 25th January Revolution coalition possessed a comparable political machine, the Muslim Brothers initially tried to appear magnanimous in offering concessions to other opposition groups (Hamid 2014: ch.6). To offset any latent suspicions of impending Muslim Brother electoral domination, the Brothers committed to contesting a plurality and not a majority of seats, while spearheading the formation of the Democratic Alliance, an electoral coalition of pro-25th January Revolution parties that would run under a single national electoral list and aim to produce a "national revolutionary majority" (*Ahram Online* 23 Mar. 2011).[9] According to this reading of the movement's intentions at this stage of the transition, the Muslim Brothers were aware that the rapidly convened "negative coalition" (Dix 1984; Beissinger 2013) of the 25th January Revolution, united primarily in its opposition to the Mubarak regime, had to be reconfigured into a positive electoral one.

However, the Democratic Alliance was a strange and imperfect vehicle for such an avuncular enterprise, one that effectively sought to "divvy up the seats in advance" (Brown 2011). The telos of this initiative, the Brothers publicly insisted, would be a competitive parliamentary system. "Everyone must act," explained Mohamed el-Beltagy, a leading Brother and former MP, "so we can reach the point where we become like the rest of the countries in the world, with three or four strong parties. We [the Brothers] will not forever remain in the position of not seeking power, the majority or the presidency. This is a temporary position until the time

---

[8] In the run-up to the 2011–2012 parliamentary elections, Essam el-Erian would boast, "We will reach voters in their homes and places of gathering and talk to them directly about the nation and its future and about the FJP and its program ... This will have the greatest impact on voting, and no competitor can compete with us in this domain. You [Muslim Brothers] are, thank God, the most organized and present in all areas of society" (*al-Hurriyya wa-l-ʿAdala* 12 Nov. 2011: 16).

[9] The Muslim Brothers initially restated their adherence to *al-mushāraka wa laysa al-mughālaba* (participation and not domination) in the political process, a position first adopted in the years following the 1992 Algerian elections when an Islamist victory provoked a military coup (see Brown 2012a). As the transition progressed, however, the number of seats the FJP planned to contest began to change, with FJP candidates going on to contest half of all the seats in the 2011–2012 parliamentary elections. The Brothers' decision to put forward a presidential candidate only served to deepen misgivings about the movement's domination of post-Mubarak politics.

there are forces that can compete" (cited in *Ahram Online* 23 Mar. 2011). However, more critical accounts of the Brothers' role in the transition (e.g., Kandil 2014: ch.4) have questioned the movement's commitment to coalition building, pointing to the insular structure of the movement and its religious mission. This fear was certainly shared by many non-Islamist members of the revolutionary coalition, who believed that the Muslim Brothers' commitment to political pluralism would not survive the movement taking power, a fear that the Brothers did too little to assuage.

What is not in dispute is that shortly after its founding in the summer of 2011, the Democratic Alliance could claim over thirty members, including the liberal Wafd, the Nasserite Karama party, and the leftist Tagammu party.[10] This, however, proved to be one of several short-lived examples of post-Mubarak revolutionary cooperation. By autumn, parties began to break away from the Democratic Alliance to form their own electoral blocs, many complaining of the Muslim Brothers' domineering leadership and its insistence on controlling seat allocations on the electoral list (e.g., *Masrawy* 3 Sept. 2011; *al-Jazeera* 6 Oct. 2011; *al-Masriyyun* 14 Oct. 2011). With the onset of the first round of the 2011–2012 parliamentary elections, the Democratic Alliance had been reduced to a core of several fairly minor parties, encompassing Islamists, centrists, liberals, and Nasserites, and headed by the FJP.

While the weight of scholarly and journalistic attention has rightly focused on the Brothers' inattentiveness to maintaining good relations with other members of the revolutionary coalition, the failure of liberal and secular forces outside of the Democratic Alliance to build political parties with meaningful links to Egypt's electoral constituencies remains one of the frequently elided dynamics undermining the transition.[11] As Nathan Brown remarked on the eve of the 2011–2012 parliamentary elections, "When such movements had a political demand, they resorted to the device that worked so well earlier [in 2011] – the public demonstration – and avoided the long task of party building" (Brown 2011). This, despite the emergence of new secular opposition groups competing in elections as early as the mid-2000s, including the aforementioned Kifaya movement (see Clarke 2011), as well as Ayman Nour's failed presidential

---

[10] For a history of the Democratic Alliance, see *Ahram Online* (2011).

[11] This is not to suggest that they were simply feckless. Rather, as Tarek Masoud (2008; 2014) has catalogued, Egyptian leftists and liberals have long struggled to negotiate Egypt's "electoral ecology," which places high entry barriers to newcomers due to the centrality of patronage in swaying electoral loyalty and the propensity for voters to support those already embedded within their social networks.

campaign in 2005 (see Oweidat et al. 2008; El-Mahdi 2009). Having provided the catalyst for the 25th January Revolution, Egypt's non-Islamist "revolutionaries" instead came to claim a moral authority to dictate the trajectory of post-Mubarak politics that was disproportionate to any democratic representation they could muster at the ballot box. Indeed, many of these figures came to reject SCAF's role and the democratic transition *in toto* as a parting imposition by the Mubarak regime designed to short circuit a revolutionary situation that still retained much of its energy, and thus negate a revolutionary outcome. With few illusions of an electoral breakthrough, anti-SCAF (and later anti-Mursi) protestors were immunized from the domesticating imperatives of democratic procedures and electoralization. This "gap" between the political demands of a cohort of protestors and activists, energized by the momentous events of the 25th January Revolution, and the possible spectrum of representation that could be produced by the infrastructure of elections, meant that large tranches of the revolutionary coalition pursued a parallel political track, mobilizing pressure from the street as a means of intervening into the formal transitional process.

This electoral landscape was made all the more uneven by the evaporation of the NDP as an electoral vehicle for old regime interests (see Menza 2012). Speaking in the spring of 2011, Hazim Kandil (2011) predicted that NDP politicians would win at least a third of seats in any new parliament, whether running under the NDP banner or as independents in the event that the party was banned. A 40 percent share of the vote, he suggested, could not be ruled out. Such a scenario remained eminently plausible when the Higher Administrative Court dissolved the NDP in April 2011, but placed no embargo on former members standing for election. The prospect of a reconstituted NDP certainly preoccupied the Muslim Brothers: they spent the transition lobbying the SCAF for a "Political Isolation Law" disbarring former NDP members from standing for parliament and the presidency for five years.[12] As it subsequently transpired, the NDP machine was only reactivated in June 2012 for the nearly triumphant presidential campaign of the Mubarak-era Prime Minister Ahmad Shafiq (Masoud 2014: 205).

---

[12] When this was not forthcoming, the Brothers championed measures to expose former regime candidates, including defacing election posters and publishing lists of *filūl* running as independent parliamentary candidates or on party lists, and running "catch a *filūl*" campaigns on social media (*al-Hurriyya wa-l-'Adala* 3 Nov. 2011: 5; *al-Hurriyya wa-l-'Adala* 11 Nov. 2011: 2).

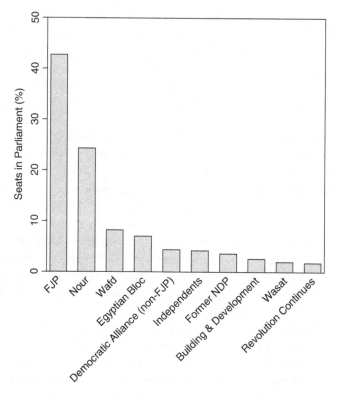

FIGURE 4.1 Results of al-Majlis al-Sha'ab elections, Nov. 2011–Jan. 2012.

In its absence, conservative forces associated with the Mubarak regime secured only a handful of seats in the parliamentary elections. This, in turn, had unforeseen consequences for the trajectory of the transition. If, in most democratic transitions, the first competitive parliamentary elections following a democratic breakthrough reveals the residual strengths and continuing entrenchment of local bosses and old regime figures (Hagopian 1996; Hite and Cesarini 2004; Robison and Hadiz 2004; Hedman 2006; Magaloni 2006), and thus compels compromises, backroom deals, and coalition-building on behalf of the pro-democratic forces, this did not occur in the Egyptian case. Instead the formal, electoral realignment that emerged following the 25th January Revolution clustered around a series of alliances in which no grouping outside of organized political Islam commanded an electoral infrastructure capable of delivering votes nationwide. It was in this context that the Muslim Brothers became the largest party in the 2011–2012 parliament (see

Figure 4.1), followed, more unexpectedly, by the ultra-religious Salafi Nour Party (see Lacroix 2012). This left the Muslim Brothers with an unusual, even excessive, level of electoral success and parliamentary (and later presidential) representation, out of sync with the political spectrum of forces that had cohered in Midan al-Tahrir. Such a result ultimately proved beyond what the revolutionary coalition could sustain, as the Brothers' claims to be countering the old regime through the ballot box quickly began to appear far more like indefinite electoral dominion and irrelevancy for the rest of Egypt's reinvigorated political scene.

MOBILIZATION AND DEMOBILIZATION

Prior to holding parliamentary and presidential elections, a timetable for the transition and several amendments to the 1971 constitution, including amendments stipulating presidential term limits and restrictions over the executive's ability to impose a state of emergency, had to be voted on in a national referendum. The Brothers campaigned for a "yes" vote, arguing that a fixed schedule for the transfer of power from the SCAF to an elected civilian government was vital to the success of the transition. The "no" vote was led by Egypt's secular revolutionaries and established liberals, who argued that a constitution should be codified before elections were held to avoid a document written by a parliament dominated by narrow party interests – a pre-emptive move that tacitly acknowledged the Brothers' electoral advantage. The tone and manner in which the referendum campaign played out has been characterized as one of the transition's "original sins ... pitting Islamists and non-Islamists against each other for the first time ... [meaning] debates that were really about the sequencing of the transition became, at least publicly, about religion" (Hamid 2014: 145). The 19 March referendum passed with 77 percent approval on a 41 percent turnout. This process saw the evaporation of much of the goodwill that had characterized relations between the different elements of the revolutionary coalition up to that point.

While the decision was never explicitly announced, for the Brothers the passing of the referendum meant that the political focus should shift from maintaining a presence in Tahrir to seeing the transition's timetable of elections and constitutional reform implemented. As one Brother recalls:

With Mubarak gone, we faced a choice: we could stay in Midan al-Tahrir and continue protesting, keep the military out of politics and start the transition later, led by the revolutionaries. But who would lead it? And how would they be chosen?

And would Egyptians accept that figure as legitimate? We did not believe that Tahrir alone had sufficient legitimacy to dictate the country's will. That's why we supported the March referendum. When the people voted "yes" and gave the transition legitimacy, we focused on the process of change: the elections and the new constitution . . . we thought that step-by-step reform was preferable to a more revolutionary path. (interview Abdullah al-Haddad 20 Feb. 2014)

Thus, the Brothers' gradualist approach was sutured to a narrow, procedural conception of democratization that the movement adhered to following the 13 March referendum. In this, there was a clear pact with the military, whether implicit or otherwise, in which the Brothers would acquiesce to the SCAF's oversight of the transitional period and a continuation of the military's Mubarak-era prerogatives in return for the "normalization" of the movement and a commitment to transfer power to an elected civilian government according to the timetable set out in the 19 March referendum. If this appears unremarkable in context of other Third Wave transitions, the Brothers' decision to demobilize did not produce the kind of conservative consolidation seen elsewhere.

By the summer of 2011 the Muslim Brothers were conspicuously absent from the *milyūniyya* (million-person) protests that were agitating for justice for the martyrs of the revolution, the reform of Egypt's Interior Ministry and security services, the prosecution of Mubarak-era regime figures, and, ultimately, the end of military rule itself. Midan al-Tahrir was intermittently reoccupied. Egypt's activists called for a second revolution against the SCAF. Hundreds of demonstrations agitating for social justice and redress for local residents were also held, as well as a massive strike wave launched by a newly emerging trade union scene (see Barrie and Ketchley 2016). The SCAF dismissed these as *fe'awi* (factional) demands and, on occasion, brutally policed the protests (Sallam 2011). In early July 2011, a *milyūniyya* planned by April 6 did elicit some concessions: elections were delayed until November to allow Egypt's new political forces to consolidate; several ministers in the transitional government were dismissed for their links to the Mubarak regime; and most spectacularly, Mubarak finally appeared in court on corruption charges and for ordering the killing of protestors during the 25th January Revolution (see Cole 2012: 490–493).

The Muslim Brothers remained aloof from the protests, arguing that further protest would drain popular support for the 25th January Revolution and lead to an electoral surge for old regime figures who promised a return to the relative stability and security of the Mubarak era (e.g., *al-Hurriyya wa-l-'Adala* 31 Oct. 2011: 3).[13] Disruptive protest, the Brothers insisted, also threatened the transition timetable and thus could prolong military rule. As the editorial of the Brothers' newspaper explained:

> The people must protect the revolution by policing the political process and ceasing unnecessary protests and strikes that can create the conditions for a counter-revolution ... Some people are expecting a crisis to occur before or during the elections; the results might be manipulated, or an incident like Maspero [when soldiers attacked a Coptic protest, killing twenty-eight] will happen, or the *filūl* will return. Everything is possible, which is why all efforts must be directed towards securing the elections ... This way, the people can visualize a safe and secure exit from the transitional period. We were capable of a revolution and deposing a dictator who ruled for thirty years, we must now protect the elections ... The revolution must carry forward its thoughts and protect its demands and gains, which is the role of the new parliament.
>
> (*al-Hurriyya wa-l-'Adala* 30 Oct. 2011: 10)

To the Brothers, protestors resembled "football hooligans ... ready to destroy the transition because their team didn't win [the 18 March referendum]. These hooligans would only recognize the referendum if the result was 'no,' but since the people said 'yes' now all they want to do is protest about poverty, unemployment, and illiteracy" (*al-Hurriyya wa al-'Adala* 2 Nov. 2011: 4). Tahrir's crowd of disorganized revolutionaries, would be best served by acting analogously to the Brothers: demobilizing and forming their own party (interview Mustafa 9 Jun. 2013). Failure to heed this advice, the Brothers' newspaper opined, would prevent the youth movements propelled to prominence during the 25th January Revolution from capitalizing on the elections; instead of occupying Tahrir and holding *milyūniyyāt*, they were better off knocking on doors and canvassing the electorate (*al-Hurriyya wa-l-'Adala* 30 Oct. 2011: 5). People power should be reserved for securing the ballot.[14] The case for demobilization was further strengthened by the calculation that Egypt's looming balance of payments crisis, lack of investor confidence, failing tourism industry, and high inflation – all problems that the Brothers looked set to inherit – were exacerbated by protests and the political

---

[13] This is a sentiment that echoes the logic of the transitology literature.

[14] One FJP proposal that was met with limited enthusiasm was the use of "popular committees" of the type formed during the 25th January Revolution; staffed by revolutionaries from across the political spectrum, they would be responsible for policing polling stations (*al-Hurriyya wa-l-'Adala* 30 Oct. 2011: 5; *al-Hurriyya wa-l-'Adala* 2 Nov. 2011: 5; *al-Hurriyya wa-l-'Adala* 4 Nov. 2011: 7).

vacuum created by the transition (*al-Hurriyya wa-l-ʿAdala* 9 Nov. 2011: 7). Economic immiseration could therefore only be alleviated by "the parliament of the revolution" (*al-Hurriyya wa-l-ʿAdala* 2 Nov. 2011: 6). In a speech to FJP members in July 2011, Mursi made the link, frequently asserted elsewhere, between the parliamentarization of politics and a return to economic growth. FJP members must bring politics indoors: competitive elections and increased productivity would solve the country's problems, not further protest (*Ikhwan Online* 17 Jul. 2011). Or, as one FJP mantra daubed on the walls of Cairo's popular quarters had it: "A true revolutionary rebels against corruption, and once he removes it, calms down to build and prosper" (cited in Youssef 3 Mar. 2013).

In the search for explanations of the Muslim Brothers' decision to demobilize, a common trope portrays the Brothers as almost congenitally risk-averse, with no stomach for chaotic street politics. An alternative reading paints the Brothers as a "counter-movement" (Alexander 2011; see also Kandil 2014) whose demobilization was evidence of their co-optation by the SCAF. The argument advanced here, by contrast, avers that the Brothers used protest strategically, depending on their reading of the political process. Accordingly, this did not preclude the movement from mobilizing. On 29 July and 18 November 2011, the Brothers went en masse to Egypt's squares in protest against what Linz and Stepan (1996: 82) call "reserve domains": conditions unilaterally imposed (or threatened) by the SCAF on the post-Mubarak constitutional order. In many ways, these mobilizations underline the limits of any deal between the Brothers and the military. The July mobilization followed several statements from the Brothers threatening to stage protests if the timetable mandated by the 19 March referendum was not adhered to (*Egypt Independent* 27 Jun. 2011). When the SCAF publicly entertained a proposal to have binding supra-constitutional principles tie the hands of any future parliament, the Brothers made good on their threat, mobilizing for the Friday protest in Midan al-Tahrir of 29 July in a show of force. For many Brothers this constituted their first return to Tahrir since the revolution. Marshalled by FJP members in high-vis jackets, the hundred thousand or so assembled protestors conveyed a simple message: the Brothers' demobilization was a matter of tactical restraint only, and was subject to review.[15] The Brothers were ostensibly behaving just as the

---

[15] The 29 July protests spectacularly backfired on the Brothers, provoking the first split in the Democratic Alliance when the Tagammu party withdrew to form a new electoral bloc after the Brothers failed to endorse the party's demand of an end to military trials for

democratization literature counsels: demobilizing to pursue their electoral ambitions, but retaining the option to protest in the event of backsliding (see Linz and Stepan 1996: 9–10).

After the supra-constitutional principles – commonly referred to as the Silmi document after its author, Deputy Prime Minister Ali El-Silmi – were belatedly published in November 2011, the Muslim Brothers again descended upon Tahrir for a *milyūniyya*, titled the "Friday of One Demand." Their grievance was Article 9, which stated that "The SCAF is the sole actor on all matters related to the SCAF and its budget and the president shall be the supreme head of the armed forces and the defense minister is the general leader of the armed forces. The president can declare war after obtaining approval from the armed forces and parliament" (*al-Hurriyya wa-l-ʿAdala* 2 Nov. 2011: 5). The Brothers' stance remained unchanged: any attempt to undermine the omnicompetence of the post-Mubarak parliament or the autonomy of the executive branch, and any restrictions imposed on the constitution writing process by the military-backed transitional government, would be countered with street protests.

Speaking in early November, Mursi had warned that the Silmi document could provoke a second revolution if it was not withdrawn, and the Brothers' leadership committed to a program of rolling protests that would continue "no matter the consequences" until the initiative was abandoned (*al-Hurriyya w-al-ʿAdala* 3 Nov. 2011: 1; 7). In an increasingly rare instance of coordination with Egypt's other revolutionary groups, the Brothers planned the protests with April 6 and other members of the Revolutionary Youth Coalition. When the day of protest arrived on 18 November, the FJP newspaper ran the headline: "Egyptians return to Tahrir to defend the gains of the revolution," pledging that: "The Muslim Brothers and its allies will engage in street protests to protect the transition and demand that the SCAF transfer power to a civilian government and cancel the supra-constitutional principles" (*al-Hurriyya wa-l-ʿAdala* 18 Nov. 2011: 1).

Following the *milyūniyya*, the Brothers continued to put pressure on the SCAF, the Brothers' usually laconic Deputy Supreme Guide and

---

civilians (*Jadaliyya* 2011). The fallout did not end there. Thousands of Nour Party Salafis defied an agreement to abstain from religious slogans by chanting for an Islamic state, leading to the protest pejoratively being known as "Kandahar Friday." As Stéfan Lacroix (2012: 4) notes, the 29 July protests presaged a growing rift between the Brothers and the Nour party, with the Brothers publicly distancing themselves from the Salafis after the event.

political powerhouse Khairat al-Shater threatening an escalation in protest if the military did not rescind the Silmi document (*al-Hurriyya wa-l-'Adala* 20 Nov. 2011: 1). "Protest," the FJP newspaper concluded, "is the only message that the military understands" (Ibid.: 7). However, an unanticipated consequence of the Brothers' mobilization was soon to test the movement's resolve to pursue a confrontational path with the military. When the Brothers vacated the Midan after the conclusion of the *milyūniyya*, families of the martyrs killed during the 25th January Revolution reoccupied Tahrir. In the early hours of Saturday morning, Interior Ministry-controlled security forces attacked the encampment. Within hours, protestors had returned to the Midan in greater numbers, provoking further clashes with police who responded with shotgun pellets, tear gas and rubber bullets.

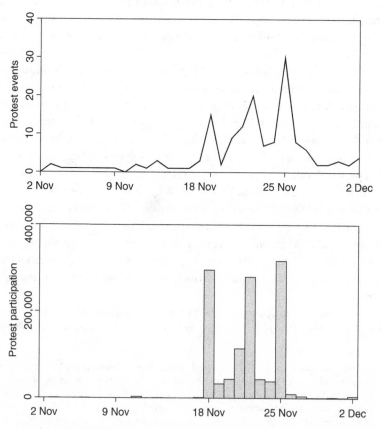

FIGURE 4.2 Anti-SCAF protest frequency and participation, 2 Nov.–2 Dec. 2011.

Finally, it seemed, Egypt's revolutionaries had the chance to bring about the second stage of the revolution that they had been agitating for since the summer. By 20 November, protestors in Tahrir were attempting to break through police lines on Muhammad Mahmoud Street to reach the Interior Ministry, demanding the return of the military to its barracks and the formation of a civilian national salvation government (see Ryzova 2011). Amid the violence, video footage circulated of Egyptian soldiers and policemen casually piling up the bodies of dead protestors. The images swelled the ranks of the protestors, leading to a series of pitched street battles known as the "Events of Muhammad Mahmoud Street," in which the momentum, for the first time since Mubarak's ousting, seemed to rest with the reinvigorated protestors. Figure 4.2 uses event data to show the scale and frequency of anti-SCAF contention during this period. As protests spread to the governorates of Alexandria, Beheira, Daqahliyya, Fayyum, Gharbiyya, Ismailia, Port Said, Sharqiyya, and Sohag, the Brothers' Guidance Bureau convened on 21 November to formulate a response (*al-Hurriyya wa-l-'Adala* 22 Nov. 2011: 1; 4). At that meeting, it appears, the Brothers' leadership resolved to gain assurances from the SCAF that the elections would be held on time before committing to going to Tahrir or not. In communicating the rationale behind this decision, Essam el-Erian, a senior Brother and FJP official insisted:

The Brothers are caught between two choices, neither of them easy: either the Brothers go down to the Midan and so risk widening the scope of the conflict and delay the elections, or we hold back and abstain from mobilizing our members while inevitably facing accusations from other political parties and the revolutionary youth that we have abandoned the revolution.   (Ibid.: 1)

El-Erian's anticipation of the opprobrium of the revolutionary coalition was to prove prescient. In a fateful decision that would cost the movement the amity and trust of many, the Brothers concluded that "Elections are the solution!" (Ibid.: 1). At the height of the most serious and sustained challenge to military rule following Mubarak's ouster, the Brothers met with SCAF and used their street presence as leverage to gain three major concessions: the rescinding of the Silmi document; a law to bar the *filūl* from competing in future elections; and a commitment that the elections would be held on time and power transferred to an elected civilian government by July 2012 (*al-Hurriyya wa-l-'Adala* 23 Nov. 2011: 1). Having secured the SCAF's assurances that the transitional timetable would be adhered to, the Brothers committed to staying out of Tahrir.

In an editorial titled "Why we went and why we didn't go" the FJP's newspaper explained:

The Brothers went to protest on 18 November to ensure the integrity of the transitional process and continue the fight against the *filūl* ... However, we will refrain from returning to the Midan as our presence will push the country into further bloody violence and delay the elections, which are the real goal of the revolution.
(Ibid.: 13)

Meanwhile, the Brothers publicly turned on the protestors. The violence in Tahrir was the work of thugs – "their goal: delay the elections" (*al-Hurriyya wa-l-'Adala* 21 Nov. 2011: 2). The *filūl* were singled out as instigators of the violence; they were "exploiting the situation to spread chaos in the country" (Ibid. 3). The Brothers' message was monotone and predictable: "Delay the election: revolutionaries beware, we will go backwards" (Ibid. 8–9). A minority of Brothers under the direction of Mohamed el-Beltagy did defy the leadership, calling on the membership to mobilize to Muhammad Mahmoud Street and continue the revolution against the SCAF (*Al-Masry Al-Youm* 23 Nov. 2011). Upon entering Tahrir, el-Beltagy was confronted by anti-SCAF protestors who accused the Brothers of selling out their fellow revolutionaries for electoral gain. Under pressure, he withdrew from the Midan.

When the parliamentary elections went ahead as scheduled, the Brothers welcomed the first round of voting, proclaiming that: "Egyptians have finally moved legitimacy from the streets to the elected institutions!" (*al-Hurriyya wa-l-'Adala* 30 Nov. 2011: 9). Egypt's youth activists, meanwhile, finding their path to the Interior Ministry blocked, decamped from Muhammad Mahmoud Street to hold a sit-in in front of the prime minister's office. Again, violent clashes broke out between protestors and soldiers. The Brothers stayed away. The movement's leadership, one senior Brother confided, feared that if the protests escalated, the SCAF might use this as a pretext to annul the election results (cited in El-Amrani 2012). In response to the violence, the Brothers adopted a more critical line, publicly condemning the SCAF for their heavy-handed policing of protest (e.g., *al-Hurriyya wa-l-'Adala* 19 Dec. 2011: 1). But this appeared almost as an afterthought, noncommittal and non-heroic.

"It was at this point," observes Chayma Hassabo, "that the revolutionaries' opposition to the Islamists, especially the Muslim Brotherhood, transcended mere ideological differences" (cited in *Ahram Online* 21 Nov. 2012). In the eyes of many, the Brothers had revealed themselves as unprincipled opportunists. As one revolutionary in Tahrir observed, "We haven't seen any Muslim Brothers, even though figures like el-Beltagy have denounced the SCAF ... This proves what we all suspected: the Muslim Brothers are only interested in power" (cited in *al-Masry al-Youm* 23 Nov. 2011: 9). Activists who had rallied in defense of the Brothers prior to the 25th January Revolution now saw the movement as willing to sacrifice them in the pursuit of their political ambitions (see Ali 2014). The Events of Muhammad Mahmoud Street, synonymous with the Muslim Brothers' betrayal, became a fixture in the revolutionary calendar, eclipsed only by 25 January itself. As one youth activist related shortly before the first anniversary of the protests:

While the military were discarding our brothers' bodies in the trash, and the police were draining their eyes [a reference to police aiming birdshot at protestors' eyes], the Brothers were preparing for parliament. While the revolutionaries were chanting "ya Tantawi [the head of SCAF], tomorrow your fate will be Gaddafi's," the Brothers were knocking on doors urging people to vote. Muhammad Mahmud will remain a black mark in the history of the Muslim Brothers. It was a shame that history will never forget and time will not erase ... That is why we won't stand with them in future protests. (cited in *Masrawy* 14 Nov. 2012)

The Muslim Brothers' demobilization was particularly damaging for the clear implication that by staying away, the Brothers had insulated the SCAF from the protestors' demands to reset the transition and have the military relinquish power there and then. Symbolically, this failure to come to the defense of Tahrir and instead privilege partisan electioneering took on an exaggerated importance in the revolutionary narrative; it was on Muhammad Mahmoud Street that the first anti-Brother chants were heard, presaging future confrontations between the movement and other members of the revolutionary coalition. Taken together, the fallout from the Brothers' failure to mobilize during this and other episodes is evidence of the "deeper effects" (LeBas 2011: 15) of protest during late Third Wave democratization: namely, in sustaining or undermining negative coalitions during parlous and prolonged democratic transitions. Notwithstanding one final act of cooperation – when many of Egypt's youth and protest movements rallied behind Mursi's candidacy as the lesser of two evils in the second round of the presidential elections to defeat the old regime candidate Ahmad Shafiq – the coalition that had ousted Mubarak was irrevocably split (see Elgindy 2012; Alim 2013).

CONCLUSIONS

The Muslim Brothers' failure to maintain good relations, memories, and linkages with other political forces in the eighteen months following the 25th January Revolution left bad legacies for Mursi's year in office. Repeated overtures to prominent liberal and secular figures, such as the Nasserist and presidential candidate Hamdeen Sabahi, to fill the position of Vice-President, and the liberal figures of Ayman Noor and Muhammad Elbaradei to head the new cabinet as Prime Minister, were rebuffed (see *Daily News Egypt* 26. Jun. 2012). Egypt's youth activists, including Ahmad Maher, one of the founders of April 6, likewise turned down positions in Mursi's government. Mursi's failure to attract a more inclusive government at this early stage ensured that he quickly became reliant on a narrow band of Islamist fellow travelers, giving succor to his opponents later on who claimed that the office of the presidency was subordinated to the Muslim Brothers' leadership.

Mursi's isolation was compounded by the Supreme Constitutional Court's dissolution of the lower house of parliament just days before the presidential run-off in a "judicial coup" (Brown 2012b), designed, so one of the court's Mubarak-appointed judges boasted, to leave only the shell of a presidency and have SCAF assume legislative powers and thereby have full control of the constitution writing process (cited in *New York Times* 3 Jul. 2012). The "parliament of the revolution" had lasted just six months. Having performed poorly in the elections, non-Islamist forces protested against SCAF's power grab, but did not mourn the passing of the legislature, reflecting a growing ambivalence felt by many in the revolutionary coalition towards the newly elected institutions.

This also marked a new and unanticipated development in the transition: the judicialization of post-SCAF politics. When Mursi wrestled legislative power from the SCAF in August 2012, judicial interventions against the legal basis of the country's newly elected institutions continued. It is against this backdrop that Mursi issued the poorly conceived 22 November 2012 constitutional declaration; a maladroit maneuver that the Brothers insisted was necessary to outflank further judicial action against the constituent assembly and the upper house of parliament (see Hamid 2014: 157). The constitutional declaration, though rescinded following the passing of the constitution in a referendum weeks later, provoked a new cycle of protest, led by many of the leading figures of the 25th January Revolution who accused Mursi of dictatorial intent. In stark contrast then to the Muslim Brothers' expectations that political contestation would telescope into democratically elected forms of civilian authority following parliamentary and presidential elections, Mursi's presidency was, instead, swiftly defined by the "deparliamentarization" of politics, the result of repeated judicial interventions into the political process and escalating protest against his rule. Having come to underestimate the power and significance of mass mobilization during the transition, Mursi and the Muslim Brothers proved to be particularly vulnerable and spectacularly inept at responding to the challenges that their erstwhile revolutionary allies mounted from Egypt's squares and streets. As Nathan Brown (2013a: 50) has argued, the Supreme Constitutional Court's refusal to ratify an electoral law for a new parliament ensured that the opposition's energies were channeled not into an electoral campaign, but rather further mobilization, as we will see in the next chapter.

In this sense, the post-Mubarak transition failed, in part, not because the Muslim Brothers eschewed procedural democracy, but because they eschewed mass mobilization and a more broadly coalitional approach to the transition. Here, a series of provisional and contingent factors – the evaporation of the NDP, the failure of Egypt's liberal and secular forces to develop a competitive political machine of their own, and the particular pathways of regime breakdown – ensured that the Brothers' electoralism and demobilization, a common theme of other Third Wave democratic transitions, magnified and exaggerated divisions within the revolutionary coalition, without ever producing a definitive outcome that could bind old regime holdovers.

However, revisiting the transitional period through the Muslim Brothers' writings, the conviction that if competitive elections were held, the will of the new parliament and the new president could not be usurped appears axiomatic in the movement's thinking. As a result, any initial constraint or attempts at coalition building soon gave way to electoral hubris and a sense of entitlement, premised on the disastrous miscalculation that democratically elected forms of civilian authority alone were sufficient both to legitimize the Brothers' corporate agenda and to reduce the power and insulation of Mubarak-era figures. As one senior Brother later conceded, "We thought that once we had the legitimacy to write a new constitution, backed up by a new parliament and new democratic institutions, any counter-revolution could be defeated" (interview Abdullah al-Haddad 20 Feb. 2014). This retreat from mass mobilization and privileging of electoral and constitutional forums is a prominent feature of Brothers' critical reappraisals of the movement's missteps following the 25th January Revolution, beginning with the movement's demobilization following the 18 March referendum. "The revolution," reflects Abdel Mawgoud al-Dardery, a leading FJP figure, "should have continued" (cited in *Jadaliyya* 15 Aug. 2013).[16]

For all the reasons outlined above – electoral ambitions, status as a privileged transitional partner, a commitment to gradualism – it nevertheless remains difficult to envisage a counterfactual scenario in which the Brothers continued to mobilize in February 2011 and force the military to cede power to an unelected civilian set of authorities in the immediate aftermath of Mubarak stepping down. Somewhat easier to imagine is some combination of the Democratic Alliance staying together, or Egypt's non-Islamist revolutionary parties performing better at the ballot box, and the Brothers mobilizing in support of a national salvation government after the SCAF signaled its intentions to remain a state within a state. In that case, the Brothers would have become a senior partner in a coalition of forces, with a presence in Midan al-Tahrir and parliament, bound by power-sharing and compromise, instead of being left with few allies to defend an isolated and unpopular president against the predations of old regime forces – forces, who, as we will see in the next chapter, would play a key role in orchestrating and ultimately capitalizing on the protests that lead to Mursi's downfall and the failure of the democratic project.

---

[16] Amr Darrag, one of Mursi's ministers echoes al-Dardery's assessment: "We underestimated the power of the deep state. We thought that just having the revolution and elections, the deep state would diminish automatically or gradually. When parliamentary elections took place and only thirteen members from *feloul* parties made it, we thought it was a strong indication that they don't have much influence. But maybe at that time they were still gathering themselves. As time passed, we found that they have much more influence. They managed to have their candidate be the second top presidential candidate. If you go through the government, as I did as minister, you find out that they are really deeply rooted everywhere. A more revolutionary path would have been necessary to expedite reform" (*Mada Masr* 8 Sept. 2013).

5

Manufacturing Dissent

I, the undersigned, of my own free will and as a member of the general assembly of the Egyptian people, have no confidence in the President of the Republic, Dr Muhammad Mursi, and call for early presidential elections, while pledging to uphold the aims of the Revolution, and committing to disseminate the Tamarrod petition among the masses, so that together we can realize a society based on the principles of dignity, freedom and justice.

Tamarrod petition

On 1 May 2013, Tamarrod officially launched its petition campaign in Midan al-Tahrir in downtown Cairo. The location ensured that Tamarrod's public debut was pregnant with revolutionary symbolism. The petition, handed out to several hundred trade unionists who had marched to Tahrir to celebrate International Workers' Day, denounced President Muhammad Mursi and the Muslim Brothers for hijacking the 25th January Revolution.[1] Only by holding new presidential elections, the petition claimed, could Egyptians realize "the Revolution's goals of bread, freedom and social justice." During an hour-long interview that aired later that night on OnTv, a satellite television channel owned by the Egyptian billionaire Naguib Sawiris, Tamarrod's spokesperson Mahmoud Badr called on the country's youth to mobilize in support of the petition and its goal of collecting 15 million signatures.[2] This was more than the total

---

[1] Despite being a relatively lowkey event, Tamarrod's launch would attract major news coverage. For footage of the launch, see YouTube video (1 May 2013) "A 'dā' Tamarrod ha-najma' 15 milyūn tawqī' li-sahb al-thiqa min Mursi wa kifaya 'alayh sana" https://youtu.be/SR5xg6JYuIM.

[2] See footage: YouTube video (1 May 2013) "Hamlat Tamarrod..al-tarīq ila sahb al-thiqa min al-ra'īs Mursi" https://youtu.be/ndtBmclbRio.

number of votes cast for Mursi in the second round of the 2012 presidential elections. The petition campaign, Badr announced, would conclude on 30 June 2013, the first anniversary of Mursi's election, with open-ended protests planned outside the presidential palace and in Midan al-Tahrir.

The number of anti-Mursi protestors who took to the streets during this period has been a matter of debate. Both Tamarrod's leadership and the nascent academic literature on the 30 June protests (e.g., Elyachar 2014; Gunning and Baron 2013: 303) cite figures ranging from 14 to 30 million anti-Mursi protestors – or roughly 25 to 50 percent of Egypt's adult population. Meanwhile, Egyptian state media has reported that over 22 million Egyptians signed the Tamarrod petition (*al-Ahram* 30 Jun. 2013). Figure 5.1 shows the frequency and size of anti-Mursi protests between 18 June and 10 July using event data culled from protest reports published in Egyptian newspapers. There is no way to independently verify the number of people who signed the Tamarrod petition.[3] However, event data suggests a more plausible upper threshold of around 1 million anti-Mursi protestors countrywide on 30 June.

This discrepancy is at least partly explained by the role played by state actors and a pliant media in inflating the level of anti-Mursi opposition in the days following the 30 June protests. While opposition movements have an obvious incentive to exaggerate the number of protestors taking to the streets, their figures tend to be counterbalanced by more conservative estimates produced by law enforcement officials (McPhail and Clark 2004: 17). This did not occur in the Egyptian case. In the days leading up to the 3 July coup, Egyptian state officials and old regime figures took to the airwaves, declaring that tens of millions of anti-Mursi protestors had taken to the streets on 30 June.[4] Speaking to journalists, one Interior Ministry official would claim that 17 million Egyptians had joined anti-

---

[3] I interviewed several leading members of the Tamarrod movement in late 2014. They insisted that the petitions were kept in storage in a flat in downtown Cairo, but that it was not possible for me to verify the number of signatures (interview Iman al-Mahdi 24 Nov. 2014; interview Ahmad Badr 26 Nov. 2014).

[4] This included interviews and media appearances with international news media. Speaking on *CNN* (3 Jul. 2013) shortly after the military seizure of power, Major General Sameh Seif El-Yezel (Ret.) claimed that 33 million Egyptians had taken to the streets on 30 June. El-Yezel, who had spent his career working in military intelligence, would later go on to lead the pro-Sisi "For the Love of Egypt" electoral list that would sweep the 2015 parliamentary elections. Egyptian journalists would later report that "For the Love of Egypt" was formed at the behest of Egypt's General Intelligence Agency, and that the first meeting of the list's founders, held at the agency's headquarters in Cairo, was attended by none other than Tamarrod's Mahmoud Badr (see Bahgat 2016).

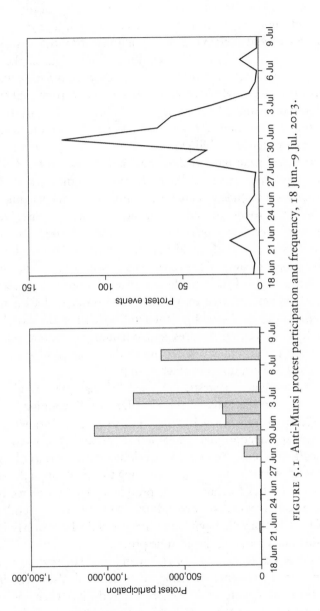

FIGURE 5.1 Anti-Mursi protest participation and frequency, 18 Jun.–9 Jul. 2013.

Mursi protests (cited in *al-Shorouk* 1 Jul. 2013: 3). So too, the military actively lobbied media outlets to report wholly unrealistic anti-Mursi protest numbers. To take one example: on the morning of the coup, the Egyptian daily newspaper *al-Masry al-Youm* (3 Jul. 2013: 1) printed a front-page corrective, claiming that "millions of [anti-Mursi] protestors" had taken to the streets on 30 June. These figures, the article explained, had been supplied by Ministry of Defence officials, who had conducted their own analysis of photography taken from military helicopters flying over anti-Mursi protests in Cairo and the governorates. "The protests," proclaimed a defence official, "were the largest in Egyptian history" (cited in Ibid.; see also *al-Shorouk* 1 Jul. 2013: 3).

Figure 5.2 uses event data to show how anti-Mursi protest frequency and protest participation varied across Egypt's governorates. By far the biggest protests on 30 June were in Cairo, with protestors packing Midan al-Tahrir and the roads around the presidential palace. Sizeable anti-Mursi protests were also held in Alexandria, Beheira, Daqahliyya, Gharbiyya, Ismailia, Kafr el-Sheikh, Luxor, Monufia, Port Said, and the Suez. These protests followed the repertoire of contention pioneered during the eighteen days of the 25th January Revolution. Between 30 June and 3 July, marches departed from mosques in residential areas to reinforce occupations, established by Tamarrod activists in the days leading up to 30 June, in central squares and outside governorate buildings. On 3 July 2013, the military seized upon the protests to suspend the recently passed constitution and stage a coup.

How did anti-Mursi protests, launched by an ostensibly grassroots social movement in the name of the 25th January Revolution, pave the way for a return to military rule? In the previous chapter, I argued that the Muslim Brothers' uncoordinated demobilization and excessive electoral victories worked against the post-Mubarak democratic project by generating a new set of grievances and precipitating the break-up of the revolutionary coalition, thus leaving Mursi's presidency fatally isolated to face old regime forces. This chapter expands on that argument by spotlighting the role played by both the Egyptian military and the Interior Ministry in orchestrating and co-opting the 30 June protests.

This requires a different angle of vision and mode of analysis from the bottom-up and agent-centered perspective adopted elsewhere in this book. In previous chapters, the object of study has been the unruly contention arising from the 25th January Revolution. By contrast, this chapter shows the 30 June protests to be conspicuously *rule-bound*, with the military and the Interior Ministry playing a key role in instigating and

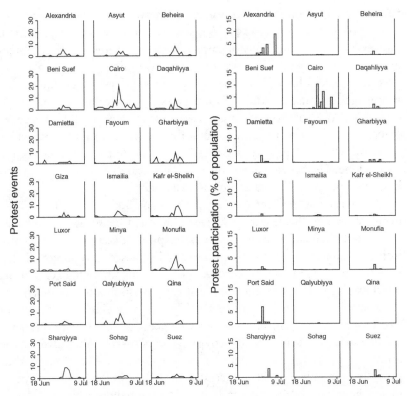

FIGURE 5.2 Anti-Mursi protest frequency and protest participation by governorate as a percentage of the population (over 10 years), 18 Jun.– 9 Jul. 2013. Notes: Dividing by population shows variation in governorates with smaller populations. Geographically distant governorates (Aswan, Matruh, Red Sea, South and North Sinai, and Wadi al-Jadid) are not shown.

then delimiting street level mobilization. Here, the "30 June Revolution" (*thawrat thalāthīn yūnyu*), as it has become known in official state discourse, can be usefully understood as belonging to a category of contentious politics increasingly seen in late Third Wave democratization: elite-facilitated contention.

ELITE-FACILITATED CONTENTION

Street protest is often thought of as being the preserve of the disenfranchised (Pettinicchio 2012, Pettinicchio 2013). This assumption is given formal expression in political process models of contentious politics, which theorize that mobilization occurs when "challengers" excluded from the formal political process make claims on established "members" of the polity (Gamson 1990 [1975]; see also Tilly 1978; Tarrow 2011). However, as a growing body of empirical research shows, political forces occupying privileged positions within state institutions, or political entrepreneurs closely linked to state actors through ties of clientelism or patronage, also use episodes of transgressive contention for their own ends (e.g., Auyero 2007; Hedman 2006; Kirschke 2000; Radnitz 2006; Robertson 2010; Chen 2014). As Scott Radnitz (2010: 15) observes in his study of "elite-led" protest in Central Asia: "protest is not a tool of the weak alone. The benefits of a show of collective public outrage ... can be harnessed by strong actors as well as weak ones."

Heartwarming moments of "people power" during late Third Wave democratization, this literature suggests, are often belied by the "obscure (and obscured) links" (Auyero 2007: 6) that protestors enjoy with powerful institutional actors. In Thailand, for example, conservative forces aligned with the military and the monarchy, and operating under the aegis of the "Yellow Shirts" movement, launched street protests in a bid to undermine successive elected governments led by Thaksin and Yingluck Shinawatra (see Ockey 2009; Ungpakorn 2009; Chambers 2010). In one infamous episode in 2008, Yellow Shirt activists were allowed, unimpeded by the army and the police, to occupy Bangkok airport for over a week, thus providing the military with a pretext to intervene in the political process under the guise of "restoring stability." We find comparable episodes of elite-facilitated dissent in Pakistan, where a pro-military political party, headed by the former international cricketer Imran Khan, manufactured and instrumentalized street protests in an attempt to oust the democratically elected government of Nawaz Sharif (see Shah and Asif 2015). That mobilization reached its apogee in 2014 when army units, tasked with protecting government buildings, stood by as protestors broke into parliament and occupied the headquarters of the state television broadcaster (Ibid.: 52).

Elite-facilitated contention is not restricted to stimulating demonstrations and sit-ins: politico-criminal configurations have also been found to be behind more serious episodes of collective violence (see e.g., Mitchell, Carey, and Butler 2014). In her study of democratization in sub-Saharan Africa, Linda Kirschke (2000: 397) found that old regime figures used "surrogate bodies such as hit squads, party youth wings, and traditional leaders" to destabilize transitional civilian governments (see also Roessler 2005; LeBas 2006; Ahram 2011; 2015). In his account of democratic transitions away from authoritarian rule in Romania and Indonesia, John Gledhill (2012) has also chronicled how state security forces use collective violence to advance their own corporate interests, often under the cover of regime proxies and agent provocateurs. "[D]uring periods of institutional ambiguity," Gledhill concludes, "contentious politics need not be enacted against the state but can, in fact, be adopted as an extra-institutional political tool of the state" (2005: 76). Similarly, Javier Auyero (2007) has shown that the 2001 food riots in Argentina, which brought down an elected president, were in part instigated and stage-managed by security forces and the Peronist opposition. Also relevant is research by Steven Wilkinson (2004) and Paul Brass (1997), who argue that politicians, local bureaucrats, and security forces in India foment and sanction episodes of ethnic violence, which they then exploit for electoral gain (see also Dhattiwala and Biggs 2010).

TAMARROD

Such "ordered disorder" (Gayer 2014) emerges from what Javier Auyero (2008) has called the "grey zone of politics": a realm of clandestine and concealed connections, in which state authorities, local bosses, and old regime figures are directly implicated in orchestrating contentious politics. As several scholars have argued, such figures were instrumental in creating the conditions for Mursi's removal and the 3 July coup; old regime hold-overs withheld key public services in a destabilization campaign designed to erode public confidence in Mursi's already divisive and unpopular presidency (see Brown 2013a, 2013b; *New York Times* 10 Jul. 2013; Pioppi 2013; Roberts 2013; Jumet 2015: ch.9; Rennick 2015: ch.9). These accounts also call attention to the decision by the police to with-draw from their routine duties in the months leading up to the 30 June protests. In the resulting security vacuum, a run on petrol stations, com-bined with prolonged power cuts and water shortages during high sum-mer and a violent insurgency led by Islamist militants in the Sinai, served to exacerbate the sense of crisis gripping the country and build momentum for the Tamarrod petition campaign and the 30 June protests. All this would play out in tandem with a sustained media campaign that sought to delegitimize the Muslim Brothers as a "terrorist" organization, and the democratic project as a foreign conspiracy (El-Amrani 30 Jun. 2013; Elmasry 2013, 2014a; *Wall Street Journal* 28 May 2014).[5]

---

[5] In the post-coup period, discussed in the next chapter, this media campaign went on to advance an eliminationist discourse, justifying the routine use of live ammunition and other repressive measures against the Muslim Brothers and anti-coup protestors.

Against this backdrop, the Tamarrod petition campaign proved to be a highly effective vehicle for uniting popular opposition to Mursi and the Muslim Brothers.[6] With its youthful leadership and revolutionary credentials, Tamarrod and the 30 June protests were seen by many members of the 25th January Revolutionary coalition as a means of reigniting a revolutionary process that had stalled under Mursi's presidency. As one veteran of the 25th January Revolution recalls:

> It [Tamarrod] was a beautiful thing – just take the spirit and the meaning of the word [i.e. rebellion]. As supporters of the 25th January Revolution, of course we were with Tamorrod and the 30 June. How could we not be? Tamarrod embodied the essence of the revolution against Mubarak – young people working together to fight dictatorship.   (interview Abdullah 4 12 Dec. 2014)

This reading is shared by many secular activists, "who speak about the 30 June protests as a second 'revolutionary wave' and relegate to the military a small assisting role" (Rennick 2015: 232). According to this analysis, Tamarrod began life as "a vehicle for the revival of the revolutionary movement" (Alexander and Bassiouny 2014: 310), only to be outmaneuvered and eclipsed by powerful state institutions in the days and weeks following Mursi's removal (see also Abdelrahman 2014: 135; Elyachar 2014).

In the absence of survey data, we can only speculate about the motivations and intentions of others who signed the Tamarrod petition and mobilized between 30 June and 3 July 2013. There is a positive and statistically significant ($p < .05$) association between anti-Mursi protest participation in the four days leading up to the coup and votes for the four main presidential candidates who came out in opposition to Mursi – the Nasserist Hamdeen Sabahi, the old regime candidate Ahmad Shafiq, the Islamist and former Muslim Brother Abdel Moneim Aboul Fotouh, and the former head of the Arab League Amr Moussa – across twenty-seven governorates in Egypt. As Figure 5.3 clearly shows, Cairo is an outlier. Excluding Cairo strengthens the association, which remains positive and statistically significant ($p < .01$). This might suggest that mobilization was significantly smaller in areas that voted for Mursi – and that

---

[6] Interestingly, the Tamarrod campaign was not the first petition to call for Mursi's resignation. Between January and March 2013, petitions were started in Asyut, Port Said, and Sharqia calling on Mursi to step aside in favor of either a military or revolutionary figure, pending new presidential elections. While these petition campaigns garnered some modest media coverage, they only managed to attract a small number of signatures. See *Daily News Egypt* (27 Feb. 2013) and *Daily News Egypt* (4 Mar. 2013).

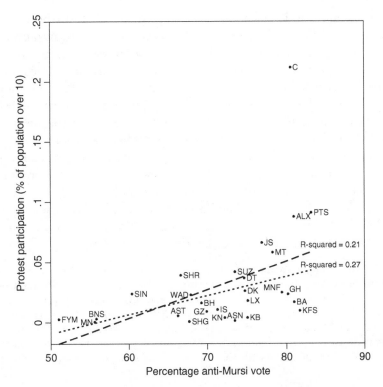

FIGURE 5.3 Anti-Mursi protest participation by governorate vote, 30 Jun.–3 Jul. 2013. Notes: R-squared for fitted values excluding Cairo (C) = 0.27.

elsewhere a broad coalition of protestors already opposed to the president took to the streets between 30 June and 3 July. Of these, no doubt some anti-Mursi protestors were motivated by a return to order and saw in the assurances of the military and the Interior Ministry a chance for the restoration of state power and a return to the relative stability of the Mubarak era. Others no doubt harbored genuine revolutionary ambitions.

What the evidence offered in this chapter unequivocally points to, however, is the background presence of powerful institutional actors and elites intent on the selective facilitation of Tamarrod and the 30 June protests in the service of definite political aims and, ultimately, state capture. Journalists in Egypt first began to document the role of the military and the Interior Ministry in funnelling material and logistical support to the Tamarrod campaign in the months following Mursi's removal. These reports, which cite senior members of Egypt's Interior

Ministry and state bureaucracy, claim that Tamarrod's leadership enjoyed substantive links with the General Intelligence Service, who saw the movement as an opportunity to redeploy "people power" against Mursi's democratically elected government (see especially *Reuters* 10 Oct. 2013; *Reuters* 20 Feb. 2014).[7] These claims have been repeated in my own interviews with serving police officers and former state security officials, as well as in statements given by several former Tamarrod members, including two of the movement's founders; they recall regular meetings with retired army officers and former regime figures acting as intermediaries for the Interior Ministry and the military leadership to coordinate protest activities in the months leading up to 30 June (see Naguib 2013; Giglio 7 Dec. 2013; Frenkel and Atef 15 Apr. 2014).[8] When asked if the Interior Ministry supported the Tamarrod movement, one informant, Hisham, a recently retired state security officer, replied:

Is it wrong to fight a virus? Of course we advised Tamarrod! We gave strategic direction so that we could trigger a crisis and then support it ... We knew that the Muslim Brothers would make mistakes and reveal themselves [referring to the Ittihadiyya clashes when Muslim Brothers clashed with secular activists protesting Mursi's constitutional declaration]. We were just waiting for the moment to act. That moment came on 30 June ... [Here], the Interior Ministry were in unity with the military. Historically, the military and the

---

[7] Seasoned activists recall being unsure of Tamarrod's origins in the run up to the 30 June protests; they referred to Tamarrod's founder Mahmoud Badr as Mahmoud *Bango* (slang for the inexpensive marijuana grown in the Sinai) because he had a reputation for being a drug dealer (personal correspondence Naglaa 28 Nov. 2014). Despite these misgivings, activists failed to make their concerns public: "we agreed amongst ourselves that we cannot be suspicious of popular initiatives" (interview Alia and Yahya 17 Dec. 2014).

[8] Despite the numerous accounts of Tamarrod's coordination with Egypt's security state, the campaign's remaining leadership continue to deny these links, although they do acknowledge that the successful courting of police sympathies was a central part of the campaign's mobilization strategy. According to Iman al-Mahdi, one of Tamarrod's earliest members, the campaign sought to: "[F]orge an alliance between anti-Mursi protestors and state institutions. We did this through public communiqués. We especially targeted the police, mentioning them positively to show that we were on their side ... Our strategy was to build a broad front against the Muslim Brothers" (interview 24 Nov. 2014). Tamarrod leaders also accept that the movement's activities were sanctioned by elements working within the state machinery. "Of course we knew that the police were on our side," Ahmad Badr, brother of founder Mahmud Badr and a Tamarrod leader himself, reflected, "They never tried to stop us from assembling and mobilizing. They never arrested or harassed our petitioners" (interview Ahmad Badr 26 Nov. 2014). Ahmed Badr also acknowledged coordinating the 30 June protests with retired army officers, but insisted that the officers were acting as private individuals, rather than as representatives of the state bureaucracy (interview Ahmad Badr 26 Nov. 2014).

Interior Ministry have been competitors – but in our time of need we united
against Mursi and the Brothers.   (interview 14 Dec. 2014)

The decision by state actors to use street protests against Egypt's first
democratically elected president appears to have been taken several
months before the coup. Ahmed Maher (2014) of April 6 has claimed
that in February 2013, he was approached by Egyptian state security to
lead protests against Mursi. He claims that when he declined, the Interior
Ministry began to cultivate Tamarrod. To facilitate the spread of the
movement, Tamarrod received significant financial backing from the
Mubarak-era business elite, and in particular from the billionaire
Naguib Sawiris, whose business interests had been pursued by Mursi's
government for tax evasion totaling several billion dollars (Kenner 10
Jul. 2013). Leaked audio recordings of conversations between senior
Egyptian military figures also reveal that Tamarrod's national leadership
drew on a bank account administered by the Ministry of Defense and
replenished by the United Arab Emirates – an implacable regional oppo-
nent of the Muslim Brothers (*New York Times* 1 Mar. 2015).[9] It has also
been reported that Mahmoud Badr, Tamarrod's spokesman, received
land from the military as a payoff for his role in leading the movement (*al-
Masry al-Youm* 17 Dec. 2014). As a result of these and other revelations,
Tamarrod quickly became a discredited political force in the post-coup
period. In October 2013, Hassan Shahin, one of Tamarrod's founders,
was assaulted in downtown Cairo by secular activists, who denounced
him for being a "pimp of the intelligence services" (*'ars al-mukhābarāt*;
see *Al-Masriyyun*19 Oct. 2013).[10]

"WE REFUSE TO PROTECT MUSLIM BROTHER HQS"

With anti-Mursi sentiment growing throughout the country in the run up
to the 30 June protests, the Muslim Brothers found themselves defending
their network of offices and charities from attack. One of the first assaults
on the Brothers' infrastructure came in December 2012 when their headquarters in Ismailia, the Suez Canal city where the movement was founded

[9] Tamarrod also received the support of entrepreneurial police officers and state officials.
To give one example, a British journalist recalled visiting the Mugamma, the vast
terracotta building on the southern edge of Midan al-Tahrir that houses the Egyptian
state bureaucracy, to find security officials and police officers using government photo-
copiers to print copies of the Tamarrod petition (interview Journalist 24 Nov. 2014).

[10] A month later, Shahin was attacked again, this time by members of 6 April as he sat in
a coffee shop in downtown Cairo (*al-Masry al-Youm* 7 Nov. 2013: 3).

TABLE 5.1 *Attacks on Muslim Brother and FJP offices, 18 Jun.–3 Jul., 2013*

Date	Location (governorate, town/city, office)
18 June	Gharbiyya, Tanta (FJP office)
19 June	Kafr el-Sheikh, Madinat Dessouq (FJP office)
25 June	Sharqiyya (FJP office)
28 June	Sharqiyya, Zagazig (MB office); Daqahliyya (MB office); Fayoum (MB office); Alexandria, Semouha (MB office); Kafr el-Sheikh, Baltim (FJP office); Kafr el-Sheikh, Baltim (FJP office); Qalyubiyya, al-Khaanka (FJP office); Beheira, Mahmoudiyya (FJP office); Madinat Basyoun (MB office)
29 June	Beheira, Housh Eissa (FJP office); Beheira, Shubra Khit (MB office); Daqahliyya, Aga (FJP office); Gharbiyya, Madinat Basyoun (FJP office); Port Said, Port Said (FJP office); Beni Suef, Madinat Beni Suef (MB and FJP offices); Port Said, Port Fuad (FJP office); Alexandria, Ibrahamiyya (FJP office)
30 June	Fayoum, Fayoum (FJP office); Cairo, Muqattam (MB HQ); Gharbiyya (FJP office); Daqahliyya, al-Sinbelawin (MB and FJP offices); Alexandria, Mintaqat al-Hadara al-Jadida (FJP office); Qalyubiyya, Tukh (FJP office); Beheira, Itay al-Barud (FJP office); Asyut (FJP office)
1 July	Gharbiyya (MB office); Gharbiyya, Madinat Basyoun (MB office); Qalyubiyya, Madinat al-Qanatir (FJP office); Sharqiyya, Zagazig (MB office); Sharqiyya, Faqus (FJP office); Sharqiyya, Abu Hamad (MB office); Sharqiyya, Qaryat al-Azaziyya (FJP office); Sharqiyya, Markaz Dirb Najm (FJP office); Sharqiyya, al-Hussayniyya (FJP office); Monufia (FJP office); Asyut (FJP office); Kafr el-Sheikh, Baltim (FJP office); Kafr el-Sheikh, Madinat Bila (FJP office); Kafr el-Sheikh, al-Burj al-Burlus (FJP office)
2 July	Beni Suef, Madinat Beni Suef (MB school); Qalyubiyya, Madinat Banha (FJP office)
3 July	Monufia, Markaz Ashmun (FJP office)

in 1928, was set on fire. Further attacks followed. On the second anniversary of the 25th January Revolution, two FJP offices in the Nile Delta cities of Mansoura and Damanhour were burnt down. It is unclear exactly who was behind these attacks, although there is some evidence to suggest that local residents, angry with what many saw as Mursi's autocratic and ineffectual presidency, played a role.[11] The Brothers, meanwhile, were

---

[11] In Ismailia, for example, opposition to the Brothers grew throughout early 2013 to culminate in residents parading through the center of the city bearing effigies of Mursi and other leading Muslim Brothers during their Spring Festival (*al-Masry al-Youm* 4 May 2013). A tradition of effigy burning dates back to the British occupation.

convinced that the attacks formed part of a destabilization campaign, sanctioned by the Interior Ministry and carried out by former members of Mubarak's National Democratic Party. The police, they noted, always failed to intervene and protect the buildings and their occupants.

Despite a massive security operation underway in the week prior to the 30 June protests, such attacks continued to escalate. Between 18 June and 3 July 2013, forty-seven headquarters and offices were gutted, most during a three-day period from 28 June to 1 July (see Table 5.1). Some buildings were attacked multiple times over successive days, and some districts saw attacks on buildings belonging to different arms of the Brothers in short succession. How could these attacks on the movement of Egypt's democratically elected president continue seemingly unimpeded? In trying to make sense of these episodes, my research suggests that anti-Muslim Brother violence was actively enabled and sanctioned by the police and the Interior Ministry's security forces.

In the days and weeks before the coup, this increase in attacks coincided with a sequence of public statements from senior police officers and Interior Ministry officials condoning the violence and telegraphing the police's commitment not to protect the buildings. This included a leaked video of a meeting in the Police Officers' Club in Giza, in which senior and mid-ranking police officers pledged not to defend Muslim Brother buildings.[12] Speaking to journalists on 29 June, Ibrahim Adeeb, a major general from the Interior Ministry, declared that "The role of security forces in the governorates on 30 June is to protect public institutions and ensure that people have the right to peaceful protest . . . we will not protect political party headquarters, including offices that belong to the FJP" (*al-Shorouk* 30 Jun. 2013: 6).

This was later reiterated by police officers in a series of interviews with Egyptian news media. In one such interview, Major Nour al-Shaykh, of the 7 March Police Officers association, insisted that no police officer would defend a building belonging to the Muslim Brothers or their political party, while pledging that officers and their families would join anti-Mursi protests (cited in *al-Shorouk* 1 Jul. 2013: 5). In another interview, Major Hisham Salih, spokesman for the General Coalition of Police Officers, declared, "We refuse to protect Muslim Brother headquarters" (cited in *al-Dostor* 2 Jul. 2013: 8). Or as another police officer put it, "We will not allow ourselves to be drawn into protecting party

---

[12] See footage: YouTube video (25 Jun 2013) *"Mawqif al-dubāt min 30 yunyu (ijtimā' al-dubāt bi-nadi al-shurta)"* https://youtu.be/cp4FBb8z7ug.

headquarters – we are the police of the people" (cited in *al-Masry al-Youm* 1 Jul. 2013: 11). This refusal to combat rising anti-Muslim Brother violence was affirmed by the Police Officers' Club in a press release stating: "Our officers will not protect Muslim Brother headquarters, they will only protect the institutions of the state" (cited in *al-Masry al-Youm* 2 Jul. 2013: 1). The Interior Ministry appeared to sanction this policy, with senior ministry officials in the governorates informing Egyptian journalists that "the police will not pander to party political interests and protect any party headquarters" (cited in *al-Masry al-Youm* 1 Jul. 2013: 10). In context, it was clear that this amounted to a refusal to protect Muslim Brother headquarters.

I interviewed two witnesses to an attack on the Muslim Brothers' national headquarters in Muqattam in Cairo on 18 March 2013 (interview Alia and Yahya 17 Dec. 2014). The interviewees lived on a street adjacent to the building. During that episode the police held back, only intervening after clashes between protestors and Muslim Brothers had gone on for several hours. Many of the "protestors," they claimed, were "*amnagī*" – literally, individuals with links to state security. In the aftermath of the March attack, a police kiosk was installed in front of the building. However, it was left unmanned on 30 June, when the building was attacked for a second time and set on fire. The failure of the police to intervene is all the more remarkable given that the district police station in Muqattam is located just a few hundred meters away from the Brothers' headquarters.

While the identities of the attackers remain elusive, the frequency and intensity of attacks nevertheless point to the complicity of Egypt's security forces in failing to prevent anti-Muslim Brother violence. As Steven Wilkinson (2004: 5) notes, the scale of collective violence often depends "not on the local factors that caused violence to break out but primarily on the will and capacity of the government that controls the forces of law and order." Large-scale collective violence "does not take place where a state's army or police force is ordered to stop it using all means necessary" (Ibid.: 5). That this did not occur in the Egyptian case underlines the very real limitations on the authority of Mursi's elected office. In the only recorded instance of state security forces interceding to stop individuals looting and setting fire to Muslim Brother offices, police in the capital are reported to have "negotiated with protestors" to withdraw from one FJP headquarters – but only because it was situated next to a building belonging to the Interior Ministry (*al-Masry al-Youm* 5 Jul. 2013: 7). No anti-Mursi protestor has been prosecuted for these episodes of collective violence, several of which resulted in the deaths and wounding of the buildings' occupants. On the other hand, violence by Muslim Brothers in defense of their property (and lives) has been used as a key legal pretext for the imprisonment of the Brothers' national and regional leadership in the post-coup period.

"THE ARMY IS WITH YOU AND WILL PROTECT YOU"

Deliberate and coordinated police inaction in the face of rising anti-Muslim Brother violence appears to have served another purpose. In the weeks leading up to the coup, senior officials in the Ministry of Defense spotlighted these attacks, and Muslim Brother counter-mobilization, as evidence that the country was irrevocably sliding towards civil war. These warnings were repeated in the days leading up to 26 June, when Egyptian army units left barracks for the second time in two years and were deployed to the streets of Cairo, Giza, and Alexandria. By the early evening, army units had taken up positions in public squares and outside of local government buildings in fourteen governorates. The decision to deploy was taken by the Defense Minister Abdel Fattah al-Sisi. Justifying the decision to leave barracks, senior army officers and Ministry of Defense officials insisted that a military presence on the streets was necessary to protect Egypt's state institutions in the lead up to the 30 June protests.

By prepositioning their forces in strategically sensitive spaces prior to the 30 June protests, the military ensured that anti-Mursi contention could never break out and scale up into a truly revolutionary situation, as had occurred during the eighteen days of the 25th January Revolution. The decision to pre-deploy does, however, appear to have created a dilemma for Egypt's military hierarchy. The sight of APCs and tanks taking up positions prior to 30 June could have been interpreted as a move to insulate the President from street protests, and thus might have served to demobilize anti-Mursi opposition. To dispel any ambiguities in regard to the military's intentions, Ministry of Defense officials were quick to issue a series of statements to Egyptian news outlets in the hours following the deployment. As one Ministry of Defense official set out:

The military are not deploying to protect the Mursi regime, or keep Muslim Brother governors in power, but rather to fulfil our patriotic duty in protecting the Egyptian people ... The military's role will be to protect peaceful protestors from any attack from armed militias [an oblique reference to the long disbanded

Special Section of the Muslim Brothers] opposed to the protests planned for 30 June. (cited in *al-Masry al-Youm* 27 Jun. 2013 : 5)

Meanwhile, Major General Osama Askar, head of Egypt's Third Army, met opposition figures to reassure them that the military would not repress or curtail anti-Mursi mobilization (see *al-Shorouk* 27 Jun. 2013: 4). This was followed by a statement the following day from Major General Muhammad Zaki, the head of the Republican Guard forces tasked with protecting the head of state, who declared to journalists that his forces would "defend the sons of the nation" taking to the streets in opposition to the President (cited in *al-Masry al-Youm* 28 Jun. 2013: 1, 4). Another newspaper article citing an anonymous military source was equally explicit:

The armed forces will defend the people, not the president or his *jama'a* [society; shorthand for the Society of the Muslim Brothers] ... The deployment of the armed forces to the governorates before the 30 June protests is to protect peaceful protestors from any attempt to target them by armed militias opposed to the protests. The intention is not to protect the regime of Muhammad Mursi, or to sustain Muslim Brother governors in power, as some have claimed on social media.   (cited in *al-Shorouk* 27 Jun. 2013: 1)

These statements and interviews conformed to a pattern established in the weeks prior to 30 June, in which Egypt's police and intelligence services made public their plans to safeguard anti-Mursi protestors. On 18 June, the Interior Ministry published details of a meeting involving the heads of the police, CSF and security directorates, in which they agreed to deploy 200,000 police officers, as well as 220 divisions of CSF troopers, to protect anti-Mursi protestors on 30 June (*al-Dostor* 19 Jun. 2013: 6).[13] In the days leading up to 30 June, the Interior Ministry announced plans to increase this number to 300,000 police officers (*al-Shorouk* 30 Jun. 2013: 5). On 1 July, Interior Ministry officials claimed that all leave had been cancelled, and that 440,000 police had been deployed to "protect protestors" and defend government buildings (*al-Masry al-Youm* 2 Jul. 2013: 9). In a move that seems to have been designed to reassure those planning to take to the streets, senior police officers pledged that CSF units would not approach Midan al-Tahrir or attempt to disperse anti-Mursi protestors (see *al-Masry al-Youm* 29 Jun. 2013: 7). In this, Interior Ministry officials were unequivocal in their support for the 30 June protests. When asked if the police would

---

[13] Note that this is up to ten times the number of police officers that are reported to have been deployed during the first days of the 25th January Revolution.

safeguard anti-Mursi protests on 30 June, one official replied, "Yes – that is our responsibility … They [the police] will stand with the majority of the Egyptian people" (cited in *al-Dostor* 24 Jun. 2013: 11).

The purpose of these statements seems clear. By publicly distancing themselves from Mursi's presidency, and by pledging to protect anti-Mursi protests and not disperse protestors, the military and the Interior Ministry were attempting to solve a collective action problem. Since there was a risk that Egyptians might be reluctant to take to the streets because the outcome was uncertain and the act inherently risky, signaling by the Interior Ministry and the military was designed to alleviate any such concerns. This even extended to the head of the General Intelligence Services, who informed journalists that his forces had erected CCTV cameras along the advertised protest routes to monitor and secure anti-Mursi marches heading to Midan al-Tahrir and the presidential palace (*al-Masry al-Youm* 30 Jun. 2013: 3). Above all, security officials were keen to stress, there would be no repeat of the chaos and lawlessness of the early days of the 25th January Revolution: Egypt's prisons and police stations would be reinforced and private property protected (*al-Masry al-Youm* 30 Jun. 2013: 3, 7; *al-Shorouk* 30 Jun. 2013: 3). This included practical measures on the ground. In Beheira, for example, in the days leading up to the protests, police vehicles were emblazoned with the logo: "your security is important to us; ensuring your safety is our goal" (*al-Shorouk* 30 Jun. 2013: 6).

This interpretation – that the Egyptian military and Interior Ministry used public statements to maximize participation on 30 June – is consistent with other episodes of elite-facilitated contention, where government officials and regime intermediaries use interviews, speeches and statements to encourage and stimulate collective action (see e.g., Auyero 2007: 122; LeBas 2006: 427; Wilkinson 2004: 62, 65). This was certainly how the President's opponents understood such messages in the run up to the 30 June protests. Following a speech by Defense Minister al-Sisi on 23 June, demanding that Mursi make political concessions to the Tamarrod campaign and the National Salvation Front, the front-page of the opposition newspaper *al-Dostor* declared: "Go into the streets for the army is with you and will protect you! Sisi's speech was clear, comprehensive and understood: it could not be read any other way" (*al-Dostor* 25 Jun. 2013: 1).[14] Reflecting on their experiences participating in the

[14] Sisi's speech marked the first public rift between Mursi and the military, and the first indication that the military were primed to move against the President. Ministry of

protest outside of the presidential palace on 30 June, two activists who had participated in the 25th January Revolution recall similar sentiments:

[Yahya]: It didn't seem like a real protest. There was no danger or anger. During the eighteen days of the January Revolution we went out and we didn't know what was going to happen: it was like going to war.
   [Alia interrupts]: This time was different; it was more of a party than a protest. We felt safe – safe because of all the messages from the police and the army beforehand that made it very clear that they weren't under the control of Mursi.
                                   (interview Alia and Yahya 17 Dec. 2014)

   Speaking to Egyptian journalists in the build-up to the 30 June protests, Ahmad Sa'd, a prominent liberal politician, agreed: "the message has been received from the army and the police – they will protect the protestors and side with the people" (cited *al-Masry al-Youm* 29 Jun. 2013: 8).

"THE POLICE AND THE PEOPLE ARE ONE HAND"

According to my argument, old regime holdovers used street level mobilization and episodes of collective violence to roll back the gains of the 25th January Revolution. In this, it is important to remember that protest was never solely the prerogative of the 25th January revolutionary coalition. As we saw in Chapter 3, pro-Mubarak figures also took to the streets during the eighteen days of the 25th January Revolution, in what was ultimately a doomed attempt to rally support for Egypt's embattled dictator. A second round of counter-revolutionary protest began during the Events of Muhammad Mahmoud Street (discussed in the previous chapter). Between 23 and 25 November 2011, several thousand pro-military protestors occupied Midan al-Abassiyya, located close to the Ministry of Defence, for the *milyūniyya* of "Support the Military Council," chanting: "O Field Marshal, O Field Marshal, Egypt isn't in Midan al-Tahrir!" and: "The army, the police and the people are one hand!" (*al-Dostor* 26 Nov. 2011: 1, 5; see also *al-Masry al-Youm* 26 Nov. 2011: 6; *al-Shorouk* 26 Nov. 2011: 4). During that episode, pro-military protestors hung banners from the 6th October Bridge, denouncing the 25th January Revolution as a foreign conspiracy. A petition was also circulated, calling

---

Defense officials subsequently boasted to Egyptian journalists that Sisi had not consulted Mursi prior to giving the speech, a move seemingly designed to signal that the military hierarchy was now taking decisions independently of the country's political leadership (see *al-Dostor* 25 Jun. 2013: 3). This was soon followed by press briefings in which senior officers warned that "soldiers and officers would be uncontrollable" if Mursi attempted to replace Sisi as Minister of Defence (*al-Shorouk* 26 Jun. 2013: 4).

on the SCAF to remain in power indefinitely (*al-Masry al-Youm* 26 Nov. 2011: 1). One eyewitness reported that many of the protestors were off-duty police officers and soldiers (Armbrust 2013b: 839). Smaller pro-SCAF protests were also held in Alexandria outside of the presidential palace (*al-Shorouk* 26 Nov. 2011: 5).

Taufiq Ukasha, a former NDP politician and the host of the satellite television talk show *al-Fara'een*, was instrumental in organizing the Abassiyya protests and in drumming up support for the 30 June protests (see Armbrust 2013b). Beginning on 26 June 2013, Ukasha organized an open-ended sit-in before the Ministry of Defense, where he was joined by several hundred protestors who chanted: "Come on Sisi, Mursi isn't my president; come on Sisi, make your move, the Egyptian people are waiting!" (*al-Masry al-Youm* 28 Jun. 2013: 4). Instead of violently dispersing the protest, as had occurred during previous demonstrations outside of the Ministry, units of military police were deployed to safeguard the protestors (*al-Masry al-Youm* 1 Jul. 2013: 4; 6). This was typical of the military's stance to anti-Mursi contention in the days leading up to the 30 June protests.

FIGURE 5.4 "Invitation to all retired policemen to assemble today at 6pm at Bab al-Opera in Midan Saad al-Zaghlul and head towards Midan al-Tahrir to express our solidarity with the glorious Egyptian people. Major General Hani al-Kamuni." (Author's photo; from *al-Masry al-Youm* 30 Jun. 2013: 7.)

Against this backdrop, the role of security personnel on 30 June was not limited to creating opportunities for collective action; they also actively participated in the mobilization. Between 30 June and 3 July, both serving and retired police officers took part in highly choreographed anti-Mursi marches, sit-ins, and demonstrations. In one blatant example of old regime forces mobilizing against the President, high-ranking former Interior Ministry officials placed advertisements in national newspapers, calling on retired police officers to march in solidarity with anti-Mursi protestors (see Figure 5.4; *al-Masry al-Youm* 30 Jun. 2013: 7). This was followed by further advertisements published on the morning of 3 July – that is, before Mursi was ousted and the constitution suspended – applauding the military's decision to move against the President, this time signed by a SCAF-appointed Interior Minister and two senior police officers (see Figure 5.5; *al-Masry al-Youm* 3 Jul. 2013: 4).

Nor was participation in anti-Mursi protests restricted to former tribunes of the Mubarak-era security state. Video footage of the 30 June protests

FIGURE 5.5 "Thanks and gratitude. Major General Mansour Aysawi, the former Minister of Interior, Major General Fuad Alaam and Major General Hani al-Kamuni thank God for the retired police officers who participated in Egypt's glorious protests to restore the rights of Egyptians. They support the constructive steps taken by the armed forces to protect Egypt from evil" (Author's photo; from *al-Masry al-Youm* 3 Jul. 2013: 4.)

shows serving police officers in uniform heading anti-Mursi marches to Midan al-Tahrir and the presidential palace, held aloft on the shoulders of ostensibly civilian protestors, chanting and waving Egyptian flags.[15] In one video of a march departing for Tahrir from outside the Police Officers' Club in Giza, one plainclothes police officer, identifiable by the pistol under his arm, instructs the assembled crowd of civilian protestors, "If you've got a uniform, go and put it on."[16] On the same day, Egyptian newspapers recorded several thousand police officers and army officers marching on the Ministry of Defense and the presidential palace to call on the army to intervene and remove Mursi (*al-Masry al-Youm* 1 Jul. 2013: 6; *al-Shorouk* 1 Jul. 2013: 6). In Beheira, Qalyubiyya, and North Sinai, police officers were also reported to have joined protest marches calling for Mursi's ousting (*al-Shorouk* 1 Jul. 2013: 6; *al-Shorouk* 2 Jul. 2013: 7). In another video from 30 June, uniformed police officers can be seen stewarding an anti-Mursi march in Alexandria, while their colleagues denounced the President from atop police vans interspersed in the crowd.[17] The following day, a funeral procession for a police officer killed by Islamist militants in the Sinai was transformed into an anti-Mursi demonstration, with several hundred police officers, led by the head of Alexandria's security directorate, chanting: "Hurry up Sisi, Mursi isn't my president!" (cited in *al-Shorouk* 2 Jul. 2013: 2; see also *al-Masry al-Youm* 2 Jul. 2013: 3, 19). A common scene relayed in videos and newspaper reporting was the use of the chant, "The police and the people are one hand!"[18]

[15] See, e.g., video footage of marches departing from three suburbs in Cairo and Giza to Midan al-Tahrir and the presidential palace, e.g., YouTube video (3 Jul 2013) "*Shararat thawrat 30 yunyu talahum al-shurta ma' al-sha'b kān al-athar al-wādih fi taghyīr shu'ūr al-muwātinīn*" https://youtu.be/4lu1s6u67BQ; (30 Jun 2013) "*Al-shurta fi muzāharāt 30 yunyu ma' al-sha'b*" https://youtu.be/DtW6ObSp3jc; (30 Jun 2013) "*Muzāharāt al-dākhi-liyya 30 yunyu fi kul shawāri' Misr – al-zāwiya al-hamrā'*" https://youtu.be/ikNdaOT4oEU.

[16] See footage: YouTube video (30 Jun 2013) "*30 yunyu al-shurta al-misriyya alati tahtarim sharaf al-mihna tahtif irhal*" http://youtu.be/cCMojekxoDU.

[17] See footage: YouTube video (1 Jul 2013) "*Al-shurta ma' al-sha'b fi muzāharāt yunyu 2013*" https://youtu.be/9OwBW6FYoRo.

[18] Interestingly, the "one hand" metaphor was also used by pro-Mursi supporters in the streets near the Raba'a al-Adawiyya occupation (discussed in the next chapter). When news of the coup broke, many chanted, "The army and the people are one hand," as army officers wrestled with Mursi supporters trying to climb aboard their vehicles (*The Guardian* 3 Jul. 2013). Of course, the different valences of the "one hand" metaphor belie a common heritage: as we saw in Chapter 3, both draw on the repertoire of claim making employed during the 25th January Revolution, while illustrating how different actors and coalitions draw on the same modalities of protest, even as power configurations change.

For some activists who had mobilized during the 25th January Revolution, the visibility and prominence of police participation in anti-Mursi protests was especially alarming. One informant recalled how, on his way to join a march to Midan al-Tahrir on 30 June, he encountered a police checkpoint manned by plainclothes officers, who directed him to the protest assembly point outside of the Mustafa Mahmud mosque in Giza:

[It] was weird. I don't like the police – I don't trust them. The Revolution was against the police, so it was strange to be protected by them. Normally, when you encounter the police, even if they don't fuck with you, they let you know that they own you. This time was different. They were kind, even gentle. It was very clear that they were on our side.   (interview Muhammad 24 Nov. 2014)

While it is impossible to gauge the extent of police participation in anti-Mursi protests, one British journalist received several eyewitness reports of hundreds of CSF troopers, stationed behind the Carlton Hotel in downtown Cairo, changing into civilian clothes and joining anti-Mursi protestors in Tahrir (interview Journalist 12 Dec. 2014). Hisham, the retired state security officer, also confirmed the presence of large numbers of police officers, both in plainclothes and in uniform, in Tahrir and in the streets outside of the presidential palace (interview 14 Dec. 2014). While none of these examples are intended to suggest that all anti-Mursi protestors were undercover police agents or old regime stooges, these episodes do underline the degree to which elements affiliated with the Interior Ministry took part in anti-Mursi protests.

"CLOSED BY ORDER OF THE PEOPLE"

Attacks on Muslim Brother offices provide just one example in which the presence and absence of state security forces determined the sites and timings of anti-Mursi contention. This dynamic is rendered all the more visible when considering the ways in which anti-Mursi protestors were allowed, unobstructed by security forces, to occupy and blockade government buildings in the days and weeks leading up to the coup. Returning to this period and examining such occupations provides a useful window into the role played by the police and the military in both enabling and then delimiting episodes of anti-Mursi contention.

The first anti-Mursi occupation occurred on 5 June when several dozen cultural figures, intellectuals and activists, in protest at the appointment of a Muslim Brother to head the Ministry of Culture, occupied the ministry's building in Zamalek and barred the new minister from entering (*al-Ahram Online* 5 Jun. 2013). Police stationed outside the ministry left the occupiers inside unmolested.[19] The Ministry of Culture occupation would go on to be an important staging point and organizing space for anti-Mursi activism. Encouraged by the Interior Ministry's inaction, more anti-Mursi occupations followed. On 16 June, Mursi announced his second gubernatorial reshuffle in a year, replacing several governors appointed by the SCAF during the first eighteen months of the post-Mubarak transition. Mursi's attempt to shore up control over local government was greeted with fierce denunciations from Tamarrod and the National Salvation Front, who accused the President of dictatorial intent and enacting an Islamist takeover. In response, Tamarrod activists declared their intention to blockade local government buildings and cripple Mursi's ability to govern (*al-Dostor* 19 Jun. 2013: 6). Between 18 and 24 June, several thousand anti-Mursi protestors attempted to blockade the entrances of governorate buildings in Ismailia, Gharbiyya, Monufia, Daqahliyya, and Luxor. During those episodes, CSF units were deployed to keep the buildings open (*al-Dostor* 21 Jun. 2013: 3).

TABLE 5.2 *Anti-Mursi Protest Occupations by Governorate*

	Mursi Governors	Military/Interior Ministry Governors
Protestors occupy local government buildings	Monufia, Beheira, Damietta, Daqahliyya, Gharbiyya, Fayoum, Kafr el-Sheikh, Sohag, Sharqiyya, Luxor, Minya, Beni Suef, Qalyubiyya, Qina, Asyut	Ismailia, Port Said
Police/army secure local government buildings		Suez, Matruh, Wadi al-Jadid, Aswan, Red Sea, North Sinai, South Sinai

[19] This point was not lost on the occupiers. As one intellectual who joined the protest later reflected, "The state was in favor of the sit-in because they wanted to remove the Brotherhood. Some protestors did gain later on and became ministry consultants and some were writers who unconditionally supported the [military] regime and now still keep silent about the oppression of young people" (cited in *Mada Masr* 1 Jul. 2016).

Event data illustrates of the ways in which anti-Mursi protests were facilitated or delimited by state security forces in the days before the coup. Table 5.2 divides Egypt's governorates by the political affiliation of their governor. Governors identified by the title *liwā'* (major general) were appointed by the SCAF during the post-Mubarak transition, from either the military or the Interior Ministry. The one exception was in Damietta governorate, where the governor, a former Interior Ministry general, was also a leading member of Ayman Nour's al-Ghad al-Thawra party. All other governors, with the exception of Cairo, Giza, and Alexandria which were headed by technocrats, were political affiliates of the Mursi regime.[20]

In governorates where the governor was drawn from the military and Interior Ministry, police and military forces pre-deployed, securing local government buildings in the days before 30 June. Black uniformed CSF troopers and army units established exclusion zones and checkpoints on roads leading to governorate buildings. In Matruh, for example, 11,000 anti-Mursi protestors were forced to coordinate their march with the governorate's military governor, who banned protestors from encroaching on the security cordon thrown up around the governorate building (*al-Dostor* 30 Jun. 2013: 5; *al-Masry al-Youm* 2 Jul. 2013: 13). In Suez, the scene of some of the most violent and sustained assaults on the symbols and infrastructure of state power during the 25th January Revolution, the streets around the governorate building were sealed off by Egypt's Third Army (see *al-Masry al-Youm* 28 Jun. 2013: 3; *al-Shorouk* 28 Jun. 2013: 3; *al-Masry al-Youm* 2 Jul. 2013: 10). It seems that comparable precautions were taken in other governorates where the governor hailed from one of Egypt's security ministries (see *al-Dostor* 30 Jun. 2013: 5).

In governorates nominally under the control of President Mursi, the police and the army left local government buildings – including city councils (*majlis al-madīna*) and governorate buildings (*al-diwān*) – conspicuously undefended on 30 June. In Asyut, al-Beheira, Damietta, Daqahliyya, Gharbiyya, Kafr el-Sheikh, Luxor, Minya, Monufia, and Qalyubiyya, all governorates with Mursi-appointed governors, police and military forces, either failed to deploy in front of local government buildings, or withdrew from their posts upon the arrival of anti-Mursi

---

[20] Governorates headed by technocrats are dropped from the comparison. This is because protestors in these areas focused on more symbolic sites, such as Midan al-Tahrir and the presidential palace. This is reflected in the relatively small number of anti-Mursi protests staged in Giza during this period. Of those protests that did begin in Giza, anti-Mursi marches traveled the relatively short distance to downtown Cairo, where they joined the Tahrir occupation.

protestors. This allowed protestors to lock the doors with heavy metal chains (*al-janāzīr*) and erect banners declaring "closed by order of the people" (*al-Masry al-Youm* 1 Jul. 2013: 8–9; *al-Masry al-Youm* 2 Jul. 2013: 11–13; *al-Masry al-Youm* 3 Jul. 2013: 10, 12; *al-Shorouk* 2 Jul. 2013: 7). In Beni Suef, for example, the governor was reduced to pleading with the army and the police to intervene and break the siege of the governorate building, after anti-Mursi protestors locked him and his staff inside (*al-Masry al-Youm* 1 Jul. 2013: 9). By 3 July, protestors had blockaded governorate buildings and city councils across governorates headed by a political ally of President Mursi.

By contrast, in governorates with governors from the military and the Interior Ministry, security forces secured local government buildings. Through the selective policing of protest, the military and the Interior Ministry were able to channel and direct contention against local manifestations of Mursi's presidential authority, while limiting disruption in areas already under the control of allies of the national security state. In Ismailia and Port Said, governorates with governors hailing from Egypt's security ministries, secular revolutionaries and activists did stage protests outside of local government buildings, seemingly with the help of government employees, only for security forces to deploy in large numbers (see *al-Masry al-Youm* 2 Jul. 2013: 10; *al-Shorouk* 2 Jul. 2013: 8). During these and other episodes, it appears that anti-Mursi contention was quickly contained and undermined if it threatened to spill over and challenge old regime interests.

This dynamic was not lost on veterans of the 25 January Revolution who were opposed to both the Muslim Brothers and the military. On 1 July, the military issued its final ultimatum, demanding that Mursi reach a political compromise with Tamarrod and the National Salvation Front or face being removed. Two days later, with a coup seemingly inevitable, activists opposed to a military takeover, and who had led calls for Mursi's ousting, attempted to occupy the presidential palace (see *al-Masry al-Youm* 4 Jul. 2013: 8). The plan failed when other protestors rounded on the revolutionaries, forcing them to withdraw.

CONCLUSIONS

In the official state narrative that has grown up around the events of 30 June, the military and the Interior Ministry are portrayed as reluctant arbiters in the face of two competing and irreconcilable political factions. According to this narrative, the decision to remove Mursi reflected the democratic aspirations of the Egyptian people, as evidenced by the "33 million" anti-Mursi protestors who mobilized on 30 June. This is mirrored in the accounts of many anti-Mursi activists, who insist that the 30 June protests occurred with very little outside help. However, as I have shown in this chapter, not only were anti-Mursi protests likely to have been significantly smaller than these actors claim, but Egypt's security ministries, far from being uninvolved in the 30 June protests, and in ways reminiscent of elite-facilitated protest in other contexts, deliberately exploited the divisions between the Brothers and other members of the 25th January coalition, by impelling anti-Mursi protests. Here, a close examination of the Egyptian case deepens our understanding of the role played by powerful institutional actors in using mass mobilization and collective violence to undermine elected governments during democratic transitions away from authoritarian rule, and the ways in which actors from across the Middle East and North Africa came together to roll back the gains of the Arab Spring in the region's most populous country.

That secular revolutionaries continued to mobilize against Mursi has been well captured by Thanassis Cambanis (2015: 227), who notes that for Tamarrod's supporters, the 30 June protests "combined two inaccurate dictums from Egypt's revolutionary period: that vast crowds outweighed the authority of a ruler, and that the people's will would restrain the military." This miscalculation ensured that anti-Mursi contention, instead of having a democratizing effect, paved the way for the return of the Mubarak-era security state. This, in turn, has important implications for Egypt's democratic trajectory. A new literature suggests that post-Cold War, military coups tend to strengthen democratization in the long run, as military regimes have become more susceptible to Western pressure to hold competitive elections (Marinov and Goemans 2014; see also Ritter 2014). Whether military coups that are engineered under the cover of mass street protests follow the same trajectory will be an important question for future research.

What this episode does underline is that, just as elections are typically conceived as important mechanisms for legitimating the exercise of state power during democratic transitions, mass street protests can equally serve to legitimate authoritarian state capture (see Ketchley 2016). In the process, anti-democratic forces co-opt potential challengers, and undermine independent citizen organizing. In Egypt, this has seen the military-backed government extol and eulogize the large crowds on 30 June in an attempt to legitimize its seizure of power and thus rebuff

Western demands for the inclusion of the Muslim Brothers in the political process. At the same time, the military have failed to progress the democratic transition triggered by Mubarak's ousting in the heady days of 2011, while passing a draconian anti-protest law that criminalizes dissent. And as we will see in the next chapter, having invoked and defended the right to protest during Mursi's presidency, the post-coup government would quickly move to contain and demobilize any further opposition in the streets, launching an unprecedented wave of repression against the Muslim Brothers and their allies.

6

Anti-Coup Mobilization

Squares are the symbol of the revolution. But now if you go there on
a march, it's a suicide mission. They fill the square with informants who
report to security if more than ten people gather. So we have made squares
out of the side streets.

Anti-coup activist, 26 Feb. 2014

On 28 June 2013, members of the Muslim Brothers and supporters of
Egyptian president Muhammad Mursi occupied Midan Raba'a al-
Adawiyya, a public square in eastern Cairo, in anticipation of the
30 June protests calling for Mursi's resignation. The choice of Raba'a
was not coincidental. The Muslim Brothers have a long association,
dating back to the Sadat era (interview Ibrahim Munir 19 Jun. 2014),
with the Raba'a al-Adawiyya mosque, which gives its name to the Midan.
A week earlier, on 21 June, there had been a dress rehearsal for the
occupation: supporters of President Mursi held a large demonstration in
Raba'a anointed the "Friday of Rejecting Violence."[1] In the days and
weeks following Mursi's removal, pro-Mursi occupations were established in public squares in Alexandria, Asyut, Aswan, al-Bahr al-Ahmar,
Beni Suef, Daqahliyya, Giza, Minya, North Sinai, Sohag, and Qina.[2]

---

[1] The Muslim Brothers had previously staged other protests in Raba'a: on 4 and
6 June 2013, for instance, they held demonstrations in the Midan in solidarity with
Syrian opposition to the regime of Bashar al-Assad.
[2] Occupations were established in Midan al-Qa'id Ibrahim in Alexandria, Midan Omar
Makram in Asyut, Midan al-Shuhada' in Aswan, Midan al-Mudiriyya in Beni Suef, Midan
al-Nahda in Giza, Midan al-Dahar in Hurghada, outside the Olympic Stadium in
Mansoura, Midan al-Balas in Minya, Midan Masjid al-Nasr in North Sinai, Midan al-
Thaqafa in Sohag, and Midan al-Sa'a in Qina.

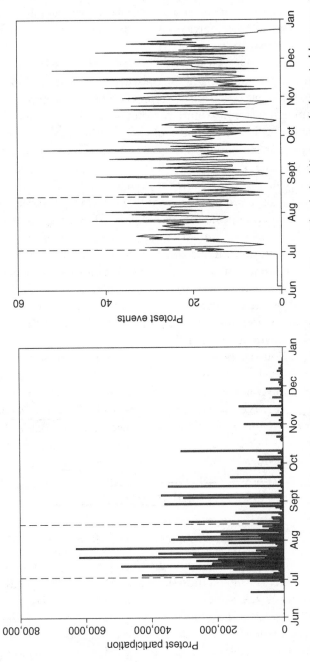

FIGURE 6.1 Anti-coup protest participation and frequency, Jun.–Dec. 2013. Notes: The dashed lines mark the period between the 3 July 2013 coup and the 14 August Raba'a massacre.

In governorates without an occupation, hastily assembled convoys of cars, buses, and coaches, from as far away as Gharbiyya, Monufia, Port Said, Suez, and Wadi al-Jadid, ferried several hundred protestors at a time to reinforce the Raba'a occupation.

Thus began a countrywide mobilization that has seen daily protests against the coup continue in the face of what Amnesty and Human Rights Watch (2014a) have described as "repression on a scale unprecedented in Egypt's modern history." Figure 6.1 shows the extent of anti-coup protests during the first six months of the mobilization. Two trends are discernible: protests became markedly smaller, but seemingly no less frequent over time. Repression peaked on 14 August 2013, when several anti-coup occupations, including the occupation at Raba'a al-Adawiyya, were violently dispersed by the new military-backed government: at least a thousand anti-coup protestors were killed (EIPR 2014; Human Rights Watch 2014b). The 14 August massacres would establish a precedent whereby soldiers and Interior Ministry-controlled security forces routinely used live ammunition, tear gas, and birdshot to disperse anti-coup protests. According to one widely cited estimate, in the year following the coup over three thousand anti-coup protestors were killed and nearly forty thousand regime opponents arrested by the military-backed government (WikiThawra 2014a; 2014b).

In the previous chapter, we saw how a reinvigorated elite saw fit to pursue street-level mobilization as a means of facilitating state capture. This chapter looks at the aftermath of this highly consequential episode, examining how protest took on new and emergent forms in a context of escalating repression. In doing so, it speaks to a large body of literature that attempts to discern the linkages between repression and mobilization. The empirical evidence offered in this final chapter points to the need to pay attention to the shifting modalities of protest, and not just protest size and frequency, when evaluating the effects of repression

REPRESSION-MOBILIZATION NEXUS

How can we explain the pattern of mobilization in Egypt since the coup? The effects of repression on protest – what the contentious politics literature refers to as the repression-mobilization nexus – are notoriously indeterminate (Davenport, Johnston, and Meuller 2004). Studies have found that repression leads to a decline in protest because of the additional 'costs' of repression (Olzak, Beasley, and Olivier 2003; Tilly 1978: 100). Alternatively, repression has been shown to generate an increased incidence of post-repression protest, known as "backlash" (Francisco 1995, 1996, 2004a, 2004b). Particularly violent repression can figure as a "transformative event" in the life story of a mobilization, leading to a higher incidence of backlash over time (Hess and Martin 2006; Martin 2007). Others have argued that there is non-monotonic relationship between repression and mobilization. Rasler's (1996) study found that mobilization resembles a U shape, in which repression has a short-term negative effect and a long-term positive effect on protest participation (see also Opp and Roehl 1990). Brockett (1995; 2005), meanwhile, has argued that the relationship between repression and protest participation takes on an inverted U shape: limited repression incentivizes protest, while higher levels encourage demobilization. As David Cunningham concludes, "the most notable finding has been the fact that seemingly all possible relationships have been supported by empirical work in this area" (2003: 47).

Faced with this indeterminacy, scholars have started to look beyond protest quantity as the dependent variable, instead asking a very different set of questions about the qualitative impact of repression on the dynamics of contentious politics (e.g., Alimi 2009; Bishara 2015; Boudreau 2009; Davenport and Eads 2001; Chang and Kim 2007; Chang 2008; 2015; Moss 2014; Titarenko et al. 2001). In taking a leaf out of the revisionist repression literature, this chapter considers how repression has influenced the timings, sites and modalities of anti-coup mobilization.[3] By shifting the focus of enquiry from the quantity of protest to its qualities, we can better understand how repression conditions the variability and viability of street politics. Such is the premise of this chapter.

In outline, we find that anti-coup protests "moved" in response to state violence during the first six months of the anti-coup mobilization. Following the clearing of the anti-coup occupations on 14 August, pro-testors relocated: from squares, outside government buildings and main arterial roads, to side streets and university campuses.[4] As repression

---

[3] The definition of "repression" requires some preliminary remarks. I adopt a fairly conventional measure of state-centric repression as including overt, coercive force (e.g., violence, killings, and arrests). There are other kinds of repression (e.g., sexual harassment, surveillance, repression by private individuals) that certainly apply in the Egyptian case, but which I do not properly consider for lack of data (see Earl 2011: 265–266).

[4] Here, I am expanding the repression-mobilization debate to address questions of concern to a literature on space and contentious politics (for a review, see Tilly 2000).

continued, the horizontal linkages between associational spaces and sites of protest became harder to sustain, contributing to the parochialization of contention. Coeval to this shift in the sites of contentious claim making was a corresponding change in the repertoire of contention. Protest became mobile, more ephemeral and less disruptive. Static occupations and demonstrations outside government buildings were superseded by *farāsha* (butterfly) sit-ins and human chains. Repression dictated the timings of protest, too. Anti-coup protestors became familiar with police shift patterns; they began mobilizing early in the morning and late at night, allowing them to mount longer actions in high-traffic areas unavailable to them during the daytime. This was not without consequence. Night time protests were safer, but less conspicuous; early morning protests increased visibility, but limited participation.

Taken together, the relationship between repression and anti-coup mobilization followed a process of "tactical interaction and innovation" (McAdam 1983; see also Johnston 2012). Absent a mechanical relationship between episodes of state violence and incidents of protest, anti-coup protestors and the military-backed government interacted through an iterative and dialogic process of move and countermove, which power disparities between challenger and regime prevented from achieving equilibrium.[5] In this, anti-coup protestors were able to sustain their high risk activism by mobilizing at the interstices of regime power – in mosques, side streets and universities – but the form and quality of their contention was impaired as a result. Protest became shorter, localized and more nimble; thus we might theorize, contention's ability to inspire and encourage was diminished as protest became less visible and "positive feedback" (Biggs 2003; 2005) was inhibited. Repression does not just raise the "costs" for individuals engaging in collective action, this argument suggests, but may also shape the locations and trajectories of "how," "where," and "when" contention can and cannot emerge and unfold in authoritarian contexts.

RETURNING TO THE STREETS

To explain the origins of the 2013 anti-coup mobilization, it is necessary to think back to the crucial decisions made by the Muslim Brothers

---

[5] This recalls Sidney Tarrow's (2011: 3) observation that "much of the history of movement-state interaction can be read as a duet of strategy and counterstrategy between movement activists and power holders."

following the 25th January Revolution that removed Husni Mubarak. As we saw in Chapter 4, with the departure of Mubarak, the Muslim Brothers demobilized, boycotting further protests calling for social justice and an end to military rule, equating the revolution's goals rather with constitutional reform and democratic authority achieved through the ballot box. That first protest cycle culminated in the "Friday of the Last Change" and the events of Muhammad Mahmoud Street in November 2011. On the streets, Egyptians were calling upon the Supreme Council of the Armed Forces (SCAF) to relinquish executive authority to a civilian-led, national salvation government. But the Brothers decided to sit out these and other contentious episodes, insisting that further protest would destabilize the country and that "elections are the solution."

The Muslim Brothers endorsed the SCAF's rule during the first year of the transitional period; their victories in parliamentary and presidential elections paved the way for the second protest cycle of the post-Mubarak era in which they found themselves the objects of protest. The Brothers' decision to mobilize dates back to violent clashes outside the Ittihadiyya presidential palace in early December 2013, when pro-Mursi supporters, led by Muslim Brothers, confronted a sit-in calling for his resignation organized by the National Salvation Front. Amid scenes of hand-to-hand fighting and accusations of both sides torturing detained protestors, eleven died, eight of them Muslim Brothers. "Following Ittihadiyya," one Muslim Brother recalls, "whenever there was an anti-Mursi protest, we aimed to hold a counter-demonstration. We decided that we had to show Egyptians, the army and the media, that there was support for Mursi in the streets" (interview Abdullah al-Haddad 20 Feb. 2014).

Meanwhile, the 30 June protests called for by the Tamarrod petition campaign were gathering momentum, encouraged by statements from the military calling on Mursi to make concessions. The Brothers, who had long threatened to mobilize their supporters if the movement's electoral authority was threatened, fell back on a repertoire pioneered during the 25th January Revolution, formulating plans to occupy public squares across the country and forming units of "ultras" to lead street protests should the military intervene.[6] As we saw in the previous chapter, on 30 June 2013 the twenty-fifth *milyūniyya* (million-person protest) in eight

---

[6] Launched in May 2013, pro-Mursi ultras mimic the hyper-masculine, high-octane performances of Egypt's football firms and are tasked with leading chants and motivating the crowd. The original ultras, the Ultras Nahdawi, have since spawned several regional

months saw mass protests outside the Presidential Palace and on the streets of downtown Cairo demanding early elections to end the presidency of Muhammad Mursi. The military, led by then Defense Minister (now president) Field Marshall Abdel Faibidttah al-Sisi, seized the protests as a pretext to launch a coup on 3 July.

Despite this setback, Muslim Brothers were initially optimistic that the coup could be reversed through protest. One informant recalls Brothers watching the documentary film *The Revolution Will not be Televised* (2002) in the days following the coup (interview Abdullah 5 10 Jun. 2014). The documentary, which recounts how a military coup against Venezuelan president Hugo Chavez was defeated by a combination of people power and a loyal presidential guard, was shared on the Brothers' closed social media pages, complete with Arabic subtitles. With Raba'a occupied, a document circulated among senior Brothers and pro-Mursi supporters outlining several possible scenarios (interview Mona 30 Apr. 2014). Included in the analysis were lessons to be drawn from previous coups, including case studies of coups in Chile, Spain, Turkey, and Venezuela. The Brothers' strategy of rolling protests was premised on a best case scenario in which Mursi could be returned to the presidential palace if elements within the military aligned with anti-coup protestors on the street. This scenario also anticipated pressure from the United States and the European Union on the military leadership to respect the democratic process. An alternative scenario envisaged Mursi being reinstated on an interim basis pending fresh presidential elections.[7] The most pessimistic scenario, and one that the Brothers increasingly prepared for, was of a violent crackdown comparable to that suffered in 1954 when Gamal Abdel Nasser suppressed the movement.

This early period was characterized by intense organization. That the anti-coup movement was able to sustain a daily protest presence is thanks in large part to a series of organizational innovations enacted by the Muslim Brothers and other members of the anti-coup movement (under the umbrella of the National Alliance to Support Legitimacy) at this stage

---

spinoffs, whose members wear specially printed T-shirts, play drums, and let off fireworks during protests.

[7] The interim reinstatement of Muhammad Mursi was the primary demand of the anti-coup movement in the period addressed by the present study. This was dropped in May 2014 when the National Alliance to Support Legitimacy endorsed the "Brussels declaration" – a ten-point political program seeking to build a broad front against the military-backed government (see *IkhwanWeb* 2014).

of the mobilization.[8] Historically a highly centralized, cadre-based social movement organization *par excellence* (Lia 1998; Wickham 2013), the Brothers' response to the arrest of large numbers of the movement's leadership immediately following the military's seizure of power was to adopt a greatly decentralized structure in which Brothers and non-Brothers organized alongside one another in anti-coup occupations, and later, in several "against the coup" movements (*ḥarakāt didd al-inqilāb*).[9] The formation of these movements – Youth Against the Coup, Students Against the Coup, Women Against the Coup, and others – in Raba'a in early July 2013 amounted to a kind of "strategic prepositioning" of what Dieter Rucht (2013) has classified as "action groups": small, informal movements that rely on face-to-face interaction and that are capable of organizing autonomously at the local level whilst simultaneously operating as components in a larger network.[10] By September, these "against the coup" movements had become semi-independent of the Muslim Brothers' organizational hierarchy, even if their core memberships were young Muslim Brothers and Muslim Sisters.[11] For example, in the first months

[8] The National Alliance to Support legitimacy was officially comprised of fifteen Islamist parties, including the Muslim Brothers' political wing, the FJP. However, informants insist that the Alliance existed in name only, issuing press releases and statements, but having little to no role in organizing protests (interview Belal 22 Jun. 2014).

[9] With Mursi detained, the new government set about rounding up the Muslim Brothers' leadership. By 5 August, 228 Muslim Brothers had been arrested, many of them senior and mid-ranking members. They included Saad al-Katatni, the chairman of FJP; the Deputy Supreme Guide, Khairat al-Shatir; and several members of the Guidance Bureau, the movement's executive decision-making body. On 20 August, General Guide Muhammad Badie was detained. Several of the prominent Brothers who remained at large took refuge in Midan Raba'a al-Adawiyya and Midan al-Nahda, while others fled the country for exile in London, Doha and Istanbul.

[10] The first "against the coup" movement was Youth Against the Coup. Formed on 5 July following an onstage conference at Raba'a, its organizational model called for flat networks of activists each working in one of three areas: media (to publicize the protests); political (to organize the protests); and social work (*al-Hurriyya wa al-'Adala* 22 Jul. 2013: 7). Social work was subsequently dropped to focus on protest activities. Addressing the crowd at Raba'a, Emad Shahin, a professor of political science at the American University in Cairo, outlined the rationale for these new protest movements: "The coup is still in a fluid state. It has not been consolidated. This conflict will be resolved on several fronts – the most important of which will be protest from the street. For this, we need to build new movements that can overcome the violence of the police and their thugs" (*al-Hurriyya wa al-'Adala* 21 Jul. 2013: 7).

[11] An online survey (n=287) conducted in April 2014 and posted in the closed Facebook groups and social media forums used by "against the coup" movements to coordinate protest strategy, found that over a third (37 percent) of survey participants who had taken part in an anti-coup protest self-identified as a Muslim Brother or Muslim Sister (see Ketchley and Biggs 2014). Respondents were also asked which party they supported in

of the mobilization local branches of Students Against the Coup were assigned a senior Muslim Brother supervisor (*mushrif*) to coordinate protest actions. This system of formal oversight was, however, almost immediately abandoned due to youth members rebelling against a controlling hand that they saw as out of touch with the realities on the ground (interview Belal 22 Jun. 2014).[12] Informants suggest that the Brothers' formal organizational role in the "against the coup" movements quickly became financial – putting up bail money for detained anti-coup protestors and providing financial support to the families of "martyred" protestors – though they also took charge of publicizing protests through the movement's various media platforms (Ibid.).[13]

ANTI-COUP REPERTOIRE OF CONTENTION

How the anti-coup movement mobilized has changed over time in response to repression. Figure 6.2 shows the frequency of marches (*masīrāt*), sit-ins (*waqafāt*), human chains (*salāsil bashariyya*), occupations (*i'tisāmāt*), and demonstrations (*muthāharāt*) as a proportion of anti-coup protest events between July and December 2013, with trend lines before and after the 14 August killings. Anti-coup demonstrations and marches were both kinetic and disruptive modes of contention and may appear indistinguishable but for their focus. Demonstrations made direct claims on regime power and either began or concluded outside of government buildings; marches, meanwhile, moved from point A to point B and aimed to mobilize anti-coup sentiment while contesting the government's control over the streets.[14] A sub-type of march not shown in Figure 6.2 is a *masīra hāshida* (gathering march). This was a protest that visited several mosques, "gathering" the faithful and passers-by, before moving on to a pre-agreed destination. Sit-ins, human chains, and occupations were all static forms of protest that varied in terms of timing and

---

the 2011–2012 parliamentary elections. 94 percent of respondents indicated support for an Islamist party.

[12] This system also extended to coordinating protests with Muslim Sisters. If Muslim Brother members of Students Against the Coup wanted to coordinate university campus protests with Muslim Sisters, they had to do so via their respective supervisors. This system proved so unwieldy that it was quickly replaced by male and female members organizing together (interview Sarah 21 Feb. 2014; interview Belal 22 Jun. 2014).

[13] The Brothers' local branches (*maktab idārat al-shu'ab*) continued to play a key role in organizing non-"against the coup" movement protests, especially the larger Friday protests and protests held on nationally-coordinated days of dissent.

[14] In rural areas, marches frequently involve participants riding motorcycles or tuk-tuks.

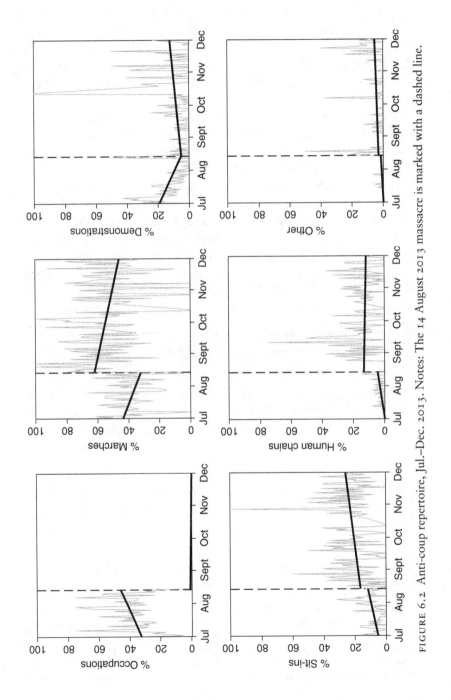

FIGURE 6.2. Anti-coup repertoire, Jul.–Dec. 2013. Notes: The 14 August 2013 massacre is marked with a dashed line.

size. Sit-ins were temporary, lasting at most a few hours. Occupations were more permanent and required an infrastructure to support them. Human chains were the smallest and least disruptive mode of protest, typically involving around ten protestors who stood by the side of a high traffic road or major building, chanting anti-coup slogans and holding posters and banners.[15]

What is immediately striking about the anti-coup mobilization is how recursive the repertoire is; providing empirical confirmation for Charles Tilly's (1978, 1995, 2008) insight that when people protest, they do so in only a limited number of ways. We only find some small deviation away from these five tactics period after the 14 August massacres, when protestors began to experiment with a limited range of new tactics.[16] There is also little evidence to support a mechanical relationship between repression and "radicalization." Beginning with Lichbach's (1987) essay on the subject, several scholars have argued that the violent repression of nonviolent protest will cause a movement to adopt more violent tactics. This thesis has been applied to the study of Islamist mobilization in Mohammed Hafez's *Why Muslims Rebel* (2003). Hafez theorizes that 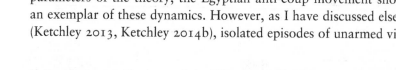Islamist movements pursue violence when they are subject to reactive, indiscriminate repression, while simultaneously being excluded from the political process. A corollary claim is that under these conditions we should expect to see the adoption of highly centralized, exclusivist organizational structures (see also della Porta 1995). Given the scope parameters of the theory, the Egyptian anti-coup movement should be an exemplar of these dynamics. However, as I have discussed elsewhere (Ketchley 2013, Ketchley 2014b), isolated episodes of unarmed violence

---

[15] Outside of major cities, human chains differ considerably. Planned at a village-level, often a week in advance (interview Youssef 2 20 Apr. 2014), they tend to be much larger, attracting participants from several villages who line the sides of one of the major highways connecting Cairo with Alexandria, Upper Egypt, and the Nile Delta cities. Because the state's coercive apparatus is concentrated in urban areas, participants face little threat of punitive action.

[16] In August there was also a call to boycott household products produced in military-owned factories in addition to brands, companies, and media outlets operated by pro-coup figures. The boycott never gained traction and was quietly dropped. Another failed innovation was a "petrol protest" which called on drivers to fill up their tanks at government-owned petrol stations, before turning off their engines and abandoning their vehicles, effectively blockading the forecourt. More successful, albeit little-used, innovations included a petition campaign, blockading roads, "protest marathons" in which young men run through major thoroughfares, theatrical retellings of the coup and its aftermath, and "data shows" – projecting images or video footage of regime violence on the sides of public buildings.

attributed to pro-Mursi supporters notwithstanding – including attacks on police stations, government buildings and churches in the immediate aftermath of the 14 August massacres, as well as the use of Molotov cocktails and improvised weapons on protests[17] – the anti-coup movement did not transform into an armed Islamist insurgency.

Instead, repression came to reconfigure a repertoire of non-violent contention. The 14 August massacres therefore represent a clear discontinuity, both in terms of the unprecedented scale of the killing, and also in their bringing to a close a phase of the mobilization in which large occupations featured prominently. By occupying squares in thirteen governorates, the anti-coup movement drew on a modality of protest pioneered during the 25th January Revolution. The occupation of Midan al-Tahrir, David Patel (2014) has argued, solved a fundamental problem of mass mobilization by communicating to would-be protestors how, where and when people were protesting. This model, Patel suggests, is especially effective in making public and conspicuous the scale of contention in authoritarian contexts where information is otherwise tightly controlled and disinformation rife.[18]

As in the 25th January occupations, anti-coup protestors, often accompanied by their families, continuously occupied squares, with other protestors reinforcing the occupations on coordinated days of protest and the largest protests held after Friday prayers or during specially-called *milyūniyya* (million-person) protests.[19] These occupations also provided important logistical functions in towns and neighborhoods where the Muslim Brothers' network of offices and headquarters had been attacked. In this sense, an anti-coup occupation operated in the tradition of a long history of protest camps, keeping protestors fed and cared for by a well-staffed infrastructure of workshops, kitchens, pharmacies, and field hospitals (see Feigenbaum, Frenzel, and McCurdy 2013). Occupations were also spaces in which previously unconnected people could come together and plan ways to challenge the coup, for instance with the

---

[17] In December anti-coup protestors began to bring fireworks, powerful gas-powered potato guns, and Molotov cocktails on marches, either to confront the police (firebombing empty police cars was a popular tactic), or to form a rearguard should the protest be attacked.

[18] This argument draws on preference falsification models in which would-be protestors calculate the risk of protesting as a function of the size of the crowd (Kuran 1991; Lohmann 1994).

[19] And like the largest protests of the 25th January Revolution, these were given names: the 5 July "Friday of Yes to Legitimacy, No to the Military Coup"; the 12 July "Friday of Marching"; the 19 July "Friday of the People will Break the Coup"; the 2 August "Friday of Egypt Against the Coup"; and so on.

formation of the "against the coup" movements. The Raba'a occupation even had its own FM radio station, followed on 15 July by a television station, 25 Ahrar, broadcasting from the Midan. Despite the arrest of the Brothers' leadership and several attacks on anti-coup protests, the anti-coup movement began life as a well-resourced and sophisticated mobilization, capable of sending several hundreds of thousands of protestors onto the streets during the largest Friday protests in the weeks following the 3 July coup.

The first instance of regime forces using live ammunition against anti-coup protestors came on 8 July when Republican Guard units attacked a pro-Mursi sit-in outside the Republican Guard Officers' Club where it was believed Mursi was being held: sixty-seven anti-coup protestors were killed. Several anti-coup protestors were also killed on 19 July when police opened fire on an anti-coup occupation in Mansoura and on 27 July police and soldiers attacked a march that had departed from the Raba'a al-Adawiyya occupation as it was passing the Tomb of the Unknown Soldier (known locally as al-Manassa) on its way towards downtown Cairo, killing over a hundred protestors. Though serious and tragic, these episodes look to have had little effect on the mobilization as a whole. Protestors continued to mobilize outside the Republican Guard building, the anti-coup occupation in Mansoura still attracted tens of thousands of participants during Friday protests, and marches left Raba'a al-Adawiyya for downtown Cairo with the same frequency. In informant testimony, these early instances of regime violence are highlighted as formative episodes in the forging of an activist mentality, with greater consideration given to the provision of first aid and to new techniques to deal with tear gas and shotgun pellets (interview Belal 22 Jun. 2014).

When it was attacked on the morning of 14 August, the Raba'a occupation had lasted forty-seven days, longer than any previous occupation of Midan al-Tahrir.[20] Occupations in Alexandria, Giza, Beni Suef, Qina, Aswan, and Assiut were also cleared. The immediate effect of the crackdown was to further decentralize the mobilization. This saw local branches of "against the coup" movements take on an increasingly important role in organizing protests as coordination moved online and into offline associational spaces such as university dorms, mosques, and private households.[21]

---

[20] For an analysis of the social backgrounds of those killed during the Raba'a massacre, see Ketchley and Biggs (2015).

[21] In early August, around 10 percent of all anti-coup protests were organized under the banner of an "against the coup" movement. By mid-September, these groups were

Following 14 August, anti-coup protestors adopted a four-fingered salute on a yellow background – a gesture deriving from Rabiʿa (fourth), the first name of the female Sufi saint who is the Midan's namesake. It quickly became synonymous with opposition to the military-backed government.

Static occupations fell out of the repertoire entirely when security forces began routinely using live ammunition against large crowds.[22] Demonstrations outside of heavily defended government buildings, which had become increasingly dangerous over July, also declined. Demonstrations began to be held with greater frequency in after October with the start of the new academic year. However, as discussed below, these were primarily held outside administrative and security offices on public university campuses. Almost immediately, then, the effects of repression following the 14 August killings can be seen to have made contention less disruptive. The frequency of marches, protestors' favored tactic for their maneuverability and impact, increased after the killings, but their form was altered in response to the threat of regime attack. Gathering marches became impossible as large numbers of protestors drew the attention of security forces. Marches also sped up. Informants recall that anti-coup marches prior to the 14 August typically lasted for several hours, traveling long distances to reach a pre-agreed terminus. By November, marches in most Cairo neighborhoods frequently dispersed after twenty minutes in anticipation of regime violence (interview Sarah and Hoda 26 Feb. 2014).

The proportion of sit-ins and human chains also increased after the clearing of the anti-coup occupations. Human chains became the default tactic on weekdays when there was a low turnout. The high frequency of human chains after September thus reflected and reproduced declining protest numbers, as local iterations of the anti-coup movement struggled

---

responsible for over half of all anti-coup protests. Anti-coup activists relied heavily on closed social media groups, some of which, informants suggest, had several thousand members, to share tactics and coordinate national days of protest. To avoid detection (when anti-coup protestors are arrested police often search their mobile phone or laptop for evidence of protest activity on social media leading many anti-coup activists to leave their smart phones at home and carry older models instead [interview Sara 15 Mar. 2014; interview Hend 17 Dec. 2014]) these groups were given innocuous names. Two examples of now defunct groups used to plan marches in Cairo were, "I love Cristiano Ronaldo" and "Buy second-hand cars" (interview with Muslim Brother 20 Mar. 2014; interview Hend 17 Dec. 2014).

[22] There were several attempts to re establish an occupation, beginning on 16 August in Midan Ramses in downtown Cairo. All were thwarted by security forces using live ammunition and birdshot.

to sustain a daily protest presence in the face of a wave of targeted arrests. Sit-ins were held primarily in university faculty buildings and on the roads in front of mosques. A more risky form of sit-in, pioneered in Assiut governorate in September and quickly adopted elsewhere, was the *waqfat al-farāsha* (butterfly sit-in). Combining a sit-in with a flash mob, butterfly sit-ins allowed protestors to temporarily take over highly symbolic spaces, such as main roads or public squares, assemble long enough to record the protestors chanting against the military and the Interior Ministry, and then move on (see *al-Jazeera* 10 Sept. 2013). One anti-coup protestor explained the butterfly sit-in's popularity: "The *farāsha* pisses off the police. You go to a place and stay there for ten minutes or just long enough that the security forces are alerted, and then you leave for another location" (interview Muhammad 26 Feb. 2014). But these insurgent tactics had an impact on the efficacy of anti-coup protest. Given their speed, necessary to outmaneuver the authorities, protestors were only visible momentarily and were afforded few opportunities to interact with people on the street. As one organizer later reflected, butterfly sit-ins allowed protestors to regain a sense of agency and momentum, but as tools for challenging the coup, they soon proved to be a "tactical dead end" (interview Belal 22 Jun. 2014).

As the anti-coup repertoire became more nimble in response to regime violence, protests themselves became the preserve of young men and women. Qualities that mattered less in sustaining occupations, i.e., being able to run fast, became essential attributes. In turn, the opportunities for many Muslim Brothers and pro-Mursi supporters to participate in demonstrations, marches, and sit-ins narrowed considerably. While the military-backed government could not stop anti-coup protestors from protesting entirely, it could strongly influence where those protests unfolded.

SPACES OF CONTENTION

Anti-coup event data allows us to present a stylized illustration of the ways in which sites of contention shifted as a consequence of repression over the first six months of the mobilization. Figure 6.3 maps recurring protest start locations (shown as weighted white nodes) and protest end locations (weighted grey nodes). Connections between nodes (shown as directed edges) show the tendency for protest to move from one space to the other. To give an example, between 28 June and 14 August over three hundred anti-coup protests began in a mosque, of which over a third

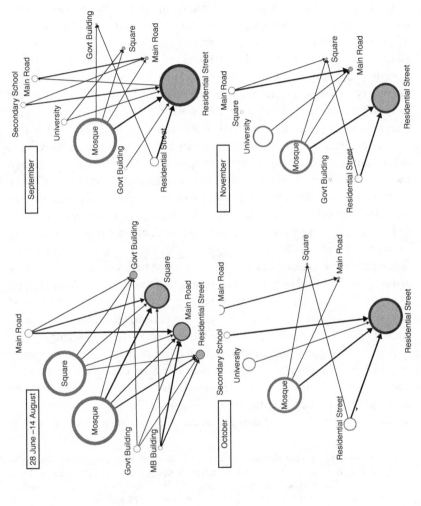

FIGURE 6.3 Anti-coup protest start and end locations, Jun.-Nov. 2013. Notes: Directed edges show horizontal linkages between start (white nodes) and end locations (gray nodes).

145

ended in a public square. The thickness of the edge connecting the "Mosque" and "Square" nodes is weighted to reflect this proportion. By contrast, in the month after the crackdown began, less than one per cent of all mosque-originating protests departed for a square. Instead, the overwhelming majority of marches moved through residential side streets. By November, this had developed into a clearly discernible trend: anti-coup marches were avoiding main roads, squares and government buildings where security forces were most heavily concentrated and where the possibility of repression was highest.

In Figure 6.3, isolated nodes or nodes with few or light edges, reflect a high proportion of static protests. Consider here the frequency of university protests. Beginning with the start of the new academic year in September, these protests escalated in early October in response to the heavy-handed policing of an anti-coup sit-in at al-Azhar University. Solidarity demonstrations, sit-ins, and strikes soon spread to al-Azhar's other campuses and tertiary institutes, as well as at the universities of Cairo, Ain Shams, Assiut, Zagazig, Mansoura, and several others. These protests bucked the general trend, growing in frequency and size as students began coordinating their actions across several faculties. In November, there were over a hundred protests on Egyptian university campuses. Crucially, however, these protests rarely left university gates. When protests increased in October, the regime had responded by posting armed police and soldiers at campus entrances with orders to open fire on any march or demonstration attempting to leave.[23] The effect of repression was to confine and isolate student contention, ensuring that protests could neither scale up nor make common cause with other sectors.[24]

Another way to visualize how repression can shape the sites of protest is to spotlight one neighborhood and consider how the routes of marches and demonstrations changed over time. Figure 6.4 shows the path taken by a "gathering march" that set off following the Friday Sermon from Muhandiseen in Giza to Midan al-Nahda, a public square located next to

[23] This represented the evolution of a tactic honed under the Mubarak regime. Writing in 2003, Asef Bayat (2010: 212) noted: "Students at Cairo University, for example, often stage protest marches inside the campus. However, the moment they decided to come out into the street, riot police are immediately and massively deployed to encircle the demonstrators, push them into a corner away from public view and keep the protest a local event."

[24] In March 2014, this saw al-Azhar students use sledgehammers and crowbars to fashion temporary exits in the campus perimeter walls, from which they surged out onto Mustafa Nahas Street. See footage: YouTube video (28 Mar 2014) "*Hasri hadm sūr jāmiʿat al-Azhar*" http://youtu.be/uwZWVXKCPOM.

Cairo University, for the 9 August protest anointed the "Friday of the Eid of Victory." Elsewhere in Giza, marches were also heading off to Midan al-Nahda from the neighborhoods of Umraniyya and al-Haram.[25] The Muhandiseen march begins outside of the Khalid Ibn al-Walid mosque, before moving on to the al-Maghfira mosque and then the Mustafa Mahmud mosque. The protestors' ranks had swelled to several thousand before the march turned down al-Batal Ahmad 'Abd al-'Aziz Street to arrive at Midan al-Nahda. The march lasted for several hours and concluded with speeches delivered from the stage erected in the Midan. This use of space perfectly mirrors the repertoire of the 25th January Revolution, with Midan al-Tahrir replaced by Midan al-Nahda.[26] Indeed, these were often the same mosques from which marches were launched on the pivotal "Friday of Anger" of 28 January 2011. Near identical anti-coup protests – with marches leaving mosques after Friday prayers for squares and main roads – were held that day in towns and cities in Alexandria, Assiut, al-Bahr al-Ahmar, Beni Suef, Cairo, Damietta, Luxor, Sharqiyya, and Ismailia.

After the 14 August massacres, anti-coup protestors continued to use mosques as staging points, but the destinations of their marches had changed. Figure 6.5 traces the route of a march departing from al-Mahrusa mosque in Muhandiseen. The date is 13 September. At this point, nearly a month has passed since the occupation of Midan al-Nahda was violently dispersed. As on every Friday since 14 August, the square was sealed off by army APCs and plainclothes police fanned out into the side streets alert to any approaching marches. Knowing this, protestors set off instead for Gami'at al-Duwal al-'Arabiyya Street, the busiest street in Giza. The march made it halfway down Gami'at al-Duwal before the protestors found their path blocked by black-uniformed Central Security Forces, who fired tear gas into the crowd. The march quickly dispersed. Prior to the 14 August, nearly a quarter of all protests leaving mosques arrived at a main arterial road. These protests were public and disruptive, with participants holding aloft posters of the deposed president Muhammad Mursi, chanting: "we are the people and these are our words: when Mursi comes back, we'll go home" (*ihna al-sha'b, wa- di kilmitna:*

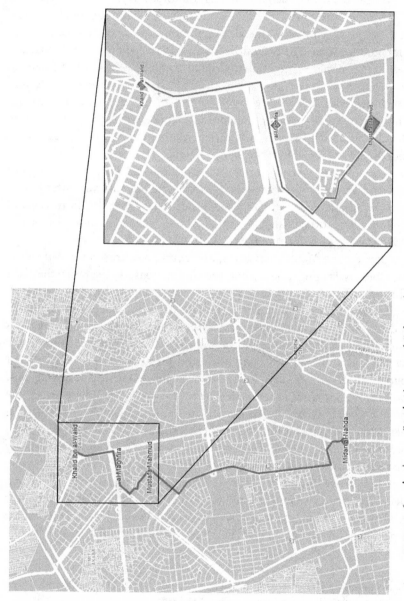

FIGURE 6.4 Anti-coup "gathering march" from three mosques to Midan al-Nahda, 9 Aug. 2013.

FIGURE 6.5 Anti-coup march from al-Mahrusa mosque to Gamiʿat al-Duwal al-Arabiyya Street, 13 Sept. 2013.

Mursi yirgaʿ nirgaʿ baytna).[27] By contrast, in September, only six marches (less than 1 percent) departing from a mosque arrived at a main road.

The use of mosques as associational spaces for organizing and launching anti-coup protests was a constant of this phase of the mobilization. As well as providing a natural constituency for the Islamist-dominated movement, mosques offered an additional advantage in the urban ecology of contention: in many Egyptian neighborhoods particular mosques have a reputation for playing host to protests following the conclusion of prayer. This meant that would-be protestors did not need access to formal

---

[27] Following 14 August, this chant changed to, "we are the people and these are our words: military rule over our dead bodies" (*ihna al-shaʿb wa-di kilmitna, ʿaskar yahkum ʿala guthitna*).

protest networks to participate; they simply needed to turn up (see here also Butt 2016). As one informant, Youssef, relates,

For Friday protests, I don't check online. All week social media is telling us what to do. But for Fridays I don't need to think about it. It's a part of your life. If you want to protest after prayer you know which mosque to go to. So you go and protest and then hang out with your friends. I don't like to say this, but protest has even become a part of the prayer itself. People start chanting in the mosque the second the prayer has finished. It's always the same chant first: "*hasbuna allah wa ni'ma al-wakil*" [literally, God is our sole and best representative, akin to: God will punish those responsible]. Then we chant "*yasqut, yasqut hukm al-'askar!*" [down with military rule!] and go out into the streets. *(interview 20 Apr. 2014)*

These low coordination costs ensured that marches departing from mosques on Friday afternoons consistently drew the largest crowds, despite the regime's attempts to deny the anti-coup movement this space.[28]

Figure 6.6 also concerns al-Mahrusa mosque. By early November the security presence in Muhandiseen had increased considerably. Following the conclusion of the Friday sermon, protestors assembled outside the nearby al-Radwan mosque and marched through residential side streets before arriving at al-Mahrusa mosque, where one would imagine the protestors offered prayers before heading home. The march would have been over within minutes and otherwise avoided detection. By December, the number of anti-coup marches in Muhandiseen setting off following Friday prayer dropped almost to zero. Muhandiseen had become what anti-coup protestors called a "closed area" (interview Sara 15 Mar. 2014) due to the high probability that a protest would be attacked. Driving this development was a new regime tactic which involved stationing CSF units every five hundred meters or so along major roads. Armed with shotguns and tear gas grenades, they stood guard beside their "boxes" alert to the

---

[28] Following the 14 August crackdown, police raided hundreds of mosques associated with the Muslim Brothers and their affiliates. Another regime tactic was to station security detachments at mosque entrances on Friday mornings, or else prohibit imams from giving the Friday sermon. In September 2013, the Ministry of Religious Endowments announced that only graduates of the state-run al-Azhar University would be allowed to deliver sermons, while optimistically pledging to close the tens of thousands of unlicensed mosques that have proliferated in recent decades (see Gaffney 1991). According to the government's own statistics, there were over ninety-five thousand mosques in Egypt at the last count in 2008 (Arab Republic of Egypt – Central Agency for Public Mobilization and Statistics 2009). Twenty thousand were unlicensed *zāwiya* (corner) mosques. Anecdotal evidence suggests that this number increased significantly in the subsequent period.

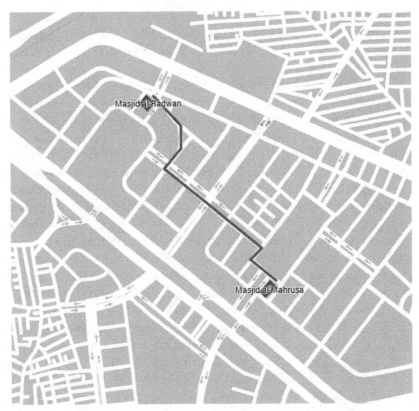

FIGURE 6.6 Anti-coup march from al-Radwan mosque via residential streets to al-Mahrusa mosque, 8 Nov. 2013.

approach of any protest. Paid *baltagiyya* and police informants reported back if they detected protestors passing through the side streets. It was still possible to protest in these areas, but only at night and always outside of the Friday afternoon slot when the security presence was especially heavy. The result was that would-be anti-coup protestors living in the area either traveled to another neighborhood where there were less police, or they stayed at home (Ibid.).[29] This tactic of striating public space with armed

[29] Another frequently reported connection between repression, participation and protest location was the reputation of the local police station. In certain neighborhoods, police acquired a reputation for sexually harassing and sometimes raping, female anti-coup protestors. The police station in Nasr City in northeast Cairo was particularly infamous for using sexual violence against detained protestors. As a result, female anti-coup protestors in Nasr City traveled to al-Matariyya, a nearby suburb, where the police

police was rolled out across Egypt's major cities. Four months after the dispersal of the Raba'a and al-Nahda occupations, anti-coup protestors celebrated any protest held in the "closed" neighborhoods of Giza, Cairo, and Alexandria.

But just as the Egyptian state struggled to regulate places of worship (churches being a notable exception), it had only a shaky grip over large tranches of urban space outside of central metropolitan areas. As Salwa Ismail (2006) has documented, since the 1980s neo-liberal economic reforms have precipitated the retreat of a distributive state and the reen-gagement of a security state whose primary purpose is regime survival.[30] As a result, Egypt's popular quarters, home to millions of Egyptians, have become increasingly autonomous and characterized by their informality, with the state's will enforced by hired thugs. As I documented in Chapter 2, during the early phase of the 25th January Revolution, many of the police stations in these districts were attacked by local residents and burnt to the ground (see also Ismail 2012, 2013). Security has never fully returned. Because of the unevenness of the regime's presence in these areas, the anti-coup movement enjoyed far more room to maneuver.

Of course, where a protest occurs matters a great deal, both in symbolic terms and in terms of the material structures that shape the protest environment. In interviews, anti-coup protestors often put a gloss on this dynamic: one anti-coup activist in Alexandria insisted, "Squares are the symbol of the revolution. But now if you go there on a march, it's a suicide mission. They fill the square with informants who report to security if more than ten people gather. So we have made squares out of the side streets" (interview Muhammad 26 Feb. 2014). But side streets are not squares.[31] As Navid Hassanpour (2014) has argued, the narrow vistas common to Egypt's popular quarters and suburbs – the result of an

were known not to arrest women (interview Sarah 20 Feb. 2014; Sarah and Hoda 26 Feb. 2014; Sara 15 Mar. 2014). This was not out of charity or misplaced benevolence: informants report that in al-Matariyya, as in Helwan and Shubra, local residents had surrounded and threatened to burn down police stations on previous occasions when female protestors had been detained, prompting their release (interview Youssef 2 6 Feb. 2014).

[30] Beginning with Janet Abu-Lughod's (1971) account of the "City Victorious," there have been several excellent histories and social anthropologies of the development of urban space in Egypt. See variously, Singerman (1995), Rodenbeck (1999), and Abaza (2001).

[31] This is a point tacitly acknowledged by other anti-coup protestors who rue the missed opportunities that such spaces afforded. "We didn't know how lucky we were having a square," says one, "we took it for granted. We always thought that we would be able to go back" (interview Youssef 2 6 Feb. 2014).

architectural style that promotes high density living – impede the flow of information and encourage network disruption. It was for this reason, he suggests, that Mubarak's decision to cut mobile phone and internet access on 27 January 2011 so spectacularly backfired. In the absence of information from other sources, residents had to leave their neighborhoods to find out what was going on – a process that saw many chance upon marches en route to Midan al-Tahrir. However, the nature of this urban space has similarly contributed to a parochialization of anti-coup protests and therefore diminished the impact of the hundreds of marches that were launched following the 14 August massacres. With squares and main roads mostly out of reach, the potential audience for these anti-coup actions was limited to shopkeepers, *bawwābīn* (doormen) and the relatively low density foot and vehicle traffic that moves through these areas.[32] As the Egyptian media scholar Muhammad ElMasry (2014b) has observed, by pushing contention into the side streets, anti-coup protests were rendered "invisible," to the vast majority of Egyptians.

TIMING OF CONTENTION

Conscious of this dynamic, and in a bid to circumvent security forces and reach a wider audience, anti-coup protestors experimented with the timings of their protests. The "7 al-Subh" (7 in the morning) movement, in particular, is accredited with pioneering the tactic of protesting in the early morning. Founded in Alexandria in September 2013, and with branches in Cairo and the Nile Delta governorates of Beheira, Sharqiyya, Kafr el-Sheikh, and Menoufiya, 7 al-Subh are known for holding sit-ins outside schools and forming human chains beside main roads during the rush hour.[33] According to Muhammad,

---

[32] Conversely, Cairo's narrow residential side streets are frequently invoked as contributing to the success of the first days of protest in the 25th January Revolution. As marches moved through side streets in a bid to avoid the police, it is argued, crowd sizes were amplified, appearing larger and more impressive than perhaps they actually were, and thus encouraging bandwagon effects as would-be protestors saw security in numbers (Gunning and Baron 2013: 156). But given the high frequency of anti-coup protests in precisely these spaces and the overall decline in protest numbers, one might conclude that this urban context actually contributed little to an outgrowth in protest participation in early 2011. Instead, it was more likely the destination and the novelty of these protests that lent a great deal more to their success.

[33] In October 2013, the arrest of twenty-one female members of 7 al-Subh members gained international media attention after they were given lengthy prison sentences (later suspended) for participating in an anti-coup protest in Alexandria.

one of 7 al-Subh's founders, the movement emerged out of a realization that regime attacks on anti-coup protests intensified in the late afternoon, especially around 5 p.m. when security forces were most active: "Protests lasted for ten minutes before the police came," he recounts, "so we started going out in the mornings. Suddenly we found that we could protest for over an hour because the police were only just coming on duty and the *baltagiyya* were still sleeping off that night's tramadol [a prescription pain killer] and hashish" (interview Muhammad 26 Feb. 2014). The number of early morning protests grew steadily, taking off in late December after the Muslim Brothers were designated a terrorist movement. In the second week of January alone, forty-six anti-coup protests – over half of all protests mounted that week – were held before 8 a.m. with protestors lining the sides of major roads chanting to passing commuters, "*Dihku 'alayku wa qālu irhāb, wa ihna girān al-bāb fi al-bāb*" (they fooled you and called us terrorists, but we are your next-door neighbors).

The decision to protest at 7 a.m underlines how repression both confined and constrained the possibilities for contentious politics. Morning protests in high traffic areas still carried risks and thus required planning via a closed network. Usually protests were planned in advance with a message sent out the night before via peer-to-peer smartphone apps, usually Viber or WhatsApp, to a trusted list of anti-coup protestors (interview Sara 15 Mar. 2014). With the protestors assembled, there were few opportunities for sympathetic onlookers to participate, save for beeping a car horn in support, as most were on their way to work or taking children to school. In this sense, 7 a.m human chains and sit-ins were the antithesis of post-Friday sermon "gathering marches." Whereas gathering marches in the first months of the mobilization aimed to build a critical mass of anti-coup sentiment in the streets, 7 a.m protests could only hope to communicate a message of ongoing struggle.

Night time protests are another example in which the regime's capacity to control urban space changed depending on the time of day. Protests beginning after 9 p.m began in mid-July during Ramadan, a period that coincided with a steep decline in crowd sizes. With most anti-coup protestors fasting, actions were moved to after the *Tarāwīh* prayer, a time when large numbers of Egyptians visit friends and relatives, or stay at home to watch specially produced television soaps (*musalsalāt*). Following the clearing of the anti-coup occupations in August, weekday marches again switched timings, with many beginning after the *'Isha* prayer, when the majority of police come off their shift. These "night marches" (*masīrāt layliyya*) and night sit-ins (*waqafāt layliyya*), measured by the frequency of attacks over time, were proportionally the safest protests and thus consistently attracted large numbers of women, middle-aged men, and children. However, this did not mean that night time protests were completely out of reach of the regime. Police stations, if they heard reports of a night protest, would instruct the state electricity company to shut off the grid to that particular neighborhood, leaving the protestors to march in the dark (interview Youssef 2 6 Feb. 2014).

CONCLUSIONS

In this chapter, we have seen how the repression-mobilization nexus can be illuminated by studying shifts along the different axes – modalities, sites and timings – of contention in response to regime violence. Here, neither repression nor mobilization appears as a unitary phenomenon. Rather, a dialogical cycle of tactical innovation, regime countermeasure, and further innovation saw a diminution in the variability and viability of anti-coup contention over time, as anti-coup protestors struggled to negate the regime's monopoly over the apparatus of coercion. This dynamic saw protest becoming increasingly mobile, but also less visible, as the sites and times available for protest became circumscribed, boxing the mobilization into increasingly smaller social spaces. Protestors could hold butterfly sit-ins in strategically sensitive areas or hold a human chain by a high traffic road in the morning – but they couldn't occupy a public square or blockade the entrance to a government building without risking heavy casualties.

Consequently, anti-coup protest rapidly became concentrated in those spaces where the regime enjoyed less influence, with contention becoming less spectacular and less disruptive as a result. In this, the unevenness of the regime's presence in wider Egyptian society and the anti-coup movement's ability to evade and outmaneuver the security forces speak to the organic relationship between power and contention; in turn, evoking political geographies of protest, repression, and space found elsewhere in the region (Schwedler 2012; 2013; Tripp 2013). Driving this process was the effect of repression on the horizontal linkages between associational spaces and sites of protest. Prior to the 14 August crackdown, anti-coup marches left mosques and squares, and traveled long distances to arrive at their pre-agreed destination, often a public space that resonated with the mobilization's demands. The scale and ferocity of regime repression after the 14 August ensured that protestors moved to mosques in outlying neighborhoods and popular quarters and stayed there, marching through residential side streets before dispersing. University campus protests were similarly contained.

Far from being outright defeated, opposition to the 3 July coup and the new military-backed government was instead delimited in ways that recall Asef Bayat's (2010: 212) observation that, "The metaphorical [Arab] street is not deserted, so much as it is controlled." Having stimulated the 30 June protests that legitimized the military takeover, repression has, in effect, created the veneer of consent. Here, as the Egyptian case vividly illustrates, the "where" of protest appears especially critical, as daily protests in backstreets and comparable spaces, staged with the intention of sidestepping regime violence, failed to build and sustain a level of mobilization necessary to topple an entrenched adversary. As such, repression should be understood not only in terms of its effects on individuals and on the extent of collective action, but also in terms of claims and effects on social space, in ways reminiscent of the "Haussmannization" of the mid-nineteenth century European city and its impact on the possibilities for popular mobilization (see variously Gould 1995; Harvey 2006; Traugott 2010).

In the process, the Muslim Brothers have been transformed into a street protest movement. This has interesting, and as yet not fully revealed, implications for the movement's future. With the Brothers' senior leadership languishing in jail or abroad and many of its middle-ranking members in hiding, the movement is increasingly being represented by its female and youth members mobilizing in some of the poorest and most deprived areas of Egypt. They are the generation of the 25th January Revolution. In their early twenties, many study elite subjects at university (Ketchley and Biggs 2017) and came of age in the initial occupation of Midan al-Tahrir. They have, though, failed to build a mass movement along the lines that emerged in early 2011. This is partly due to the anti-coup movement's inability to transcend institutional and social differences; a legacy of Mursi's disastrous presidency and the Muslim Brothers' culpability in siding with the military during many of the early exchanges of the democratic transition. But more fundamentally, authoritarian regime learning has ensured that the 25th January Revolution repertoire of occupying squares and disrupting urban space is, in the short-to-medium term at least, no longer viable.

7

Conclusion

How can we explain the 25th January Revolution, its trajectories and legacies? From a series of vantage points, this book has pursued an analytical and empirically grounded account of the particular ways in which Egyptians have mobilized (or demobilized) in the three years that followed Mubarak's ousting in 2011. Writing against top-down, structuralist, and culturally essentialist explanations, my approach has shown how the patterns of political change in Egypt, and the long-term prospects for the Arab Spring more broadly, can be powerfully illuminated by an interactive political sociology of the new modes and dynamics of contentious politics arising from the events of early 2011.

With a view to explaining how anti-regime protestors were able to best Mubarak's formidable national security state during the critical opening exchanges of the 25th January Revolution, the book began by developing a focused account of anti-police violence, which started in the Suez and then proliferated nationwide during the afternoon of the Friday of Anger. These episodes of collective violence, which were primarily a response by residents to the killing of local protestors, served the function of facilitating nonviolent protest in Egypt's main roads and squares, protecting protestors from repression and fatally undermining the coercive reach of Mubarak's vaunted Interior Ministry. With police forces in disarray in several key governorates, protestors in Midan al-Tahrir and elsewhere then sought to contain and neutralize the threat posed by the military, making immediate, emotional claims on the loyalty of newly deployed armoured units. But fraternization, as John Chalcraft (2016: 515) notes, while tactically clever, "was strategically problematic, as it helped to propel an army to power that had no answer to the protestors' problems."

After Mubarak resigned on 11 February 2011, the initial revolutionary situation quickly subsided into a conventional democratic transition, with key members of the 25th January revolutionary coalition retreating from mass mobilization and putting their faith in a transition administered by the SCAF, electoral mechanisms and the authority of a new parliament and president. This was to have particular significance for the Muslim Brothers, whose fading out of street protests left the movement with a problematic status in Midan al-Tahrir and with those activists agitating for a truly revolutionary outcome. Despite performing well – perhaps too well – on election day, the Brothers' uncoordinated demobilization meant that the movement had few allies willing to defend Egypt's newly elected democratic institutions against old regime holdovers opposed to new forms of elected civilian authority.

Politically isolated, and with only a titular grip on Egypt's state institutions, Mursi's fumbling and divisive presidency was fatally undermined by a concerted destabilization campaign that was impelled and enabled by Egypt's unreformed security ministries. This campaign culminated in mass protests on 30 June 2013, when old regime forces and revolutionaries took to the streets in tightly controlled protests that were supervised and directed by the Interior Ministry and the military. Following Mursi's ousting, the Muslim Brothers and members of an anti-coup movement launched daily protests in the streets and squares of Egypt's cities, and these continued in spite of massive and unprecedented repression. But while anti-coup protestors were able to creatively adapt to regime violence, their contention was nevertheless circumscribed in ways that led to the effective marginalization of the mobilization and allowed the new military-backed government to achieve a degree of dominance.

Some readers will no doubt object to what this account leaves out. Three silences in particular should be acknowledged. In the enormous output of journalistic and academic writing that followed 2011, it has become obligatory to invoke the role of Facebook and Twitter as platforms for coordinating and inspiring offline mobilization in Egypt. Yet, with several notable exceptions, these social media platforms have barely figured in my account of the 25th January Revolution and its aftermath. Here, I tend to concur with Marc Lynch (2011), who has argued that while social media was an important source of information in the run-up to 25 January 2011, and for those following events from afar, it played little role in shaping the dynamics of mobilization on the ground. Indeed, as Navid Hassanpour (2014) points out, Egyptians only began to take to the streets in significant numbers in the period *after* these technologies were switched off by the regime. There is little evidence to suggest that the action was coordinated over social media during the key moments and battles in Midan al-Tarir and elsewhere.[1] As a result, for close observers and participants alike, the idea of a social media revolution in Egypt is "a swear-word, by which nobody is swearing" (Chalcraft 2014: 157).

A second silence is Tunisia. It is undeniably the case that the overthrow of Ben Ali in Tunisia at the hands of ebullient people power captured the attention of millions of Egyptians, inspiring many to take action against their own ageing and calcified autocrat when the opportunity arose. Events in Tunisia were front-page news in Egyptian newspapers and the subject of rolling coverage on *al-Jazeera* in the days and weeks leading up to the first day of protest. When protestors took to the streets on 25 January, they chanted, "Tunisia is not the end but the beginning" (cited in *al-Masry al-Youm* 26. Jan 2011: 4, 6). They were prescient. As an example of "non-relational diffusion" (Tarrow 2005), the Tunisian Revolution was clearly formative in shaping the possibilities for purposeful mobilization in Egypt and other Arab Spring countries, especially in lowering individuals' revolutionary thresholds. Here, the positive example of Tunisians ousting Ben Ali set in motion what Mark Beissinger (2002: ch.4) has called "thickened" history – when the once impossible thought of ousting Mubarak became the inevitable telos of protestors' accelerating demands and street level mobilization. In turn, protestors from elsewhere in the region and beyond took inspiration from the anti-Mubarak mobilization. Bahrainis, Jordanians, Libyans, Moroccans, Syrians, and Yemenis launched street protests and occupied squares, demanding the downfall of their own autocrats (see Patel 2014). But the putative demonstration effects of the Tunisian Revolution for Egyptians, and the diffusion of the Tahrir model to other contexts, do not translate into commensurate assistance for the analyst trying to explain the specific modes and tactics adopted during the eighteen days of Egyptian mass mobilization, and the particular pathways of state breakdown and reconstitution after the initial revolutionary situation had been averted. While we await the first systematic account of the Tunisian Revolution, the patterns of protest and democratization appear

---

[1] Parenthetically, there is good reason to be critical of empirical accounts of the 25th January Revolution that rely on "tweets from Tahrir." As several of my informants pointed out, even after the regime restored mobile phone and internet access, the cellular network in Midan al-Tahrir frequently crashed during large protests due to the high demand. On these occasions, observers had to leave the area to receive news or share information about events in the Midan.

sufficiently distinct to conclude that the 25th January Revolution quickly followed its own path, driven by local dynamics of contention.

A third silence relates to the absence of organized labor from my explanation of Mubarak's overthrow. Several scholars working in a Marxian vein have argued that strikes were the key catalyst for Mubarak's ousting (e.g., Achcar 2013; Abdelrahman 2014; Alexander and Bassiouny 2015). The problem with these accounts is that labor protests during the 25th January Revolution were largely uncoordinated, only rarely advanced anti-systemic demands, and began too late to have been singularly decisive (see Bishara 2012). While the frequency of labor protests increased from 7 February 2011 onwards, these actions were dwarfed in size by non-labor protests and only really took off on 10 February, by which time Mubarak had already appointed a successor and was getting ready to depart Cairo for self-imposed exile in Sharm al-Sheikh (see Barrie and Ketchley 2016). This is not to deny the agency and grievances of Egyptian workers. Numerous newspaper accounts record workers and state employees as being present on some of the earliest anti-Mubarak protests. But this was almost always alongside other political forces. The event catalogue does not record particularly large or sustained labor protests in Egypt's industrial heartlands during the first two weeks of the anti-Mubarak mobilization. By the time that workers began to mobilize in significant numbers, the repressive presence of the Interior Ministry had been significantly reduced in Egypt's major cities, and military officers were openly defecting to the protest occupation in Midan al-Tahrir and elsewhere. This leads me to advance a different and arguably more compelling explanation for what brought about the revolutionary situation that sealed Mubarak's fate: anti-police violence, a repertoire of ever-larger protests in Egypt's public squares and main roads, and fraternization with military units.

It is also apparent that the trajectories and dynamics identified in this book represent only a point of departure. As I write this conclusion, Egypt's squares and main roads are quiet again. Protest in these spaces is too risky, so long as police and security forces fire live ammunition and birdshot with impunity. This is backed up by a campaign of intimidation: in the days leading up to the fifth anniversary of the 25th January Revolution, state security agents, on the lookout for seditious activists and Muslim Brothers plotting a return to Midan al-Tahrir, reportedly searched 3,000 apartments in downtown Cairo. Meanwhile, the military-backed government of Abdel Fatah El-Sisi has disappeared thousands of regime opponents, many of them students and journalists. Once taken, they are held in black sites, only to resurface months later in one of Egypt's overflowing prisons. Often they are tortured. In February 2016, the mutilated corpse of Giulio Regeni, an Italian doctoral student researching labor activism in the country, was found on the Cairo-Alexandria road. While Egyptian authorities initially speculated that Regeni had been involved in a road traffic accident, or else was the unfortunate victim of a highway robbery, an independent autopsy revealed that Regeni had been electrocuted and suffered cigarettes stubbed out on his body before he died, suggesting that this was the handiwork of Egyptian state security.

There are still pockets of opposition and redoubts of institutional disruption. Small numbers of Muslim Brothers and Muslim Sisters continue to take to the streets, but their protests have become even faster and take place in ever more socially closed and geographically isolated locations. Meanwhile, the Brothers' leadership has struggled to control the movement's youth members, who have launched their own "local operations" targeting police officers and state officials implicated in the killing of protestors. Still, the Brothers have not morphed into an armed insurgent group. Similarly, football ultras, long an independent center of power and organization in Egyptian street politics, continue to take to the terraces and chant against the hated Interior Ministry, despite a court ruling that they be designated terrorist movements. So too, workers continue to mobilize and withdraw their labor, albeit at a much diminished rate to the strike wave of 2011. In February 2016, an off-duty police officer killed a taxi driver in Darb al-Ahmar in Cairo, provoking angry demonstrations by local residents who witnessed the district police station, as well as police stations in two neighboring districts, being evacuated in anticipation of anti-police violence.

So what is next for Egypt? It is a recurring theme of scholarship on the 25th January Revolution, when moving from specific, assertive explanations for the dynamics of mobilization to more hesitant, informed speculation about the future trajectories of contentious politics in Egypt, to conclude that despite the defeats, the massive repression and the retrenchment, Mubarak's national security state will continue to face significant, popular challenges from below. I am inclined to continue this tradition. As of this writing, Egypt looks to have returned to its Mubarak-era situation, one in which "coercion outweighs consent in the political order at large" (Chalcraft 2014: 165). Genuinely popular authoritarian regimes have few problems motivating regime supporters to go to the ballot box, even when the result is a foregone conclusion. And yet, while Egyptian media has promoted a narrative of "Sisi mania," and despite the concerted efforts of state actors, local bosses, and the business elite, voter participation in post-coup elections has been pitifully low, especially when compared to elections held during the post-Mubarak transition. Egyptians have proven so reluctant to electorally endorse the new military-backed government that the country's electoral authorities during both the 2014 presidential and 2015 parliamentary elections, fearful that turnout would not reach double digits, were forced to declare impromptu national holidays and keep polling stations open for an unscheduled extra day of voting. This is a far cry from the votes of 2011 and 2012, when voters queued in huge numbers to cast their ballots in the first competitive elections since the founding of the modern Egyptian republic. And just as the regime has struggled to turn its dominance into electoral legitimacy, so a violent Islamist insurgency in the Sinai continues to erode public confidence in the military, as do Egypt's economic woes, which remain unaddressed by vanity projects such as the new extension to the Suez Canal, or calls to build a new capital city (the initial plans for which, tellingly, have no provision for public squares).

If and when the next episode of mass mobilization occurs, Egyptians will be able to draw on a readymade repertoire for making public their defiance, even if their methods of dissent are now problematically familiar to the forces. As this book has hopefully demonstrated, an analysis that takes seriously the interactive, conjunctural, and creative nature of social and political life, and which draws on both qualitative and quantitative data, will offer a powerful lens through which to understand and explain those future "times of revolution" in Egypt and elsewhere.

Appendix

The event data that I analyze primarily derives from protest reports published in four Egyptian national newspapers, *al-Masry al-Youm, al-Dostor, al-Shorouk*, and the Muslim Brothers' Freedom and Justice Party (FJP) newspaper, *al-Hurriyya wa-l-ʿAdala*. Events were handcoded by myself and two Arabic-speaking research assistants. Where appropriate, I also consulted other Egyptian newspapers and social media sources.

Due to the labor and resource intensive nature of handcoding event data, I decided to focus on three salient subperiods between January 2011 and January 2014. The largest portion of the catalog extends from 1 January 2011 to 1 January 2012 and contains detailed information on 4,917 protest events. This section of the catalog primarily draws on protest reports published in Egypt's largest independent newspaper *al-Masry al-Youm*. To combat possible "news holes," when the high incidence of protest lead to underreporting, I also coded protest events reported in *al-Dostor* and *al-Shorouk* during major episodes of contention (including the 25th January Revolution and the Events of Muhammad Mahmoud Street), and consulted YouTube videos and other social media.

The second portion of the event catalog charts the anti-Mursi mobilization, which reached its apogee on 30 June 2013. This portion of the event catalog covers from 18 June to 18 July 2013 and contains 445 protest events. Due to the high number of protests events during this period, I coded protest reports published in *al-Masry al-Youm, al-Shorouk* and, more selectively, *al-Dostor*.[1] I also consulted YouTube videos and other Egyptian newspapers.

---

[1] By 2013, *al-Dostor's* protest coverage had become increasingly unreliable, with reports sometimes claiming unrealistic protest participation on anti-Mursi protests, e.g.

The final section of the event catalog records anti-coup protests launched by the Muslim Brothers and their allies. This catalog extends from 4 June to 24 December 2013, and encompasses 3,039 events. Event data was derived from protest reports published in the print edition of the Muslim Brothers' Freedom and Justice Party (FJP) daily newspaper, *al-Hurriyya wa-l-ʿAdala*. Note that the Egyptian authorities totally suppressed the newspaper between 13 and 18 October. After analyzing other Egyptian newspapers and media sources, I concluded that *al-Hurriyya wa-l-ʿAdala* was the most reliable and systematic source for coverage of the anti-coup mobilization in the six months following the coup. This was gauged by comparing video footage uploaded to dedicated anti-coup channels on YouTube and Bambuser.[2] Most governorates had a YouTube and Bambuser (for live streaming) account, which acted as aggregators for anti-coup protest footage and photographs. These accounts were maintained by one of several "against the coup" movements.[3] Sampling longitudinally and latitudinally, I matched over 10 percent of protests recorded in the event catalog to videos.

One representative protest report in *al-Hurriyya wa-l-ʿAdala* reads as follows:

The city of Damietta witnessed a march that began in front of the al-Matbuli mosque following Friday prayer, in which thousands of residents participated. The rally toured Abdulrahman Street, arriving at the Nile Corniche, where the participants formed a human chain by the side of the road, holding photographs and posters denouncing the coup. (*al-Hurriyya wa-l-ʿAdala*, 14 Sept. 2013: 1)

I found video footage of the Damietta protest on the Damietta anti-coup movement YouTube channel.[4] Comparing the article with the video record gives a sense of the accuracy of the reporting. The video has

---

"millions" of protestors. On these occasions, I either deferred to the reporting in *al-Masry al-Youm*, or reviewed the reporting on a case-by-case basis.

[2] I coded protest events in the six months of the coup from *al-Masry al-Youm*, but decided not to use the data due to the poor quality of the reporting – a result of restrictions on press freedom imposed following the military's seizure of power.

[3] One reason for the anti-coup movement's meticulous recording and uploading of protests is to generate video footage for Al Jazeera Mubashir Misr, the Egypt-focused channel of the Qatar-based satellite network. Mubashir Misr provides anti-coup protestors with pre-paid 3G-enabled smart phones (usually Galaxy Samsung S4s), which come with high quality cameras that can be used to record and stream the protests (interview Youssef 2 6 Feb. 2014; interview Belal 22 Jun. 2014).

[4] See YouTube video (13 Sep 2013) "*Damietta – masīrat masjid al-matbūlī – 13/9/2013*": http://youtu.be/Z7KwI1-lk3Q.

been clearly edited for length and lasts for eight minutes. In the bottom right-hand corner of the video is a date stamp and a banner that reads "Damietta – March al-Matbuli mosque – 13/09/2013." In the video we see protestors assemble outside of a mosque before marching down a main road until they reach the Nile Corniche, where the protestors form a human chain, holding banners and chanting anti-coup slogans. The number of protestors appears consistent with the reporting. The most significant discrepancy is a failure to note the large number of women in the crowd. Other protest reports do record female participation, including for protests in Damietta, suggesting that this is an issue of underreporting, but not a systematic reporting bias. Tallied against the video footage, the Damietta protest report otherwise appears highly accurate, with date, protest location, size, and repertoire faithfully relayed.

VARIABLES

In total, twenty-seven variables were collected and coded for each protest event. The following is a list of the most important variables. A complete codebook is available from the author upon request.

Date (*date*). The beginning date of a protest event. Events for which a specific date could not be determined were excluded. In rare cases, event dates were interpolated from newspaper reporting. For example, a protest event that lasted three days is first reported on the third and final day. In this situation, events would be entered for the two previous days taking the values of the reported event.

Governorate (*governorate*). The governorate in which the protest occurred. Protests that could not be located in their governorate were excluded. Governorate boundaries in Egypt have undergone extensive changes in the period under study. I used the 2011 governorate boundaries.

Census district (*census_district*). The census district in which the protest started. Protest events were located in their 2006 census district (the last census conducted). Protest events that could not be located in their census district are dropped from any statistical analysis.

Protest size (*protest_size*). The number of participants in a protest event. To record protest size, I followed the inferential coding convention used in the European Protest and Coercion Dataset (Francisco n.d.). Newspaper reports frequently described protest size using terms such as "thousands," "tens of thousands," and "hundreds of thousands," instead of definite numbers. Following Francisco, for protest participation reported in *al-Masry al-Youm, al-Dostor, al-Shorouk*, I coded "tens" as "30"; "hundreds" as "300"; "thousands" as "3000"; and so forth. For protest reports published in the Muslim Brothers newspaper, I followed a slightly different coding convention for crowd sizes. In the absence of a second newspaper to compare reporting, and after having checked reports against the video evidence, I decided to use a more conservative inference in which "tens" would be coded "10"; "hundreds" would be coded "100"; thousands would be coded "1000"; tens of thousands" would be coded "10,000"; and "hundreds of thousands" would be coded "100,000."[5] To distinguish inferences from reported numbers, I recorded the inference with a final 1, e.g., 11, 101, 1001, and so on. Protest reports in *al-Hurriyya wa-l-'Adala* from Minya governorate often claimed unrealistic protest sizes (e.g., "millions"). I also struggled to match reports from Minya to videos of anti-coup protests. As a result, I decided to exclude that governorate from reported protest participation. When nominally independent newspapers, e.g., *al-Dostor* reported similarly implausible crowd sizes during the anti-Mursi mobilization, I reviewed the reported protest size on a case-by-case basis. On some occasions, protest participation was not reported in a newspaper. Checked against other media sources and video footage, the failure to report protest participation usually meant that the protest was small (less than 1,000 participants). On these occasions an imputed value was entered: strikes were coded as "301"; marches were coded as "301"; demonstrations were coded as "301"; sit-ins were coded as "31"; human chains were coded as "31"; occupations were coded as "1001"; and blockades were coded as "301," etc.

Repertoire (1st) (*first_repertoire*). The primary protest tactic employed on a protest event. Includes march, demonstration, occupation, sit-in, human chain, blockade, strike, attack, and petition.

Repertoire (2nd) (*second_repertoire*). Protest events sometimes employed two tactics. For example (as with the example of an anti-coup protest in Damietta given above), a protest could set off from one location

---

[5] Of note, I coded the maximum size of protests in Midan al-Tahrir as "300,001." This is in line with analysis carried by Egyptian news media following the initial occupation of Tahrir in early 2011, which put the maximum capacity of Midan al-Tahrir in the low hundreds of thousands.

and arrive at its destination, whereupon protestors would employ a different tactic. Includes march, demonstration, occupation, sit-in, human chain, blockade, strike, attack, and petition.

Protest start location (*protest_start*). The departure point or location of a protest event. Includes mosque, public square, government building, factory, university, main road, residential street, political party building, and police station.

Protest end location (*protest_end*). The destination or end point of a mobile protest event. Includes mosque, public square, government building, factory, university, main road, residential street, political party building, and police station. For some mobile protests, protest end locations went unreported. This was a problem for protest reports in *al-Hurriyya wa-l-ʿAdala*. Anti-coup protest marches that began in mosques located in residential areas would move through the streets of the immediate neighborhood before disbanding. This was often reported in the newspaper as a protest touring "the local streets of the neighborhood" (*fi shawāriʿa al-hayy*) and was distinct from a protest occurring on one of the district's "main roads" (*turuq raʾīsiyya*). However, this was sometimes judged as not sufficiently newsworthy and so only the protest start location (almost always a mosque) was reported. This became apparent when checking reports against video footage of protests. When protest end location was unreported and a video was not available, "residential streets" was imputed from the protest start location (e.g., a mosque), the size of the protest, and the census district in which the protest took place.

Protest organizer (*organizer*). A social movement or actor who participated in a protest event.

Repression (*repression*). A binary variable to denote if a protest event was repressed. The minimum definition of repression is the use of force.

Repressive actor (*repressive_actor*). The actor repressing a protest event. Includes the police (Central Security Forces, State Security, Traffic Police, etc.), military (Soldiers, Republican Guard, Military Police, etc.), thugs, and civilians.

Type of repression (*repression_type*). The method of repression. Includes live ammunition, birdshot, tear gas, crowd control/batons, and other (describe).

Number killed (*no_killed*). The number of protestors killed. Newspaper reports were checked against human rights reporting and where disagreements existed, I deferred to the later.

Number arrested (*no_arrested*). The number of protestors arrested. The number arrested were sometimes reported using terms such as "several"; "tens"; "hundreds"; and so forth. I decided to use a conservative inference and coded "several" as "3"; "tens" as "11"; "hundreds" as "101."

Performance (*performance*). Chants or slogans used by protestors, as well as any other notable contentious performances.

Bibliography

Abaza, Mona. 2001. "Shopping Malls, Consumer Culture and the Reshaping of Public Space in Egypt." *Theory, Culture & Society* 18 (5): 97–122.

Abdelrahman, Maha. 2009. "'With the Islamists? – Sometimes. With the State? – Never!' Cooperation between the Left and Islamists in Egypt." *British Journal of Middle Eastern Studies* 36 (1): 37–54.

Abdelrahman, Maha. 2013. "In Praise of Organization: Egypt between Activism and Revolution." *Development and Change* 44 (3): 569–585.

Abdelrahman, Maha. 2014. *Egypt's Long Revolution: Protest Movements and Uprisings.* London: Routledge.

AbuKhalil, As'ad. 2011. "How to Start a Revolution: Or the Delusions of Gene Sharp," *Al-Akhbar.* 2 Dec. At: http://web.archive.org/web/20160304000520/http://english.al-akhbar.com/node/2169 (accessed 24 Sept. 2013).

Abul-Magd, Zeinab. 2012. "Occupying Tahrir Square: The Myths and the Realities of the Egyptian Revolution." *South Atlantic Quarterly* 111 (3): 565–572.

Abu-Lughod, Janet. 1971. *Cairo: 1001 years of the City Victorious.* Princeton, NJ: Princeton University Press.

Abu-Lughod, Lila. 2012. "Living the 'Revolution' in an Egyptian Village: Moral Action in a National Space." *American Ethnologist* 39 (1): 21–25.

Achcar, Gilbert. 2013. *The People Want: A Radical Explanation of the Arab Uprising.* London: Saqi Books.

Adams, Julia, Elisabeth S. Clemens, and Ann Shola Orloff. 2005. "Introduction: Social Theory, Modernity, and the Three Waves of Historical Sociology." in Julia Adams, Elisabeth S. Clemens, and Ann Shola Orloff, eds. *Remaking Modernity: Politics, History, and Sociology.* London and Durham: Duke University Press.

Ahram, Ariel I. 2011. *Proxy Warriors: The Rise and Fall of State-Sponsored Militias.* Stanford: Stanford University Press.

Ahram, Ariel I. 2015. "Pro-Government Militias and the Repertoires of Illicit State Violence." *Studies in Conflict & Terrorism* 39 (2): 207–226.

Al-Ahram. 2011. "Ayqūniyyat al-Jaysh wa al-Shaʿb: al-Naqīb Maged Boules ... Asad al-Tahrir." 6 Oct. At: http://web.archive.org/web/20120104030631/http:// www.ahram.org.eg/Al-Ahram%20Files/News/105257.aspx (accessed 20 Jun. 2013).

Al-Ahram. 2013. "Tamarrod tastaʿid li-naql 22 milyūn tawqiʿ li-amākin siriyya." 30 Jun. At: http://web.archive.org/web/20150624195713/http://www.ahram.org.eg/ News/866/25/218197/%D8%A7%D9%84%D8%A3%D9%88%D9%84%D9 %89/%D8%AA%D9%85%D8%B1%D8%AF-%D8%AA%D8%B3%D8%A A%D8%B9%D8%AF-%D9%84%D9%86%D9%82%D9%84-%D9%85% D9%84%D9%8A%D9%88%D9%86-%D8%AA%D9%88%D9%82%D9% 8A%D8%B9-%D9%84%D8%A3%D9%85%D8%A7%D9%83%D9%86-% D8%B3%D8%B1%D9%8A%D8%A9-%D8%AA%D8%AC%D8%B1%D8 %AF-.aspx (accessed 20 Jun. 2016).

Ahram Online. 2011. "Muslim Brotherhood Won't Cap Ambitions Forever." 23 Mar. At: http://english.ahram.org.eg/NewsContent/1/64/8451/Egypt/Politics-/M uslim-Brotherhood-wont-cap-ambitions-forever.aspx (accessed 20 Jun. 2016).

Ahram Online. 2011. "Democratic Alliance (Freedom and Justice)." 18 Nov. At: http://web.archive.org/web/20160620214547/http://english.ahram.org.eg/Ne wsContent/33/103/26895/Elections-/Electoral-Alliances/Democratic-Alliance-Freedom-and-Justice-.aspx (accessed 20 Jun. 2016).

Ahram Online. 2013. "Fall of a Strongman, 2 Years On: Untold Stories of Egypt's Revolution." 11 Feb. At: http://web.archive.org/web/20160620214901/http:// english.ahram.org.eg/News/64471.aspx (accessed 20 Jun. 2016).

Ahram Online. 2013. "Wild Rumours of Hamas Interference in Egypt Find Audience." 12 May. At: http://english.ahram.org.eg/News/71258.aspx (accessed 20 Jun. 2016).

Ahram Online. 2013. "Artists break into Egypt's culture ministry building, declare sit-in." 5 Jun. At: http://english.ahram.org.eg/NewsContent/5/35/7324 9/Arts–Culture/Stage–Street/-Artists-break-into-Egypts-culture-ministry-build i.aspx (accessed 20 Jun. 2016).

al-Ahram Weekly Online. 2011a. "Islam in the Insurrection?" 3–9 Mar. At: http:// weekly.ahram.org.eg/2011/1037/sc70.htm (accessed 20 Jun. 2016).

al-Ahram Weekly Online. 2011b. "Tactical Gains." 10–16 Feb. At: http://weekly .ahram.org.eg/2011/1034/sc51.htm (accessed 20 Jun. 2016).

Alexander, Anne. 2011. "Brothers-in-Arms? The Egyptian Military, the Ikhwan and the Revolutions of 1952 and 2011." *Journal of North African Studies* 16 (4): 533–554.

Alexander, Anne and Mostafa Bassiouny. 2014. *Bread, Freedom, Social Justice: Workers and the Egyptian Revolution.* London: Zed Books.

Alexander, Jeffrey. 2011. *Performative Revolution in Egypt: An Essay in Cultural Power.* London and New York: Bloomsbury.

Ali, Nagat. 2014. "The Road to Mohamed Mahmoud Street." *Yalla Italia.* At: http://web.archive.org/web/20160621102958/http://www.yallaitalia.it/2014/04/ the-road-to-mohamed-mahmoud-street/ (accessed 20 Jun. 2016).

Alim, Frida. 2013. "The Politics of the Brotherhood Democracy: How the Muslim Brotherhood Burned Their Bridges." *Jadaliyya.* At: http://www.jadaliyya.com/

pages/index/13062/the-politics-of-the-brotherhood-democracy_how-the- (last accessed 20 Jun. 2016).

Alimi, Eitan Y. 2009. "Mobilizing Under the Gun: Theorizing Political Opportunity Structure in a Highly Repressive Setting." *Mobilization: An International Journal* 14 (2): 219–237.

Alimi, Eitan Y., Lorenzo Bosi, and Chares Demetriou. 2015. *The Dynamics of Radicalization: A Relational and Comparative Perspective.* Oxford: Oxford University Press.

Anderson, Benedict. 2006. [1972] *Java in a Time of Revolution: Occupation and Resistance, 1944–1946.* Jakarta: Equinox Publishing.

Anderson, Benedict. 1998. *The Spectre of Comparisons: Nationalism, Southeast Asia and the World.* London: Verso.

Arab Barometer. 2011. "Wave II Stata-Data file." At: http://www.arabbarom eter.org/sites/default/files/ADBII_Merged_Data_file_English_FINAL_0.dta (accessed 20 Jun. 2016).

Arab Republic of Egypt – Central Agency for Public Mobilization and Statistics. 2009. "Number of Mosques & Zawaya by Gov 07/2008." At: http://web.arc hive.org/web/20160620220245/http://www.sis.gov.eg/newVR/egyptinnum ber/egyptinfigures/arabictables/164.pdf (accessed 20 Jun. 2016).

Armbrust, Walter. 2013a. "The Ambivalence of Martyrs and the Counter-revolution." *Cultural Anthropology.* At: http://production.culanth.org/field sights/213-the-ambivalence-of-martyrs-and-the-counter-revolution (accessed 20 Mar. 2016).

Armbrust, Walter. 2013b. "The Trickster in Egypt's January 25th Revolution." *Comparative Studies in Society and History* 55 (4): 834–864.

Ashour, Omar. 2012. "From Bad Cop to Good Cop: The Challenge of Security Sector Reform in Egypt." *Brookings Doha Center Paper Series.*

Ashworth, Tony. 1968. "The Sociology of Trench Warfare, 1914–1918." *British Journal of Sociology* 19 (4): 407–420.

Ashworth, Tony. 2000. [1980] *Trench Warfare 1914–18: The Live and Let Live System.* London: Pan.

Associated Press. 2011. "Egypt Military Deploys after Day of Riots." 28 Jan. At: http://www.youtube.com/watch?v=xmcGZEkM9TU (accessed 20 Jun. 2016).

Atlantic. 2011. "A General's Unnerving Visit to Tahrir Square." 5 Feb. At: http://web.archive.org/save/_embed/http://www.theatlantic.com/international/archive/2011/02/a-generals-unnerving-visit-to-tahrir-square/70822/ (accessed 20 Jun. 2016).

Auyero, Javier. 2007. *Routine Politics and Violence in Argentina: The Gray Zone of State Power.* Cambridge: Cambridge University Press.

Axelrod, Robert. 1984. *The Evolution of Cooperation.* New York: Basic Books.

Bahgat, Hossam. 2016. "Anatomy of an Election: How Egypt's 2015 Parliament was Elected to Maintain Loyalty to the President." *Mada Masr.* At: http://web.archive.org/web/20160621101822/http://www.madamasr.co m/sections/politics/anatomy-election (accessed 20 Jun. 2016).

Barany, Zoltan. 2011. "Comparing the Arab Revolts: The Role of the Military." *Journal of Democracy* 22 (4): 28–39.

Barrie, Christopher. 2016. "The Contentious Politics of Nationalism and the Anti-Naturalization Campaign in Tunisia, 1932–33." *Nations & Nationalism.*

Barrie, Christopher and Neil Ketchley. 2016. "Opportunity without Organization: Labour Mobilization in Egypt after the 25th January Revolution." unpublished working paper.

Bassiouni, M. Cherif. 2016. "Egypt's Unfinished Revolution." in Adam Roberts, Michael J. Willis, Rory McCarthy, and Timothy Garton Ash, eds. *Civil Resistance in the Arab Spring Triumphs and Disasters.* Oxford: Oxford University Press.

Bayat, Asef. 2010. *Life as Politics: How Ordinary People Change the Middle East.* Stanford: Stanford University Press.

BBC. 2012. "Egypt's President Mursi Assumes Sweeping Powers." 22 Nov. At: http://web.archive.org/web/20160621101915/http://www.bbc.co.uk/news/world-middle-east-20451208 (accessed 20 Jun. 2016).

Beissinger, Mark R. 2002. *National Mobilization and the Collapse of the Soviet State.* Cambridge: Cambridge University Press.

Beissinger, Mark R. 2013. "The Semblance of Democratic Revolution: Coalitions in Ukraine's Orange Revolution." *American Political Science Review* 107 (3): 574–592.

Beissinger, Mark R. 2014. "The Changing Face of Revolution as a Mode of Regime-Change, 1900–2012." unpublished manuscript.

Beissinger, Mark R., Amaney A. Jamal and Kevin Mazur. 2015. "Explaining Divergent Revolutionary Coalitions: Regime Strategies and the Structuring of Participation in the Tunisian and Egyptian Revolutions." *Comparative Politics* 48 (1): 1–44.

Bennani-Chraïbi, Mounia and Olivier Fillieule. 2015. "Towards a Sociology of Revolutionary Situations: Reflections on the Arab Uprisings." *Revue française de science politique* 62: 1–29.

Bermeo, Nancy. 1997. "Myths of Moderation: Confrontation and Conflict during Democratic Transitions." *Comparative Politics* 29 (3): 305–322.

Bermeo, Nancy. 2003. *Ordinary People in Extraordinary Times: The Citizenry and the Breakdown of Democracy.*, Princeton, NJ: Princeton University Press.

Biggs, Michael. 2003. "Positive Feedback in Collective Mobilization: The American Strike Wave of 1886." *Theory and Society* 32 (2): 217–254.

Biggs, Michael. 2005. "Strikes as Forest Fires: Chicago and Paris in the Late 19th Century." *American Journal of Sociology* 110 (6): 1684–1714.

Biggs, Michael. 2013. "How Repertoires Evolve: The Diffusion of Suicide Protest in the Twentieth Century." *Mobilization: An International Quarterly* 18 (4): 407–428.

Bishara, Dina. 2012. "The Power of Workers in Egypt's 2011 Uprising." in Bahgat Korany and Rabab El-Mahdi, eds. *Arab Spring in Egypt: Revolution and Beyond.* Cairo: American University in Cairo Press.

Bishara, Dina. 2015. "The Politics of Ignoring: Protest Dynamics in Late Mubarak Egypt." *Perspectives on Politics* 13 (4): 958–975.

Blaydes, Lisa. 2011. *Elections and Distributive Politics in Mubarak's Egypt.* Cambridge: Cambridge University Press.

Boudreau, Vincent. 2009. *Resisting Dictatorship: Repression and Protest in Southeast Asia*. Cambridge: Cambridge University Press.

Brass, Paul R. 1997. *Theft of an Idol: Text and Context in the Representation of Collective Violence*. Princeton, NJ: Princeton University Press.

Brockett, Charles D. 1995. "A Protest-Cycle Resolution of the Repression/ Popular-Protest Paradox." in Mark Traugott, ed. *Repertoires and Cycles of Collective Action*. Durham and London: Duke University Press.

Brockett, Charles D. 2005. *Political Movements and Violence in Central America*. Cambridge: Cambridge University Press.

Brown, Nathan. 2011. "The Muslim Brotherhood's Democratic Dilemma." *National Interest*. At: http://web.archive.org/web/20160621102231/http://nationa linterest.org/commentary/the-muslim-brotherhoods-democratic-dilemma-6205 (accessed 20 Jun. 2016).

Brown, Nathan. 2012a. *When Victory Is Not an Option: Islamist Movements in Arab Politics*. Ithaca, NY: Cornell University Press.

Brown, Nathan. 2012b. "Cairo's Judicial Coup." *Foreign Policy*. At: http://web .archive.org/web/20160621102412/http://foreignpolicy.com/2012/06/14/cairos-judicial-coup/ (accessed 20 Jun. 2016).

Brown, Nathan J. 2013a. "Egypt's Failed Transition." *Journal of Democracy* 24 (4): 45–58.

Brown, Nathan J. 2013b. "Egypt's Wide State Reassembles Itself." *Foreign Policy*. 17 Jul. At: http://web.archive.org/web/20160621102614/http://foreignpolicy.com/ 2013/07/17/egypts-wide-state-reassembles-itself/ (accessed 20 Jun. 2016).

Brownlee, Jason. 2012. *Democracy Prevention: The Politics of the U.S.-Egyptian Alliance*. Cambridge: Cambridge University Press.

Brownlee, Jason. 2013. "Morsi Was No Role Model for Islamic Democrats." *Middle East Institute*. At: http://web.archive.org/web/20160621102719/http:// www.mei.edu/content/morsi-was-no-role-model-islamic-democrats (accessed 20 Jun. 2016).

Bunce, Valerie and Sharon L. Wolchik. 2006. "Favorable Conditions and Electoral Revolutions." *Journal of Democracy* 17 (4): 5–18.

Butt, Ahsan I. 2016. "Street Power: Friday Prayers, Islamist Protests, and Islamization in Pakistan." *Politics and Religion* 9 (1): 1–28.

Cambanis, Thanassis. 2015. *Once Upon a Revolution: An Egyptian Story*. London: Simon and Schuster.

Canel, Eduardo. 1992. "Democratization and the Decline of Urban Social Movements in Uruguay: A Political-Institutionalist Account." in Arturo Escobar and Sonia E. Alvarez, eds. *The Making of Social Movements in Latin America: Identity, Strategy, and Democracy*. Boulder, Co.: Westview Press.

Chabot, Sean and Majid Sharifi. 2013. "The Violence of Nonviolence: Problematizing Nonviolence Resistance in Iran and Egypt." *Societies Without Borders* 8 (2): 205–232.

Chalcraft, John. 2012. "Horizontalism in the Egyptian Revolutionary Process." *Middle East Report* 262 (Spring): 6–11.

Chalcraft, John. 2014. "Egypt's 25 January Uprising, Hegemonic Contestation, and the Explosion of the Poor." in Fawaz A. Gerges, ed., *The New Middle East:*

Protest and Revolution in the Arab World. Cambridge: Cambridge University Press.

Chalcraft, John. 2016. *Popular Politics and the Making of the Modern Middle East.* Cambridge: Cambridge University Press.

Chambers, Paul. 2010. "Thailand on the Brink: Resurgent Military, Eroded Democracy." *Asian Survey* 50 (5): 835–858.

Chang, Paul Y. 2008. "Unintended Consequences of Repression: Alliance Formation in South Korea's Democracy Movement (1970–1979)." *Social Forces* 87 (2): 651–677.

Chang, Paul Y. 2015. *Protest Dialectics: State Repression and South Korea's Democracy Movement.* 1970–1979, Stanford: Stanford University Press.

Chang, Paul Y. and Byung-Soo Kim. 2007. "Differential Impact of Repression on Social Movements: Christian Organizations and Liberation Theology in South Korea." *Sociological Inquiry* 77 (3): 326–355

Chen, Jessica. 2014. *Powerful Patriots: Nationalist Protest in China's Foreign Relations.* Oxford: Oxford University Press.

Chenoweth, Erica. 2011. "Armed Wing in Syria: To What Effect?" *Rationalinsurgent,* 10 Oct. At: http://web.archive.org/save/_embed/https://ratio nalinsurgent.com/2011/10/10/armed-wing-in-syria-to-what-effect/ (last accessed 20 Jun. 2016).

Chenoweth, Erica and Kathleen Gallagher Cunningham. 2013. "Understanding Nonviolent Resistance: An Introduction." *Journal of Peace Research* 50 (3): 271–276.

Chenoweth, Erica and Kurt Schock. 2015. "Do Contemporaneous Armed Challenges Affect the Outcomes of Mass Nonviolence Campaigns?" *Mobilization: An International Quarterly* 20 (4): 427–451.

Chenoweth, Erica and Maria J. Stephan. 2011. *Why Civil Resistance Works: The Strategic Logic of Nonviolent Conflict.* New York: Columbia University Press.

Chorley, Katherine. 1973. [1943], *Armies and the Art of Revolution.* Boston: Beacon Press.

Clarke, Killian, 2011, "Saying "Enough": Authoritarianism and Egypt's Kefaya Movement," *Mobiliation: An International Journal* 16, 4: 397–416.

Clarke, Killian. 2014. "Unexpected Brokers of Mobilization: Contingency and Networks in the 2011 Egyptian Uprising." *Comparative Politics* 46 (4): 379–397.

CNN. 2013. "Transcript: Egyptian President Ousted by Military; Interview with Former Egyptian Army General Sameh Seif Elyazal." 3 Jul. At: http://web.arc hive.org/web/20160621102853/http://transcripts.cnn.com/TRANSCRIPTS/13 07/03/cg.01.html (accessed 20 Jun. 2016).

Cole, Juan. 2012. "Egypt's New Left versus the Military Junta." *Social Research* 79 (2): 487–510.

Cole, Juan. 2014. "Egypt's Modern Revolutions and the Fall of Mubarak." in Fawaz A. Gerges, ed., *The New Middle East: Protest and Revolution in the Arab World.* Cambridge: Cambridge University Press.

Colla, Elliot. 2012. "The People Want." *Middle East Report* 263 (Fall): 8–13.

Collier, Ruth. 1999. *Paths Towards Democracy.* Cambridge: Cambridge University Press.

Collins, Randall. 2004. *Interaction Ritual Chains*. Princeton, NJ: Princeton University Press.

Collins, Randall. 2008. *Violence: A Micro-Sociological Theory*. Princeton, NJ: Princeton University Press.

Cunningham, David. 2003. "State versus Social Movement: FBI Counterintelligence against the New Left." in Jack Goldstone, ed. *States, Parties and Social Movements*. Cambridge: Cambridge University Press.

Daily News Egypt. 2012. "Morsi Set to Pick Vice Presidents, Prime Minister, and Cabinet." 26 Jun. At: http://web.archive.org/web/20160621094618/http://www.dailynewsegypt.com/2012/06/26/morsi-set-pick-vice-presidents-prime-mi nister-cabinet/ (accessed 20 Jun. 2016).

Daily News Egypt. 2013. "Port Said residents want army to manage state." 27 Feb. At: http://web.archive.org/web/20160621094717/http://www.daily newsegypt.com/2013/02/27/port-said-residents-want-army-to-manage-state/ (accessed 20 Jun. 2016).

Daily News Egypt. 2013. "More governorates call on army to manage state." 4 Mar. At: http://web.archive.org/web/20160621094757/http://www.dailynew segypt.com/2013/03/04/more-governorates-call-on-army-to-manage-state/ (accessed 20 Jun. 2016).

Davenport, Christian and Marci Eads. 2001. "Cued to Coerce or Coercing Cues? An Exploration of Dissident Rhetoric and Its Relationship to Political Repression." *Mobilization: An International Quarterly* 6 (2): 151–171.

Davenport, Christian, Hank Johnston and Carol Mueller. 2004. *Repression and Mobilization*. Minneapolis: University of Minnesota Press.

Della Porta, Donatella. 1995. *Social Movements, Political Violence and the State: A Comparative Analysis of Italy and Germany*. Cambridge: Cambridge University Press.

Della Porta, Donatella and Sidney Tarrow. 1986. "Unwanted Children: Political Violence and the Cycle of Protest in Italy, 1966–1973." *European Journal of Political Research* 14 (5–6):607–632.

Diamond, Larry. 2002. "Thinking About Hybrid Regimes." *Journal of Democracy* 13 (2): 21–35.

Dhattiwala, Raheel and Michael Biggs. 2010. "The Political Logic of Ethnic Violence: The Anti-Muslim Pogrom in Gujarat, 2002." *Politics & Society* 40 (4): 483–516.

Dix, Robert H. 1984. "Why Revolutions Succeed and Fail." *Polity* 16 (3): 423–426.

Al-Dostor. 2011a. "Jum'at al-Ghadab." 28 Jan. At: http://web.archive.org/web/20110211030308/http://dostor.org/politics/egypt/11/january/28/35813 (accessed 24 Sept. 2013).

Al-Dostor. 2011–2023. Print ed. Cited by date.

Al-Dostor. 2011c. "Al-Jaysh wa-l-Sha'b ... Qaddamū Shuhadā' fi al-Thawra." 22 Feb. At: http://web.archive.org/web/20110308080012/http://dostor.org/society-and-people/variety/11/february/22/36760 (accessed 24 Sept. 2013).

Dzenovska, Dace and Iván Arenas. 2012. "Don't Fence Me In: Barricade Sociality and Political Struggles in Mexico and Latvia." *Comparative Studies in Society and History* 54 (3): 644–678.

Earl, Jennifer. 2011. "Political Repression: Iron Firsts, Velvet Gloves, and Diffuse Control." *Annual Review of Sociology* 37: 261–284.

Earl, Jennifer, Andrew Martin, John D. McCarthy, and Sarah A. Soule. 2004. "The Use of Newspaper Data in the Study of Collective Action." *Annual Review of Sociology* 30: 65–80.

Egypt Independent. 2011. "Brotherhood Party to Confront Ruling Military Council if Constitution Drafted." 27 Jun. At: http://web.archive.org/web/201 60621094838/http://www.egyptindependent.com/news/brotherhood-party-co nfront-ruling-military-council-if-constitution-drafted (accessed 20 Jun. 2016).

Egypt Independent. 2011. "Anan Denies Military Were Ordered to Kill Protestors." 8 Oct. At: http://web.archive.org/web/20130330064537/http://www.egyptinde pendent.com/news/anan-denies-claim-military-was-ordered-kill-protesters (accessed 20 Jun. 2016).

Egypt Independent. 2012. "Was the Egyptian Revolution Really Non-Violent?" 24 Jan. At: http://web.archive.org/web/20160201122145/http://www.egyptin dependent.com/news/was-egyptian-revolution-really-non-violent (accessed 20 Jun. 2016).

Egypt Initiative for Personal Rights (EIPR). 2014. "Weeks of Killing: State Violence, Communal Violence and Sectarian Attacks in the Summer of 2013." At: http://web.archive.org/web/20160621095117/http://eipr.org/en/report/2014/ 06/18/2124 (accessed 20 Jun. 2016).

Egyptian Gazette. 2011a. No. 42442, 6 Feb. Print ed.

Egyptian Gazette. 2011b. No. 42447, 11 Feb. Print ed.

Ekiert, Grzegorz and Jan Kubik. 1999. *Rebellious Civil Society: Popular Protest and Democratic Consolidation in Poland, 1989–1993*. Ann Arbor: University of Michigan Press.

El-Amrani, Issandr. 2011. "The Army and the People." *The Arabist*, 29 Jan. At: http://web.archive.org/save/_embed/http://arabist.net/blog/2011/1/29/the-ar my-and-the-people.html (accessed 20 Jun. 2016).

El-Amrani, Issandr. 2012. "Sightings of the Egyptian Deep State." *MERIP Online*. At: http://web.archive.org/web/20160621095245/http://www.merip.org/ mero/mero010112 (accessed 20 Jun. 2016).

El-Amrani, Issandr. 2013. "The Delegitimization of Mohamed Morsi." *The Arabist*, 30 Jun. At: http://web.archive.org/web/20160621095320/http://arab ist.net/blog/2013/6/30/the-delegitimization-of-mohamed-morsi (accessed 20 Jun. 2016).

El Chazli, Youssef. 2015. "On the Road to Revolution: How Did 'Depoliticised' Egyptians Become Revolutionaries?" *Revue française de science politique* 62: 79–101.

El Chazli, Youssef. 2016. "A Geography of Revolt in Alexandria, Egypt's Second Capital." *Metro Politics*. At: http://www.metropolitiques.eu/A-Geography-of-Revolt-in.html (accessed 20 Jun. 2016).

El-Ghobashy, Mona. 2005. "The Metamorphosis of the Egyptian Muslim Brothers." *International Journal of Middle Eastern Studies* 37 (3): 373–395.

El-Ghobashy, Mona. 2011. "The Praxis of the Egyptian Revolution." *Middle East Report* 258 (Spring): 2–13.

Elgindy, Khaled. 2012. "Egypt's Troubled Transition: Elections without Democracy." *The Washington Quarterly* 35 (2): 89–104.

El-Hamalawy, Hossam. 2007. "Comrades and Brothers." *Middle East Report* 242 (Spring): 40–43.

El-Hamalawy, Hossam. 2011. "Friday of Anger." 6 Feb. At: http://web.archive.org/save/_embed/http://arabawy.org/24311/jan25-friday-of-anger (accessed 20 Jun. 2016).

El-Mahdi, Rabab. 2009. "Enough! Egypt's Quest for Democracy." *Comparative Political Studies* 42 (8): 1011–1039.

El-Mahdi, Rabab. 2011. "Orientalising the Egyptian Uprising." *Jadaliyya*. 11 Apr. At: http://www.jadaliyya.com/pages/index/1214/orientalising-the-egyptian-uprising (accessed 20 Jun. 2016).

Elmasry, Mohamad. 2013. "Unpacking Anti-Muslim Brotherhood Discourse." *Jadaliyya*. 28 Jun. At: http://www.jadaliyya.com/pages/index/12466/unpacking-anti-muslim-brotherhood-discourse (accessed 20 Jun. 2016).

Elmasry, Mohamad. 2014a. "The Role of the Media in Egypt's Military Coup." Roundtable: Covering Egypt: Media and Politics in the Post-Mubarak Period, Columbia University, 22 May. At: https://www.youtube.com/watch?v=7AX2uPNiRYo (accessed 20 Jun. 2016).

Elmasry, Mohamad. 2014b. "Egypt's Invisible Protesters, One Year after the Coup." *Middle East Eye*, 4 Jul. At: http://web.archive.org/save/http://www.middleeasteye.net/columns/egypt-s-invisible-protesters-one-year-after-coup-1090863626 (accessed 20 Jun. 2016).

El-Sherif, Ashraf. 2014. "The Egyptian Muslim Brotherhood's Failures." *Carnegie Endowment for International Peace.* At: http://web.archive.org/web/20150627205458/http://carnegieendowment.org/2014/07/01/egyptian-muslim-brotherhood-s-failure/hez8 (accessed 20 Jun. 2016).

Elyachar, Julia. 2014. "Upending Infrastructure: Tamarod, Resistance, and Agency after the January 25th Revolution in Egypt." *History and Anthropology* 25 (4): 452–471.

Emirbayer, Mustafa. 1997. "Manifesto for a Relational Sociology." *The American Journal of Sociology* 103 (2): 281–317.

Fahmy, Khaled. 1997. *All the Pasha's Men: Mehmed Ali, His army and the Making of Modern Egypt.* Cambridge: Cambridge University Press.

Fahmy, Khaled. 2013. "Islāh al-Shurta wa Laysa Fard al-Tawāri' Huwa al-Hall." *Al-Shorouk*. 1 Feb. At: http://web.archive.org/web/20160621100030/http://www.shorouknews.com/columns/view.aspx?cdate=01022013&id=fdd26f05-4014-44e8-91fe-6ef59d3f552c (accessed 20 Jun. 2016).

Feigenbaum, Anna, Fabian Frenzel and Patrick McCurdy. 2013. *Protest Camps.* London: Zed Books.

Foran, John. 2005. *Taking Power: On the Origins of Third World Revolutions.* Cambridge: Cambridge University Press.

Francisco, Ronald A. n.d. *Codebook for European Protest and Coercion Data. 1980 through 1995.* At: http://web.archive.org/web/20160621100226/http://web.ku.edu/~ronfrand/data/ (accessed 20 Jun. 2016).

Francisco, Ronald A. 1995. "The Relationship between Coercion and Protest: An Empirical Evaluation in Three Coercive States." *The Journal of Conflict Resolution* 39 (2): 263–282.

Francisco, Ronald A. 1996. "Coercion and Protest: An Empirical Test in Two Democratic Societies." *American Journal of Political Science* 40 (4): 1179–1204.

Francisco, Ronald A. 2004a. "After the Massacre: Mobilization in the Wake of Harsh Repression." *Mobilization: An International Quarterly* 9 (2): 107–126.

Francisco, Ronald A. 2004b. "The Dictator's Dilemma." in Christian Davenport, Hank Johnston and Carol Mueller, eds. *Repression and Mobilization*. Minneapolis: University of Minnesota Press.

Franzosi, Roberto. 1987. "The Press as a Source of Socio-Historical Data: Issues in the Methodology of Data Collection from Newspapers." *Historical Methods* 20: 5–15.

Frenkel, Sheera and Maged Atef. 2014. "How Egypt's Rebel Movement Helped Pave the way for a Sisi Presidency." *Buzzfeed*. 15 Apr. At: http://web.archive .org/save/_embed/https://www.buzzfeed.com/sheerafrenkel/how-egypts-rebel-movement-helped-pave-the-way-for-a-sisi-pre?utm_term=.vorMx8man#.jqW ye9XvQ (accessed 20 Jun. 2016).

Gaffney, Patrick D. 1991. "The Changing Voices of Islam: The Emergence of Professional Preachers in Contemporary Egypt." *The Muslim World* 81 (1): 27–47.

Gamson, William. 1990. [1975], *The Strategy of Social Protest*. Belmont, Calif.: Wadsworth Pub.

Gayer, Laurent. 2014. *Karachi: Ordered Disorder and the Struggle for the City*. London: Hurst & Co.

Gerbaudo, Paulo. 2014. "The 'Movements of the Squares' and the Contested Resurgence of the 'Sovereign People' in Contemporary Protest Culture." unpublished manuscript.

Ghonim, Wael. 2012. *Revolution 2.0: The Power of the People Is Greater than the People in Power: A Memoir*. Boston: Houghton Mifflin Harourt.

Giglio, Mike. 2013. "A Cairo Conspiracy." *The Daily Beast*. 7 Dec. At: http://web .archive.org/articles/2013/07/12/a-cairo-conspiracy.html (accessed 20 Jun. 2016).

Gledhill, John. 2005. "States of Contention: State-Led Political Violence in Post-Socialist Romania." *East European Politics & Societies* 19 (1): 76–104

Gledhill, John. 2012. "Competing for Change: Regime Transition, Intrastate Competition, and Violence." *Security Studies* 21 (1): 43–82.

Goffman, Erving. 1971. *Relations in Public: Micro-Studies of the Public Order*. London: Penguin.

Goffman, Erving. 1972. *Interaction Ritual: Essays in Face-to-Face Behaviour*. Chicago and London: Penguin.

Goldstone, Jack A. 1991. *Revolution and Rebellion in the Early Modern World*. Berkeley and Los Angeles: University of California Press.

Goodwin, Jeff. 2001. *No Other Way Out: States and Revolutionary Movements, 1945–1991*. Cambridge: Cambridge University Press.

Gould, Roger. 1995. *Insurgent Identities: Class, Community, and Protest in Paris from 1848 to the Commune*. Chicago: Chicago University Press.

Guardian. 2011. "Friend or Foe? Egypt's Army Keeps Protesters Guessing." 30 Jan. At: http://web.archive.org/save/_embed/https://www.theguardian.com/world/2011/jan/30/egypt-protesters-army-guessing (accessed 20 Jun. 2016).

Guardian. 2013. "Egyptian Army Suspends Constitution and Removes President Morsi – As it Happened." 3 Jul. At: http://web.archive.org/save/_embed/https://www.theguardian.com/world/middle-east-live/2013/jul/03/egypt-countdown-army-deadline-live#block-51d452d6e4b03a793030bb29 (accessed 20 Jun. 2016).

Gunning, Jeroen and Ilan Zvi Baron. 2013. *Why Occupy a Square? People, Protests and Movements in the Egyptian Revolution*. London: Hurst & Company.

Hafez, Mohammed M. 2003. *Why Muslims Rebel: Repression and Resistance in the Islamic World*. Boulder, CO: Lynne Rienner.

Hagopian, Frances. 1996. *Traditional Politics and Regime Change in Brazil*. Cambridge: Cambridge University Press.

Haines, Herbert. 1984. "Black Radicalization and the Funding of Civil Rights: 1957–1970." *Social Problems* 32 (1): 31–43.

Haines, Herbert. 1988. *Black Radicals and the Civil Rights Mainstream*. Knoxville: University of Tennessee Press.

Halverson, Jeffry R., Scott W. Ruston and Angela Trethewey. 2013. "Mediated Martyrs of the Arab Spring: New Media, Civil Religion, and Narrative in Tunisia and Egypt." *Journal of Communication* 63 (2): 312–332.

Hamid, Shadi. 2014. *Temptations of Power: Islamists and Illiberal Democracy in a New Middle East*. Oxford: Oxford University Press.

Harvey, David. 2006. "The Political Economy of Public Space." At: http://web.archive.org/web/20160621100716/http://davidharvey.org/media/public.pdf (accessed 20 Jun. 2016).

Hassan, Hatem M. 2015. "Extraordinary Politics of Ordinary People: Explaining the Microdynamics of Popular Committees in Revolutionary Cairo." *International Sociology* 30 (4): 383–400.

Hassanpour, Navid. 2014. "Media Disruption and Revolutionary Unrest: Evidence From Mubarak's Quasi-Experiment." *Political Communication* 31 (1): 1–24.

Hedman, Eva-Lotta E. 2006. *In the Name of Civil Society: From Free Election Movements to People Power in the Philippines*. Honolulu: University of Hawaii Press.

Hellyer, H. A. 2014. "Faking Egypt's past: The Brotherhood and Jan. 25." *al-Arabiya*. 20 Jan. At: http://web.archive.org/web/20141216094737/http://english.alarabiya.net/en/views/news/middle-east/2014/01/20/Faking-Egypt-s-past-the-Brotherhood-and-Jan-25.html (accessed 20 Jun. 2016).

Hess, David and Brian Martin. 2006. "Repression, Backfire, and the Theory of Transformative Events." *Mobilization: An International Quarterly* 11 (1): 249–267.

Heyworth-Dunne, James. 1950. *Religious and Political Trends in Modern Egypt*. Washington: Published by the Author.

Hipsher, Patricia L. 1996. "Democratization and the Decline of Social Movements in Chile and Spain." *Comparative Politics* 28 (3): 273–297.

Hipsher, Patricia L. 1998. "Democratic Transitions and Social Movement Outcomes: The Chilean Shantytown Dwellers' Movement in Comparative Perspective." in Marco G. Giugni, Doug McAdam and Charles Tilly, eds. *From Contention to Democracy*. Lanham, Maryland: Rowman and Littlefield Publishers, Inc.

Hite, Katherine and Paola Cesarini. 2004. *Authoritarian Legacies and Democracy in Latin America and Southern Europe*. Notre Dame, Ind.: University of Notre Dame Press.

Hmed, Choukri. 2015. "Abeyance Networks, Contingency and Structures: History and Origins of the Tunisian Revolution." *Revue Française de Science Politique* 62: 31–53.

Holmes, Amy Austin. 2012. "There Are Weeks When Decades Happen: Structure and Strategy in the Egyptian Revolution." *Mobilization: An International Quarterly* 17 (4): 391–410.

Human Rights Watch. 2013. "Egypt: Security Forces Used Excessive Lethal Force." At: http://web.archive.org/web/20161216163534/https://www.hrw.org/news/2013/08/19/egypt-security-forces-used-excessive-lethal-force (accessed 20 Jun. 2016)

Human Rights Watch. 2014a. "Egypt: New Leader Faces Rights Crisis." At: http://web.archive.org/save/_embed/https://www.hrw.org/news/2014/06/09/egypt-new-leader-faces-rights-crisis (accessed 20 Jun. 2016).

Human Rights Watch. 2014b. "All According to Plan: The Rab'a Massacre and Mass Killings of Protestors in Egypt." At: http://web.archive.org/save/_embed/https://www.hrw.org/report/2014/08/12/all-according-plan/raba-massacre-and-mass-killings-protesters-egypt (accessed 20 Jun. 2016).

Huntington, Samuel. 1991. *The Third Wave: Democratization in the Late Twentieth Century*. Norman: University of Oklahoma Press.

Al-Hurriyya wa al-'Adala. 2013. Print edition. Cited by date.

Idle, Nadia and Alex Nunns. 2011. *Tweets from Tahrir: Egypt's Revolution as it Unfolded, in the Words of the People Who Made It*. New York: OR Books.

Ikhwan Online. 2011. "Ra'īs al-Hurriyya wa-l-'Adala yutālib al-Misriyyīn bidaf' 'agalat al Intāj." 17 Jul. At: http://web.archive.org/web/20110820090113/http://www.ikhwanonline.com/new/Article.aspx?ArtID=87869&SecID=250 (accessed 20 Jun. 2016).

IkhwanWeb. 2014. "Muslim Brotherhood praises pro-democracy Brussels Declaration." 14 May, available at: http://web.archive.org/web/20160621120540/http://www.ikhwanweb.com/article.php?id=31653 (accessed 20 Jun. 2016)

Isaac, Larry, Steve McDonald and Greg Lukasik. 2006. "Takin' It from the Streets: How the Sixties Mass Movement Revitalized Unionization." *American Journal of Sociology* 112 (1): 46–96.

Ismail, Salwa. 2006. *Political Life in Cairo's New Quarters: Encountering the Everyday State*. Minneapolis: University of Minnesota Press.

Ismail, Salwa. 2012. "The Egyptian Revolution against the Police." *Social Research* 79 (2): 435–462.

Ismail, Salwa. 2013. "Urban Subalterns in the Arab Revolutions: Cairo and Damascus in Comparative Perspective." *Comparative Studies in Society and History* 55 (4): 865–894.

Jadaliyya. 2011. "National Progressive Unionist (Tagammu) Party." At: http://www.jadaliyya.com/pages/index/3157/national-progressive-unionist-(tagammu)-party (accessed 20 Jun. 2016).

Jadaliyya. 2013. "The Brotherhood After 30 June: An Interview with the FJP's Abdel Mawgoud al-Dardery." 15 Aug. At: http://www.jadaliyya.com/pages/index/13597/the-brotherhood-after-30-june_an-interview-with-th (accessed 20 Jun. 2016).

Al-Jazeera. 2011. "Al-Wafd Yunhi Tahālufan Intikhābiyyan maʿ al-Ikhwān." 6 Oct. At: http://web.archive.org/save/_embed/http://www.aljazeera.net/news/arabic/2011/10/6/%D8%A7%D9%84%D9%88%D9%81%D8%AF-%D9%8A%D9%86%D9%87%D9%8A-%D8%AA%D8%AD%D8%A7%D9%84%D9%81%D8%A7-%D8%A7%D9%86%D8%AA%D8%AE%D8%A7%D8%A8%D9%8A%D8%A7-%D9%85%D8%B9-%D8%A7%D9%84%D8%A5%D8%AE%D9%88%D8%A7%D9%86 (accessed 20 Jun. 2016).

Al-Jazeera. 2013. "People, Power, or Propaganda? Unravelling the Egyptian opposition." 19 Jul. At: http://web.archive.org/web/20160621121021/http://www.aljazeera.com/indepth/opinion/2013/07/201371711575564410917.html (accessed 20 Jun. 2016).

Al-Jazeera. 2013. "*Al-Farāsha . . . muthāharāt tayāra fi Assiut.*" 10 Sept., available at: http://web.archive.org/web/20160621121210/http://www.aljazeera.net/news/reportsandinterviews/2013/10/9/-%D8%A7%D9%84%D9%81%D8%B1%D8%A7%D8%B4%D8%A9-%D9%85%D8%B8%D8%A7%D9%87%D8%B1%D8%A7%D8%AA-%D8%B7%D9%8A%D8%A7%D8%B1%D8%A9-%D9%81%D9%8A-%D8%A3%D8%B3%D9%8A%D9%88%D8%B7 (accessed 20 Jun. 2016).

Johnston, Hank. 2012. "State Violence and Oppositional Protest in High-Capacity Authoritarian Regimes." *International Journal of Conflict and Violence* 6 (1): 55–74.

Jumet, Kira D. 2015. *Why Do People Protest? Explaining Participation in the 2011 and 2013 Egyptian Uprisings.* unpublished doctoral dissertation, Rutgers, The State University of New Jersey.

Kadivar, Mohammad Ali. 2013. "Alliances and Perception Profiles in the Iranian Reform Movement, 1997 to 2005." *American Sociological Review* 78 (6): 1063–1086.

Kandil, Hazem. 2011. "Revolt in Egypt." *New Left Review* 68, Mar.–Apr. At: http://newleftreview.org/II/68/hazem-kandil-revolt-in-egypt (accessed 20 Jun. 2016).

Kandil, Hazim. 2012. *Soldiers, Spies and Statesmen: Egypt's Road to Revolt.* London: Verso.

Kandil, Hazem. 2014. "Sisi's Turn." *London Review of Books* 36 (4): 15–17.

Kayfa Tathūr bi-Hadāʾa: Maʿlūmāt wa Taktikāt Hāmma. 2011. Anonymously authored Arabic-language protest handbook, Cairo.

Kenner, David. 2013. "Egypt's Bloomberg Outlasts His Islamist Enemies." *Foreign Policy.* 10 Jul. At: http://blog.foreignpolicy.com/posts/2013/07/10/egypt_sawiris_interview (accessed 20 Jun. 2016).

Kerton, Sarah. 2012. "Tahrir, here? The Influence of the Arab Uprisings on the Emergence of Occupy." *Social Movement Studies* 11 (3–4):302–308.

Ketchley, Neil. 2013. "The Muslim Brothers Take to the Streets." *Middle East Report* 269 (Winter): 12–17.

Ketchley, Neil. 2014a. "'The Army and the People Are One Hand!' Fraternization and the 25th January Egyptian Revolution." *Comparative Studies in Society and History* 56 (1): 155–186.

Ketchley, Neil. 2014b. "How Social Media Spreads Protest Tactics From Ukraine to Egypt." *Washington Post*, 14 Feb. At: http://www.washingtonpost.com/blogs/monkey-cage/wp/2014/02/14/how-social-media-spreads-protest-tactics-from-ukraine-to-egypt/ (accessed 20 Jun. 2016).

Ketchley, Neil. 2016. "Elite-led Protest and Authoritarian State Capture in Egypt." *POMEPS Studies 20*

Ketchley, Neil and Michael Biggs. 2014. "What is the Egyptian Anti-Coup Movement Protesting For?" *Washington Post*. 4 Apr. At: http://www.washingtonpost.com/blogs/monkey-cage/wp/2014/04/04/what-is-the-egyptian-anti-coup-movement-protesting-for/ (accessed 20 Jun. 2016).

Ketchley, Neil and Michael Biggs. 2015. "Who Actually Died in Egypt's Rabaa Massacre?" *Washington Post*. 14 Aug. At: https://www.washingtonpost.com/blogs/monkey-cage/wp/2015/08/14/counting-the-dead-of-egypts-tiananmen/ (accessed 20 Jun. 2016).

Ketchley, Neil and Michael Biggs. 2017. "The Educational Contexts of Islamist Activism: Elite Students and Religious Institutions in Egypt." *Mobilization: An International Quarterly*.

Khamis, Sahar and Katherine Vaughn. 2012. "'We Are All Khaled Said': The potentials and limitations of cyberactivism in triggering public mobilization and promoting political change." *Journal of Arab & Muslim Media Research* 4 (2–3):145–163.

Kirschke, Linda. 2000. "Informal Repression, Zero-Sum Politics and Late Third Wave Transitions." *The Journal of Modern African Studies* 38 (3): 383–405.

Kopecký, Petr and Cas Mudde. 2002. *Uncivil Society? Contentious Politics in Post-Communist Europe*. London: Routledge.

Kuran, Timur. 1991. "Now Out of Never: The Element of Surprise in the East European Revolution of 1989." *World Politics* 44 (1): 7–48.

Laclau, Ernesto. 2007. *On Populist Reason*. London: Verso.

Lawson, George. 2005. *Negotiated Revolutions: The Czech Republic, South Africa and Chile*. Aldershot: Ashgate.

Lawson, George. 2012. "The Arab Uprisings: Revolution or Protests?" in *After the Arab Spring: Power Shift in the Middle East?* LSE IDEAS Special Reports.

Lawson, George. 2015. "Revolution, non-violence, and the Arab Uprisings." *Mobilization: An International Quarterly* 20 (4): 453–470.

LeBas, Adrienne. 2006. "Polarization as Craft: Party Formation and State Violence in Zimbabwe." *Comparative Politics* 38 (4): 419–438.

LeBas, Adrienne. 2011. *From Protest to Parties: Party-building and Democratization in Africa*. Oxford: Oxford University Press.

Lacroix, Stéphane. 2012. *Sheikhs and Politicians: Inside the New Egyptian Salafism*. Brookings Doha Centre Publications.

Leenders, Reinoud. 2012. "Collective Action and Mobilization in Dar'a: An Anatomy of the Onset of Syria's Popular Upring." *Mobilization: An International Quarterly* 17 (3): 419–434.

Lehoucq, Fabrice. 2016. "Does Nonviolence Work?" *Comparative Politics* 48 (2): 269–287.

Lenin, Vladimir Ilyich. 1964. [1917], "The Significance of Fraternisation." in *Lenin's Collected Works*. Moscow: Progress Publishers.

Levitsky, Steven and Lucan A. Way. 2010. *Competitive Authoritarianism: Hybrid Regimes after the Cold War*. Cambridge: Cambridge University Press.

Lia, Brynjar. 1998. *The Society of the Muslim Brothers in Egypt: The Rise of an Islamic Mass Movement*. Reading: Ithaca Press.

Lichbach, Mark Irving. 1987. "Deterrence or Escalation? The Puzzle of Aggregate Studies of Repression and Dissent." *The Journal of Conflict Resolution* 31 (2): 266–297.

Lichbach, Mark Irving. 1995. *The Rebel's Dilemma*. Ann Arbor: Michigan: University of Michigan Press.

Linz, Juan J. and Alfred Stepan. 1996. *Problems of Democratic Transition and Consolidation: Southern Europe, South America, and Post-Communist Europe*. Baltimore and London: The John Hopkins University Press.

Lohmann, Susanne. 1994. "The Dynamics of Information Cascades: The Monday Demonstrations in Leipzig, East Germany, 1989–1991." *World Politics* 47 (1): 42–101.

Lust, Ellen, Gamal Soltan and Jakob Wichmann. n.d. *Islam, Ideology and Transition: Egypt after Mubarak*. unpublished manuscript.

Lynch, Marc. 2011. "After Egypt: The Limits and Promise of Online Challenges to the Authoritarian Arab State." *Perspectives on Politics* 9 (2): 301–310.

Mada Masr. 2013. "Persisting Brothers: Q&A with Amr Darrag." 8 Sept. At: http://web.archive.org/save/_embed/http://www.madamasr.com/sections/politics/persisting-brothers (accessed 20 Jun. 2016).

Mada Masr. 2016. "June 30, 3 Years on: Protesting Intellectuals Revisit their Position." 1 Jul. At: http://web.archive.org/web/20160704094238/http://www.madamasr.com/sections/culture/june-30-3-years-protesting-intellectuals-revisit-their-position (accessed 3 Jul. 2016).

Magaloni, Beatriz. 2006. *Voting for Autocracy: Hegemonic Party Survival and its Demise in Mexico*. Cambridge: Cambridge University Press.

Maher, Ahmed. 2014. "Lil-Asaf Kuntu A'lam." *Masr al-Arabia*. 14 May. At: http://web.archive.org/web/20160621134419/http://www.masralarabia.com/%D8%A7%D8%AE%D8%A8%D8%A7%D8%B1-%D9%85%D8%B5%D8%B1/113-%D8%A7%D9%84%D9%85%D9%82%D8%A7%D9%84%D8%A7%D8%AA/%D8%A3%D8%AD%D9%85%D8%AF-%D9%85%D8%A7%D9%87%D8%B1/268315-%D9%84%D9%84%D8%A3%D8%B3%D9%81-%D9%83%D9%86%D8%AA-%D8%A3%D8%B9%D9%84%D9%85 (accessed 20 Jun. 2016).

Maney, Gregory M. and Oliver, Pamela E. 2001. "Finding Collective Events: Sources, Searches, Timing." *Sociological Methods and Research* 30: 131–69.

Marinov, Nikolay and Hein Goemans. 2014. "Coups and Democracy." *British Journal of Political Science* 44 (4): 799–825.

Marshall, Shana and Joshua Stacher. 2012. "Egypt's Generals and Transnational Capital." *Middle East Report* 262 (Spring): 12–18.

Martin, Brian. 2007. *Justice Ignited: The Dynamics of Backfire.* Lanham, MD: Rowman and Littlefield.

Masoud, Tarek. 2008. *Why Islam Wins: Electoral Ecologies and Economies of Political Islam in Contemporary Egypt.* Unpublished PhD, Yale University.

Masoud, Tarek. 2014. *Counting Islam: Religion, Class and Elections in Egypt.* Cambridge: Cambridge University Press.

McAdam, Doug. 1983. "Tactical Innovation and the Pace of Insurgency." *American Sociological Review* 48, (6): 735–754.

McAdam, Doug, Sidney Tarrow, and Charles Tilly. 2001. *Dynamics of Contention.* Cambridge: Cambridge University Press.

McPhail, Clark and John McCarthy. 2004. "Who Counts and How: Estimating the Size of Protests." *Contexts* 3 (3): 12–18.

Al-Masry al-Youm. 2011–2013. Print ed. Cited by date and page number.

Al-Masry al-Youm. 2011. "al-Ikhwān tabda' rasmiyyan igra'āt ta'sīs hizb al-hurriyya wa al-'adala." 22 Feb. At: http://web.archive.org/web/20160621134621/http://today.almasryalyoum.com/article2.aspx?ArticleID=288629 (accessed 20 Jun. 2016).

Al-Masry al-Youm. 2011. "Al-Masry al-Youm Tanshur Tafāsīl Itasālāt Shurtat al-Iskandariyya Yawm Jum'at al-Ghadab." 15 Mar. At: http://web.archive.org/web/20140201002239/http://www.almasryalyoum.com/News/details/119075 (accessed 20 Jun. 2016).

Al-Masry al-Youm. 2011. "Inshiqāq Dakhil al-Ikhwān bi-Sabab al-Ghiyāb 'an al-Milyūniyya." 23 Nov. At: http://web.archive.org/web/20160621134843/http://today.almasryalyoum.com/article2.aspx?ArticleID=318448 (accessed 20 Jun. 2016).

Al-Masry al-Youm. 2012. "Kutayyib ta 'limātal-thawra: Hal yahriq al-tha'ir al-haq qism al-shurta?" 3 Mar. At: http://web.archive.org/web/20160621134945/http://www.almasryalyoum.com/news/details/53231 (accessed 20 Jun. 2016).

Al-Masry al-Youm. 2013. "al-Ismailia Tasta'id l-'ihrāq Duma al-Ikhwān fi Sham al-Nasīm." 4 Jun. At http://web.archive.org/web/20160621135708/http://today.almasryalyoum.com/article2.aspx?ArticleID=381216 (accessed 20 Jun. 2016).

Al-Masry al-Youm. 2014 "Haqiqat takhs īsal-dawla qit'at ard li-Mahmoud Badr li-binā' masna' baskawīt bi al-Qalyubiyya." 17 Dec. At: http://web.archive.org/web/20160621135805/http://www.almasryalyoum.com/news/details/603535 (accessed 20 Jun. 2016).

Masrawy. 2011. "Insihāb Hizb al-Nūr al-Salafi min al-Tahāluf al-Dimocrāti." 3 Sept. At: http://web.archive.org/web/20120105125624/http://www.masrawy.com/News/Egypt/Politics/2011/september/3/elnoor_party.aspx?; (accessed 20 Jun. 2016).

Masrawy. 2012. "Nushatā' yathkurūn "Khiyānat al-Ikhwān" fi "Muhammad Mahmud" ... wa al-Jamā'a: Radayna 'alayha Milyūn Mara." 14 Nov. At: http://web.archive.org/web/20140224025302/http://www.masrawy.com/News/reports/2012/november/14/5432856.aspx (accessed 20 Jun. 2016).

Al-Masriyyun. 2011. "Al-Hizb al-Nāssiri Yansahib min 'al-Tahaluf al-Dimocrāti'" 14 Oct. At: http://web.archive.org/web/20111015190249/http://www.almesryoon.com/backup/(S(vr2cfgrwfs4q4ozgg15aphmn)F(BACEA

A66265146F4013400370032006100630000002628 8B056D8BCC010026A8
A756C773E70172006F006C006500730000002F000000))/news.aspx?id=82011
(accessed 20 Jun. 2016).

Al-Masriyyun 2013. "ʿalaqa sākhina li-muʾasis Tamarrod bi-wasat al-balad."
19 Oct. At: https://web.archive.org/web/20131022015911/http:/almesryoon
.com/%D8%AF%D9%81%D8%AA%D8%B1-%D8%A3%D8%AD%D9
%88%D8%A7%D9%84-%D8%A7%D9%84%D9%88%D8%B7%D9%8
6/273047-%D8%B9%D9%84%D9%82%D8%A9-%D8%B3%D8%A7%D
8%AE%D9%86%D8%A9-%D9%84%D9%85%D8%A4%D8%B3%D8%
B3-%D8%AA%D9%85%D8%B1%D8%AF-%D8%A8%D9%88%D8%B3
%D8%B7-%D8%A7%D9%84%D8%A8%D9%84%D8%AF (accessed 20
Jun. 2016).

Mellor, Noha. 2014. "Who Represents the Revolutionaries? Examples from the
Egyptian Revolution 2011." *Mediterranean Politics* 19 (1): 82–98.

Menza, Mohamed Fahmy. 2012. *Patronage Politics in Egypt: The National
Democratic Party and the Muslim Brotherhood in Cairo.* London: Routledge.

Mitchell, Neil, Sabine C. Carey and Christopher K. Butler. 2014. "The Impact of
Pro-Government Militias on Human Rights Violations." *International
Interactions* 40 (5): 812–836.

Mitchell, Richard P. 1993. *The Society of the Muslim Brothers.* Oxford: Oxford
University Press.

Moss, Dana M. 2014. "Repression, Response, and Contained Escalation Under
"Liberalized" Authoritarianism in Jordon." *Mobilization: An International
Quarterly* 19 (3): 261–286.

Naguib, Ghada Muhammad. 2013. "Why I left Tamarrod." At: http://web.archi
ve.org/web/20140330184112/http://revolution-news.com/why-i-left-tamarod/
(accessed 20 Jun. 2016).

Nepstad, Sharon E. 2011. *Nonviolent Revolutions: Civil Resistance in the Late
20th Century.* Oxford: Oxford University Press.

Nepstad, Sharon E. 2013. "Mutiny and Nonviolence in the Arab Spring:
Exploring Military Defections and Loyalty in Egypt, Bahrain and Syria."
Journal of Peace Research 50 (3): 337–349.

Nepstad, Sharon. 2015. *Nonviolent Struggle: Theories, Strategies, and Dynamics.*
Oxford: Oxford University Press.

New York Times. 2011. "After First Talks, Egypt Opposition Vows New
Protest." 6 Feb. At: http://www.nytimes.com/2011/02/07/world/middleeast/07
egypt.html?pagewanted=all&_r=2&; (accessed 20 Jun. 2016).

New York Times. 2012. "Judge Helped Egypt's Military to Cement Power." 3 Jul.
At: http://www.nytimes.com/2012/07/04/world/middleeast/judge-helped-egyp
ts-military-to-cement-power (accessed 20 Jun. 2016).

New York Times. 2013. "Sudden Improvements in Egypt Suggest a Campaign to
Undermine Morsi." 10 Jul. At: http://www.nytimes.com/2013/07/11/world/
middleeast/improvements-in-egypt-suggest-a-campaign-that-undermined-mo
rsi.html?_r=2&; (accessed 20 Jun. 2016).

New York Times. 2013. "Ousted General in Egypt is Back, as Islamists' Foe."
30 Oct. At: http://www.nytimes.com/2013/10/30/world/middleeast/ousted-gen

eral-in-egypt-is-back-as-islamists-foe.html?pagewanted=1&_r=0&hp (accessed 20 Jun. 2016).

New York Times. 2015. "Recordings Suggest Emirates and Egyptian Military Pushed Ousting of Morsi." 1 Mar. At: http://www.nytimes.com/2015/03/02/wo rld/middleeast/recordings-suggest-emirates-and-egyptian-military-pushed-oust ing-of-morsi.html?_r=0 (accessed 20 Jun. 2016).

Ockey, James. 2009. "Thailand in 2008: Democracy and Street Politics." *Southeast Asian Affairs 2009*: 315–333.

O'Donnell, Guillermo, Philippe Schmitter. 1986. *Transitions from Authoritarian Rule*. Baltimore: The Johns Hopkins University Press.

Olesen, Thomas. 2013. ""We are all Khaled Said": Visual Injustice Symbols in the Egyptian Revolution, 2010–2011." Nicole Doerr, Alice Mattoni, Simon Teune, eds., *Advances in the Visual Analysis of Social Movements (Research in Social Movements, Conflicts and Change 35)*. Emerald Group Publishing Limited. pp.3–25

Olzak, Susan, Maya Beasley and Johan L. Olivier. 2003. "The Impact of State Reforms on Protest Against Apartheid in South Africa." *Mobilization: An International Quarterly* 8 (1): 27–50.

Opp, Kart-Dieter and Wolfgang Roehl. 1990. "Repression, Micromobilization, and Political Protest." *Social Forces* 69 (2): 521–547.

Oweidat, Nadia, Cheryl Benard, Dale Stahl, Walid Kildani, Edward O'Connell, and Audra K. Grant. 2008. *The Kefaya Movement: A Case Study of a Grassroots Reform Initiative*. Santa Monica, CA: Rand Corporation.

Oxhorn, Philip. 1994. "Where Did All the Protestors Go? Popular Mobilization and the Transition to Democracy in Chile." *Latin American Perspectives* 21 (3): 49–68.

Oxhorn, Philip. 1996. "Surviving the Return to 'Normalcy': Social Movements, Democratic Consolidation and Economic Restructuring." *International Review of Sociology* 6 (1): 117–134

Patel, David. 2014. "Roundabouts and Revolutions: Public Squares, Coordination, and the Diffusion of the Arab Uprisings." Unpublished manuscript.

Pearlman, Wendy. 2011. *Violence, Nonviolence, and the Palestinian National Movement*. Cambridge: Cambridge University Press.

Pettinicchio, David. 2012. "Institutional Activism: Reconsidering the Insider/Outsider Dichotomy." *Sociology Compass* 6 (6): 499–510.

Pettinicchio, David. 2013. "Strategic Action Fields and the Context of Political Entrepreneurship: How Disability Rights Became Part of the Policy Agenda." in Patrick G. Coy, ed., *Research in Social Movements, Conflicts and Change (Research in Social Movements, Conflicts and Change 36) Research in Social Movements*. Emerald Group Publishing Limited: 79–106.

Pickvance, Christopher G. 1999. "Democratisation and the Decline of Social Movements: The Effects of Regime Change on Collective Action in Eastern Europe, Southern Europe and Latin America." *Sociology* 33 (2): 353–372.

Pioppi, Daniela. 2013. "Playing with Fire: The Muslim Brotherhood and the Egyptian Leviathan." *The International Spectator* 48 (4): 51–68.

Przeworski, Adam. 1991. *Democracy and the Market: Political and Economic Reforms in Eastern Europe and Latin America*. Cambridge: Cambridge University Press.

Radnitz, Scott. 2010. *Weapons of the Wealthy: Predatory Regimes and Elite-Led Protests in Central Asia*. Ithaca, NY: Cornell University Press.

Ramadan, 'Abd al-'Azim. 1977. *Al-Jaysh al-Miṣrī fī al-Siyāsah, 1882–1936*. Cairo: al-hay'ah al-misriyah al-'ammah lil-kitab.

Raskolinikov, F. F. 1982. [1918], "Fraternisation: A Story." in *Tales of Sub-Lieutenant Ilyin*. At: http://www.marxists.org/history/ussr/government/red-ar my/1918/raskolnikov/ilyin/cho7.htm (accessed 20 Jun. 2016).

Rasler, Karen. 1996. "Concessions, Repression and Political Protest in the Iranian Revolution." *American Sociological Review* 61 (1): 132–152.

el-Refai, Nour. 2011. "A Quick Reminder for Police." 28 Jan. At: http://web.arc hive.org/web/20110819120013/http://nourelrefai.wordpress.com/2011/02/28/a-quick-reminder-for-police/ (accessed 20 Jun. 2016).

Rennick, Sarah Anne. 2015. *The Practice of Politics and Revolution: Egypt's Revolutionary Youth Social Movement*. Unpublished doctoral dissertation, Lund University.

Reuters. 2011. "Egypt Army Officer Says 15 Others Join Protestors." 11 Feb. At: http://web.archive.org/web/20130522052700/http://www.reuters.com/article/ 2011/02/11/ozatp-egypt-protest-officers-idAFJOE71A06N20110211 (accessed 20 Jun. 2016).

Reuters. 2013. "Special Report – The real force behind Egypt's 'revolution of the state,'" 10 Oct. At: http://web.archive.org/web/20160617034728/http://uk.reu ters.com/article/uk-egypt-interior-special-report-idUKBRE99908720131010 (accessed 20 Jun. 2016).

Reuters. 2014. "Activists who Backed Mursi's Fall Turn Against Military." 20 Feb. At: http://web.archive.org/web/20140222234219/http://www.reu ters.com/article/2014/02/20/us-egypt-politics-tamarud-idUSBREA1J1 E420140220?irpc=932 (accessed 20 Jun. 2016).

Ritter, Daniel. 2014. *The Iron Cage of Liberalism: International Politics and Unarmed Revolutions in the Middle East and North Africa*. Oxford: Oxford University Press.

Roberts, Hugh. 2013. "The Revolution That Wasn't." *London Review of Books* 35 (17): 3–9.

Robertson, Graeme B. 2010. *The Politics of Protest in Hybrid Regimes: Managing Dissent in Post-Communist Russia*. Cambridge: Cambridge University Press.

Robison, Richard and Vedi Hadiz. 2004. *Reorganizing Power in Indonesia: The Politics of Oligarchy in an Age of Markets*. London: RoutledgeCurzon.

Rodenbeck, Max. 1999. *Cairo: The City Victorious*. New York: Knopf.

Roessler, Philip G. 2005 "Donor-Induced Democratization and the Privatization of State Violence in Kenya and Rwanda." *Comparative Politics* 37 (2): 207–227.

Rosenberg, Tina. 2011. "Revolution U: What Egypt Learned from the Students Who Overthrew Milosevic." *Foreign Policy*. 6 Feb. At: http://www.foreignpo licy.com/articles/2011/02/16/revolution_u (accessed 19 Sept. 2012).

Rucht, Dieter. 2013. "Social Movement Structures in Action: Conceptual Propositions and Empirical Illustration." in Jacquelien van Stekelenburg, Conny Roggeband and Bert Klandermans, eds. *The Future of Social Movement Research: Dynamics, Mechanisms and Processes*. Minneapolis: University of Minnesota Press.

Ryzova, Lucie. 2011. "The Battle of Muhammad Mahmoud Street: Teargas, Hair Gel, and Tramadol." *Jadaliyya*. At: http://www.jadaliyya.com/pages/index/33 12/the-battle-of-muhammad-mahmud-street_teargas-hair- (accessed 20 Jun. 2016).

Ryzova, Lucie. 2015. "Strolling in Enemy Territory: Downtown Cairo, Its Publics, and Urban Heterotopias." Beirut: Orient-Institut Studies.

Sabaseviciute, Giedre. 2011. "Re-creating the Past: The Manipulation of the Notion of Rupture in Egyptian Revolutions." *La Révolution française*. At: http://lrf.revues.org/348 (accessed 20 Jun. 2016).

Al-Safha al-Rasmiyya li-l-Majlis al-ʾAʿla li-l-Quwwāt al-Musallaha. 2011. Facebook, messages 22, 24, 30, 35, 45, 47, 51, 52, 55, 58, 59, 72, 83, and 85. At: https://www.facebook.com/Egyptian.Armed.Forces (accessed 19 Sept. 2012).

Said, Atef. 2012. "The Paradox of Transition to 'Democracy' under Military Rule." *Social Research* 79 (2): 397–434.

Said, Atef. 2014. *The Tahrir Effect: History, Space, and Protest in the Egyptian Revolution of 2011*. Unpublished doctoral dissertation, University of Michigan.

Sallam, Hesham. 2011. "Striking Back at Egypt's Workers." *Middle East Report* 259 (Summer): 20–25.

Sandoval, Salvador A. M. 1998. "Social Movements and Democratization: The Case of Brazil and the Latin countries." in Marco G. Giugni, Doug McAdam and Charles Tilly, eds. *From Contention to Democracy*. Lanham, Maryland: Rowman and Littlefield Publishers, Inc.

Schedler, Andreas. 2002. "The Menu of Manipulation." *Journal of Democracy* 13 (2): 36–50.

Schielke, Samuli. 2015. *Egypt in the Future Tense: Hope, Frustration and Ambivalence before and after 2011*. Bloomington, Indiana: Indiana University Press.

Schock, Kurt. 2003. "Nonviolent Action and Its Misconceptions: Insights for Social Scientists." *PS: Political Science and Politics* 36 (4): 705–712.

Schock, Kurt. 2005. *Unarmed Insurrections: People Power Movements in Nondemocracies*. Minneapolis: University of Minnesota Press.

Schock, Kurt. 2013. "The Practice and Study of Civil Resistance." *Journal of Peace Research* 50 (3): 277–290.

Schwedler, Jillian. 2012. "The Political Geography of Protest in Neoliberal Jordan." *Middle East Critique* 21 (3): 259–270.

Schwedler, Jillian. 2013. "Spatial Dynamics of the Arab Uprisings." *PS: Political Science* 46 (2): 230–234.

Seidman, Gay. 2001. "Guerrillas in their Midst: Armed Struggle in the South African Anti-Apartheid Movement." *Mobilization: An International Quarterly* 6 (2): 111–127.

Selbin, Eric. 2010. *Revolution, Rebellion, Resistance: The Power of Story.* London: Zed Books.

Sewell, William H. Jr. 1979. "Corporations Républicaines: The Revolutionary Idiom of Parisian Workers in 1848." *Comparative Studies in Society and History* 21 (2): 195–203.

Sewell, William H. Jr. 2001. "Space in Contentious Politics." in Ronald R. Aminzade et al., eds., *Silence and Voice in the Study of Contentious Politics.* Cambridge: Cambridge University Press.

Sewell, William H. Jr. 2005. *The Logics of History: Social Theory and Social Transformation.* Chicago: Chicago University Press.

Shah, Aqil and Bushra Asif. 2015. "Pakistan in 2014: Democracy under the Military's Shadow." *Asian Survey* 55 (1): 48–59.

Shalaby, Tariq. 2011. "What Happened on Friday 28th." 7 Mar. At: http://web .archive.org/web/20160325220840/http://tarekshalaby.com/2011/03/what-ha ppened-on-friday-28th/ (accessed 19 Sept. 2012).

Sharp, Gene. 1980. *Social Power and Political Freedom.* Boston: Extending Horizons.

Sharp, Gene. 2005. [1973], *The Politics of Nonviolent Action: Part 2, The Methods of Nonviolent Action.* Boston: Extending Horizons.

Shehata, Samer and Joshua Stacher. 2006. "The Brotherhood Goes to Parliament." *Middle East Report* 240 (Fall): 32–39.

Al-Shorouk. 2011–2013. Print ed. Cited by date.

Al-Shorouk. 2012. "Sijn al-Rā'id Ahmad Shuman 6 Sanawāt li-l-Sulūk al-Muddir wa Mukhālafat al-Qanūn al-'Askari." 3 Apr. At: http://web.archive.org/web/ 20120405200010/http://www.shorouknews.com/news/view.aspx?cda te=03042012&id=122d01e7-8b58-40c4-b071-e3dbf8921e32 (accessed 19 Sept. 2012).

Al-Shorouk. 2013. "Ba'd ahdāth al-Shūra.<<da'm al-shar'iyya>>: hān waqt tanahiyya al-khilafāt al-siyāssiyya li-mowājahat al-inqilāb." 27 Nov. At: http://web.archive.org/web/20160621140724/http://www.shorouknews.com/ne ws/view.aspx?cdate=27112013&id=3b64c857-a70b-4ea8-8c71-52e1eb9d2df4 (accessed 20 Jun. 2016).

Sidel, John T. 2014. "Dangers and Demon(izer)s of Democratization in Egypt: Through an Indonesian Glass, Darkly." in Fawaz A. Gerges, ed., *The New Middle East: Protest and Revolution in the Arab World.* Cambridge: Cambridge University Press.

Singerman, Diane. 1995. *Avenues of Participation: Family, politics and networks in urban quarters of Cairo.* Princeton, NJ: Princeton University Press.

Skocpol, Theda. 1979. *States and Social Revolutions: A Comparative Analysis of France, Russia and China.* Cambridge: Cambridge University Press.

Slater, Dan. 2010. *Ordering Power: Contentious Politics and Authoritarian Leviathans in Southeast Asia.* Cambridge: Cambridge University Press.

Springborg, Robert. 1987. "The President and the Field Marshall: Civil-Military Relations in Egypt Today." *Middle East Report* 147 (July-August).

Star. 2011. "Protestors Stand Their Ground as Tanks Roll into Tahrir Square." 30 Jan. At: http://web.archive.org/web/20120102161127/http://www.thestar.com/news/world/article/930658-protesters-stand-their-ground-as-tanks-roll-into-tahrir-square (accessed 19 Sept. 2012).

Tarrow, Sidney. 1989. *Democracy and Disorder: Protest and Politics in Italy, 1965–1975.* New York: Oxford University Press.

Tarrow, Sidney. 1995. *"Mass Mobilization and Regime Change."* in Richard Gunther, Nikiforos P. Diamandouros and Hans-Jürgen Puhle, eds. *The Politics of Democratic Consolidation: Southern Europe in Comparative Perspective.* Baltimore: John Hopkins University Press.

Tarrow, Sidney. 2011. *Power in Movement: Social Movements and Contentious Politics.* Cambridge: Cambridge University Press.

Tarrow, Sidney. 2005. *The New Transnational Activism.* Cambridge: Cambridge University Press.

Tarrow, Sidney. 2012. *Strangers at the Gates: Movements and States in Contentious Politics.* Cambridge: Cambridge University Press.

Thompson, Mark R. 2003. *Democratic Revolutions: Asia and Eastern Europe.* London: Routledge.

Tilly, Charles. 1977. "Getting it Together in Burgundy, 1675–1975," *Theory and Society* 4 (4): 479–504.

Tilly, Charles. 1978. *From Mobilization to Revolution.* New York: Random House.

Tilly, Charles. 1993. *European Revolutions, 1492–1992.* Cambridge, MA: Blackwell.

Tilly, Charles. 1995. *Popular Contention in Great Britain, 1758–1834.* Cambridge, MA: Harvard University Press.

Tilly, Charles. 1997. "Parliamentarization of Popular Contention in Great Britain, 1758–1834." *Theory and Society* 26 (2–3):245–273.

Tilly, Charles. 2000. "Spaces of Contention." *Mobilization: An International Quarterly* 5, (2): 135–159.

Tilly, Charles. 2002. "Event Catalogs as Theories." *Sociological Theory* 20 (2): 248–254.

Tilly, Charles. 2003. *The Politics of Collective Violence.* Cambridge: Cambridge University Press.

Tilly, Charles. 2006. *Regimes and Repertories.* Chicago: University of Chicago Press.

Tilly, Charles. 2008. *Contentious Performances.* Cambridge: Cambridge University Press.

Tilly, Charles, Louise Tilly and Richard Tilly. 1975. *The Rebellious Century, 1830–1930.* Cambridge, MA: Harvard University Press.

Titarenko, Larissa, John McCarthy, Clark McPhail, and Boguslaw Augustyn, 2001, "The Interaction of State Repression, Protest Form and Protest Sponsor Strength During the Transition from Communism in Minsk, Belarus, 1990–1995." *Mobilization: An International Quarterly* 6 (2): 129–150.

Traugott, Mark. 2010. *The Insurgent Barricade.* California: University of California Press.

Trejo, Guillermo. 2014. "The Ballot and the Street: An Electoral Theory of Social Protest in Autocracies." *Perspectives on Politics* 12 (2): 332–352.

Tripp, Charles. 2013. *The Power and the People: Paths of Resistance in the Middle East.* Cambridge: Cambridge University Press.

Trombetta, Lorenzo. 2013. "More than Just a Battleground: Cairo's Urban Space during the 2011 Protests." *European Urban and Regional Studies* 20 (1): 139–144.

Trotsky, Leon. 2003. [1932], *The History of the Russian Revolution.* 3 Vols. New York: Pathfinder.

Tompkins, Elizabeth. 2015. "A Quantitative Reevaluation of Radical Flank Effects within Nonviolent Campaigns." *Research in Social Movements, Conflicts and Change* 38: 103–135.

Ungpakorn, Giles Ji. 2009. "Class Struggle between the Coloured T-Shirts in Thailand." *Journal of Asia Pacific Studies* 1 (1): 76–100.

Wall Street Journal. 2014. "Egyptian TV Swayed Public Against Morsi, in Favor of Sisi." 28 May. At: http://online.wsj.com/articles/egyptian-tv-swayed-public-against-morsi-in-favor-of-sisi-1401330765 (accessed 20 Jun. 2016).

Washington Post. 2013. "Backing Egypt's Generals, Saudi Arabia Promises to Fill Financial Void." 19 Aug. At: http://www.washingtonpost.com/world/middle_east/backing-egypts-generals-saudi-arabia-promises-to-fill-financial-void/2013/08/19/9d91384a-0901-11e3-9941-6711ed662e71_story.html (accessed 20 Jun. 2016).

Washington Post. 2014. "Influence of Moneyed Elites Rebounds in Egypt." 18 Jan. At: http://www.washingtonpost.com/world/middle_east/influence-of-mon eyed-elites-rebounds-in-egypt/2014/01/17/e7608456-7d25-11e3-93c1-0e8881 70b723_story.html (accessed 20 Jun. 2016).

Way, Lucan. 2008. "The Real Causes of the Color Revolutions." *Journal of Democracy* 19 (3): 55–69.

Way, Lucan. 2011. "The Lessons of 1989." *Journal of Democracy* 22 (4): 17–27.

Wickham, Carries R. 2002. *Mobilizing Islam: Religion, Activism and Political Change in Egypt.* New York: Columbia University Press

Wickham, Carries R. 2013. *The Muslim Brothers: Evolution of an Islamist movement.* Princeton, NJ: Princeton University Press.

WikiThawra. 2013. "Hasr Qatalat al-18 Yūm al-Aūla min al-Thawra Tafsīliyyan." At: http://web.archive.org/web/20160119182534/https://wikithawra.word press.com/2013/10/23/25jan18dayscasualities/ (accessed 20 Jun. 2016).

WikiThawra. 2014a. "Hasr al-Maqbūd 'alayhum wa al-Mulāhaqīn Qadā'iyan Khilal 'Ahd al-Sisi wa Adli Mansour, muhadath hata 15 Mayu 2014." At: http://web.archive.org/web/20160322224747/https://wikithawra.wordpress.com/2014/01/09/sisi-mansour-detainees/ (accessed 20 Jun. 2016).

WikiThawra. 2014b. "Hasr Qatala 'Ahd al-Sisi wa Adli Mansour Tafsīliyan (muhadath) hata 31 Yanayir 2014." At: http://web.archive.org/web/2016050 3073136/https://wikithawra.wordpress.com/2013/11/12/sisicasualities/ (accessed 20 Jun. 2016).

Wilkinson, Steven. 2004. *Votes and Violence: Electoral Competition and Ethnic Riots in India.* Cambridge: Cambridge University Press.

Youssef, Nour. 2013. "Clean Streets, First Sign of Elections." *The Arabist.* 3 Mar. At: http://web.archive.org/web/20160412123835/http://arabist.net/blog/2013/ 3/3/clean-streets-first-sign-of-elections.html (accessed 20 Jun. 2016).

Zunes, Stephen. 2011. "The Power of Strategic Nonviolent Action in Arab Revolutions." *Middle East Institute.* 1 Aug. At: http://web.archive.org/web/20 140725213711/http://www.mei.edu/content/power-strategic-nonviolent-actio n-arab-revolutions (accessed 20 Jun. 2016).

Index

Books in the Series (continued from p.iii)